Uneasy Sensations

UNEASY SENSATIONS

SMOLLETT AND THE BODY

Aileen Douglas

THE UNIVERSITY OF CHICAGO PRESS
Chicago & London

Aileen Douglas is lecturer in the English department
at Trinity College, Dublin.

The University of Chicago Press, Chicago 60637
The University of Chicago Press, Ltd., London
© 1995 by The University of Chicago
All rights reserved. Published 1995
Printed in the United States of America
04 03 02 01 00 99 98 97 96 95   12345
ISBN (cloth): 0-226-16051-3

Library of Congress Cataloging-in-Publication Data

Douglas, Aileen, 1961–
Uneasy sensations : Smollett and the body / Aileen Douglas.
p.   cm.
Includes bibliographical references (p.   ) and index.
1. Smollett, Tobias George, 1721–1771—Criticism and
interpretation.   2. Body, Human, in literature.   3. Smollett, Tobias
George, 1721–1771—Knowledge—Medicine.   4. Smollett, Tobias George,
1721–1771—Knowledge—Anatomy.   5. Literature and society—England—
History—18th century.   6. Literature and science—England—History—
18th century.   7. Medicine in literature.   8. Anatomy in
literature.   I. Title.
PR3698.B57D68   1995
823'.6—dc20   95-1786
                                         CIP

⊗ The paper used in this publication meets the minimum requirements of the
American National Standard for Information Sciences—Permanence of Paper
for Printed Library Materials, ANSI Z39.48-1984.

FOR MY PARENTS

Contents

ACKNOWLEDGMENTS

I am grateful to all the friends and colleagues who read parts of the manuscript, or talked with me about its concerns. Special mention must be made, however, of Margaret Doody and Richard Kroll, who have encouraged this work from its very beginnings, and of Jerry Beasley, Robert Hogan, and Claudia Johnson, who helped it along in various ways. My debt to Ian Campbell Ross, already substantial, accumulated greatly in the writing of this book. It is a pleasure to be able to thank him here. James Douglas taught me by example that writing is best accomplished sitting down. He and my mother, Eileen, have provided unstinting support over the years. This book is for them.

NOTE ON EDITIONS USED

The following are the editions of Smollett's works quoted. Page
numbers are given parenthetically in the text.

The Adventures of Roderick Random. Edited by Paul-Gabriel
Boucé. Oxford: Oxford University Press, 1979.

*The Adventures of Peregrine Pickle in Which Are Included Mem-
oirs of a Lady of Quality.* Edited by James L. Clifford. Revised by
Paul-Gabriel Boucé. Oxford: Oxford University Press, 1983.

The Adventures of Ferdinand Count Fathom. Edited by Jerry C.
Beasley. Athens: University of Georgia Press, 1988.

The Life and Adventures of Sir Launcelot Greaves. Edited by
David Evans. Oxford: Oxford University Press, 1973.

The Complete History of England. 4 vols. London, 1766.

A Continuation of the Complete History of England. 2 vols. London, 1766.

The Present State of All Nations. 8 vols. London, 1768–69.

Travels through France and Italy. Edited by Frank Felsenstein.
Oxford: Oxford University Press, 1979.

The History and Adventures of an Atom. Edited by Robert Adams
Day. Athens: University of Georgia Press, 1989.

The Expedition of Humphry Clinker. Edited by Lewis M. Knapp.
Revised by Paul-Gabriel Boucé. Oxford: Oxford University Press,
1984.

Poems, Plays, and "The Briton." Edited by Byron Gassman.
Athens: University of Georgia Press, 1993.

The Letters of Tobias Smollett. Edited by Lewis M. Knapp. Oxford:
Oxford University Press, 1970.

INTRODUCTION

All born into the world are "surrounded with Bodies, that perpetually and diversly affect them."[1] We are unlikely to quarrel with John
Locke's assertion. In a placid, commonsense way we know that we
are material beings, objects in a world of objects. We recognize too
our different senses of the bodies around us: humdrum when we
avoid them on a busy pavement or grocery aisle; acute in moments
of intimacy or intense irritation. Why draw attention to the obvious? One reason, of course, is to claim a new importance, a
greater significance, for what is taken for granted. Locke is not simply saying that bodies affect other bodies. He is also saying that
bodily experience, what we sense and feel, is primary in what we
know and what we are. Locke articulates, and in some measure in-
spires, the eighteenth-century preoccupation with the physical.

Some aspects of this preoccupation can be traced fairly easily. It has an institutional history in the foundation of medical
societies and hospitals.[2] Eighteenth-century apprehensions of
physicality are also entangled, in ways historians are just beginning
to understand, with the birth of a consumer society. Knowledge, in
a burgeoning print culture, is an opportunity for profit; enlightenment and advertisement are confounded.[3] Eighteenth-century periodicals, with their numerous and technical reviews of medical
works, testify that the "animal machine" interested general as well
as more specialized readers. Review journals such as the *Critical* or
the *Monthly* also make us aware that eighteenth-century physicality is distinct from our own. Digestion, knee joints, cancers, ve-

1. John Locke, *An Essay concerning Human Understanding,* ed. Peter H.
Nidditch (Oxford: Clarendon Press, 1979), 106.
2. See Roy Porter, "Was There a Medical Enlightenment in England?" *British Journal for Eighteenth-Century Studies* 5 (1982): 49–63.
3. Philip K. Wilson, "Acquiring Surgical Know-how: Occupational and Lay
Instruction in Early Eighteenth-Century London," in *The Popularization of
Medicine, 1650–1850,* ed. Roy Porter (London: Routledge, 1992), 42–71. For a
reader-oriented study of popularization see the essay by Mary E. Fissell,
"Readers, Texts, and Contexts: Vernacular Medical Works in Early Modern England," in the same volume, 72–96.

nereal disease—the body parts, processes, and disorders are immediately recognizable, but they combine in forms we may not, at first, make out. The culture that supported Edward Barry's *Treatise on the three different Digestions and Discharges of the human body* also absorbed Adam Smith's *Theory of Moral Sentiments,* a text in which the human body is less obtrusive, but just as vital. In fact, both works were given serious consideration in the same volume of the *Critical Review.* As twentieth-century readers we see at once that Barry's book is about the body. What we may not apprehend immediately, however, is that Smith's theories too have a material, physical basis.

Eighteenth-century letters and diaries, documents from the everyday, intimate that people dealt readily with their own physicality and were interested in talking about it. Of course, any tendency to perceive ourselves as scientific specimens increases dramatically once we experience bodily discomfort or are threatened by disease, and among the most memorable and impressive pieces of eighteenth-century writing are accounts of illness and physical pain. In a letter to her sister Esther, Fanny Burney gives a brave and completely harrowing account of her mastectomy.

> When the wound was made, & the instrument was withdrawn, the pain seemed undiminished, for the air that suddenly rushed into those delicate parts felt like a mass of minute but sharp and forked poniards, that were tearing the edges of the wound—but when again I felt the instrument—describing a curve—cutting against the grain, if I may so say, while the flesh resisted in a manner so forcible as to oppose and tire the hand of the operator, who was forced to change from the right to the left—then, indeed, I thought I must have expired.[4]

Burney's ability to confront extreme pain and bodily disintegration and give both linguistic form is one she shares with many near contemporaries, among them Tobias Smollett. A few months before his death, Smollett wrote to the surgeon and anatomist John Hunter: "With respect to myself, I have nothing to say but that if I can prevail upon my wife to execute my last will, you shall receive my poor

4. *Journals and Letters of Fanny Burney,* ed. Joyce Hemlow et al. (Oxford: Clarendon Press, 1975), 6:612.

carcase in a box, after I am dead, to be placed among your rarities. I am already so dry and emaciated that I may pass for an Egyptian mummy without any other preparation than some pitch and painted linen, unless you think I may deserve the denomination of a curiosity in my own character" (*Letters,* 140). That a dying man turns his decrepit body into a witticism, and that a woman composes her unimaginable pain into a written record, owes most to personal courage, but as Smollett and Burney acknowledge inescapable aspects of their own physicality, they also epitomize their culture's readiness to make the body a subject.

Seeing Burney and Smollett confront, in their private letters, the vulnerability of their own bodies, modern readers feel the difficulty of responding with tact and delicacy. Other aspects of the period's emphasis on the physical pose different kinds of problems. How, for example, does one demonstrate that eighteenth-century culture is also pervaded by awareness of embodiment? That writers in the period talk about the body a lot is more or less susceptible to proof, but that they make use of the reader's sense of physicality, as they might make use of the reader's knowledge of Homer, is rather more difficult to establish. William Hogarth provides an instance of what I mean when he tells the reader of *An Analysis of Beauty* (1753) that his work is one that "the sense of feeling, as well as that of seeing, hath been apply'd to." Feeling is the most physical, and least intellectual, of the senses. When Hogarth makes the reader use an awareness of touch and feeling, he appeals to the reader as an embodied creature rather than as an intellect alone. His aesthetic is one in which the reader must "feel out the nature of forms."[5]

Behind much of what I say in this study is my belief that the eighteenth-century novel offers its culture's emphasis on physicality and embodiment a formal recognition. The novel provides a space to dramatize and explore the various modifications and ramifications of what bodies are and what they are said to be. To a remarkable extent, characters in the eighteenth-century novel *are* their bodies.[6] This is to say that, when we try to define characters,

5. William Hogarth, *An Analysis of Beauty,* ed. Joseph Burke (Oxford: Clarendon Press, 1955), 107.

6. "From its outset, the novel documents the corporeal" (Pat Rogers, "Fat Is a Fictional Issue: The Novel and the Rise of Weight-Watching," in *Literature*

or to explain what happens to them, we quickly become involved in descriptions of physicality and physical events. Novels, because they minutely register the perpetual and diverse affects of body upon body, insinuate that the predicaments of human physicality are at the heart of most stories. One need only think of Samuel Richardson's circumstantial account of Pamela's fainting fits; or of Smollett's sensationalism when he gives us Roderick Random during a sea battle, "well-nigh blinded" by the brains of a marine (167–68); or of the less brutal, but no less physical, scenes in which Fanny Burney records Evelina's symptoms of social embarrassment. A commonplace of literary criticism implicates seventeenth-century philosophy in the rise of the novel. Ian Watt directly relates both Locke's insistence that knowledge results from experience and sensation, and Descartes's emphasis on the thought processes of the individual, to the formal realism that distinguishes the novel as genre. Michael McKeon claims that the novel triumphs because it can mediate, and render intelligible, problems of epistemological and social instability "central to early modern experience."[7] Empiricists, asserting that our primary knowledge of the world comes through "Sounds, Tastes, Smells, visible and tangible Qualities," place the body and its sensations at the center of their philosophy. The importance empiricists give the body is credited in the novel, where the narration of "particular individuals having particular experiences at particular times" depends on representations of physical experience.[8] From the observation that characters in the eighteenth-century novel are their bodies, we can move to the broader, more abstract assertion that physicality is one of the problems that the early novel mediates.

and Medicine during the Eighteenth Century, ed. Marie Mulvey Roberts and Roy Porter [London: Routledge, 1993], 178). A similar contention is made by Peter Brooks: "modern narratives appear to produce a semioticization of the body which is matched by a somatization of story: a claim that the body must be a source and a locus of meanings, and that stories cannot be told without making the body a prime vehicle of narrative significations" (*Body Work: Objects of Desire in Modern Narrative* [Cambridge: Harvard University Press, 1993], xii).

7. Ian Watt, *The Rise of the Novel* (Berkeley: University of California Press, 1957), 9–30; Michael McKeon, *The Origins of the English Novel* (Baltimore: Johns Hopkins University Press, 1987), 20.

8. Locke, *Essay concerning Human Understanding,* 120; Watt, *Rise of the Novel,* 31.

Grappling with human physicality, the eighteenth-century novel is much concerned with the definition, legibility, and control of the body. For example, novels often present the apparently simple act of defining or recognizing the human body as difficult and troubling. Gulliver, taking a swim, is shaken when a young female Yahoo identifies him as a desirable member of her own species. Tobias Smollett's Roderick Random suffers the indignity of being "reconnoitred" with a spyglass before his commanding officer accepts him as a "tolerable" creature (197). In Fanny Burney's *Evelina* (1777), a wag encourages a fop to wrestle with a monkey: "doff your coat and waistcoat, and swop with Monsieur *Grinagain* here, and I'll warrant you'll not know yourself which is which."[9] Granted that some of these scenes serve particular satiric purposes, they still suggest that no absolute division can be made between human and animal forms. Nor do the problems posed by the human body end with definition. A major issue in the eighteenth-century novel is the extent to which the body is legible. With how much assurance can one move from outward bodily signs to the inner disposition of the individual? How reliable is the information the body provides? Deeply involved in such problems, the novel also recognizes that they are, from a legal or a political perspective, irrelevant. In political terms the body is clearly defined as a type of property. Moreover, the unambiguous vulnerability of the human body, exploited by physical punishment, is vital to political control. Perhaps most significantly of all, the novel reminds us that it is inaccurate to speak of the "human body." The novel delineates, sometimes reinforcing and sometimes subverting, the way in which anatomy is used to justify differing social and political experiences for men and women.

When we understand the eighteenth-century novel in this way, we can appreciate that the work of Tobias Smollett (1721–71) is both representative and distinctive. Smollett is the eighteenth-century novelist most celebrated and derided for the physicality of his writing. Often, however, Smollett's preoccupation with physicality has been reduced, by critics, to mere crudity—the kind of thing that some people care for while others do not, but that every-

9. *Evelina*, ed. Edward A. Bloom (Oxford: Oxford University Press, 1968), 400.

one understands, and no one need explain. It has to be admitted
that, in certain respects, Smollett's treatment of physicality is not
subtle (I'm thinking here of his interest in perforated chamber pots
and loose bowels), but such is not always, or indeed usually, the
case.[10] Smollett's distinct contribution to the eighteenth-century
novel is his concern for bodily sentience, his attempt to summon
up the feeling body enmeshed in patterns of social and political order. What bodies feel cannot be separated from how bodies are represented, but attention to how the bodies in a particular society
"perpetually and diversly" affect one another can, and does in
Smollett, become the basis of social and political criticism. What is
most valuable about Smollett's fiction is that it stages, in many very
different ways, the central paradox of human physicality; it allows
the reader to grasp that, although our physical experience of the
world is informed and mediated by political and social pressures of
various kinds—among them the discourses of medicine, law, and
philosophy—the human body is more than signifying matter.
Bodies, whatever they are, must still be registered as authentic and
deserving of respect.

   Smollett first intended to make a living as a doctor, and the
significance of his medical background to his life and work generally is signaled by the title of Lewis Knapp's biography: *Tobias
Smollett: Doctor of Men and Manners* (1949). Apprenticed to two
well-known Glasgow surgeons in 1736, Smollett later served briefly
as a naval surgeon before trying to establish a medical practice in
London. Although the venture was not successful, Smollett's pen-
chant for medical diagnosis was not extinguished. In his letters he
gives exact accounts of his physical state (usually poor) to friends.
After he began the *Critical Review* in 1756, he was able to share his
professional interest in the human body with the general reading
public. His reviews of current medical research in that journal often (as was the practice in reviews of all subjects) contained long
and detailed extracts. They usefully remind us that at this time the
reading of the literate public could include not only technical writ-

10. Robert Adams Day collects suggestive evidence for "a deeply buried
homosexual-excremental myth" in Smollett's fictions ("Sex, Scatology,
Smollett," in *Sexuality in Eighteenth-Century Britain,* ed. P.-G. Boucé [Man-
chester: Manchester University Press, 1982], 225–43).

ings on the body but also commentary on the social and moral implications of such writings.

In his novels Smollett's major subject is the body at risk. To talk about Smollett's writing we need a vocabulary derived from physical experience: matter, energy, motion, resistance, force, impact. Reading Smollett's fiction, we feel the pressure of what John Locke calls solidity, "the Idea most intimately connected with, and essential to Body": "the Bodies which we daily handle, make us perceive, that whilst they remain between them, they do by an insurmountable Force, hinder the approach of the parts of our Hands that press them. That which thus hinders the approach of two Bodies, when they are moving one towards another, I call *Solidity.*"[11] From *The Adventures of Roderick Random* (1748) to *The Expedition of Humphry Clinker* (1771), Smollett's solid protagonists are among the most embodied in fiction. We have already alluded to the grisly experience of Roderick Random during a sea battle: "the head of the officer of Marines, who stood near me, being shot off, bounced from the deck athwart my face, leaving me well-nigh blinded with brains" (167–68). Even in the more genteel circumstances of Smollett's last novel the characters are oppressively "surrounded by Bodies, that perpetually and diversly affect them." Matthew Bramble, "as tender as a man without a skin; who cannot bear the slightest touch without flinching" (49), is overcome by the pressure of other bodies at the Bath assembly. Both Random and Bramble are material substance, resisting the other forms of matter with which they share the world. Smollett's characters painfully register the world through which they move, and the society and politics of eighteenth-century England become known through, and are measured by, the body.

Smollett's first readers recognized the centrality of physical experience to his fictional achievement when they spoke of his "just, though very wretched descriptions," and pondered his refusal to "represent Nature with a Veil."[12] Only when we reach William Hazlitt's "On the English Novelists" is Smollett's physical,

11. Locke, *Essay concerning Human Understanding,* 123.
12. Catharine Talbot, quoted in *Tobias Smollett: The Critical Heritage,* ed. Lionel Kelly (London: Routledge and Kegan Paul, 1987), 38; An Oxford Scholar, quoted in the same volume, 40.

material representation found decisively wanting. For Hazlitt, a
superior novel gives "insight into the springs of human character";
it is psychological and interior. Smollett, although he is a "first-
rate" writer, is too concerned with external, bodily reality to provide these satisfactions: "He seldom probes to the quick, or penetrates beyond the surface."[13] Whereas Hogarth and Smollett both
appeal to a "sense of feeling" that is literal and tactile, Hazlitt's
probing and penetration is metaphorical and mental. Hazlitt is decisively not preoccupied with human physicality or embodiment.
For him, the body is a surface of limited interest. The "quick" is
elsewhere. We can read in Hazlitt's remarks on Smollett the shifting
cultural attitudes towards human physicality and its representation in fiction that were mainly responsible for Smollett's
nineteenth-century decline.[14] Nor was his loss of a general reader-
ship later made good by specialized academic attention. Academic
readers in search of form, irony, and ambiguity were not captivated
by Smollett's flying heads, chamber pots, and gross descriptions of
the waters at Bath.

　　Following Foucault, contemporary critics delight in the con-
ceptual complexities of human physicality: the bodies against
which we jostle in a crowd, and the bodies to which we turn for intimacy and comfort, are alike "constructed." In either case, we approach them through complicated social categories. Foucault's
insistence that the "grip" of power extends over "bodies and their
materiality, their forces, energies, sensations and pleasures" would
seem to undermine a central assertion of this study: that Smollett's
representation of physical experience as absolute and irreducible
becomes the basis of his social and political criticism.[15] That materiality is in the grip of power does not necessarily rule out its usefulness as an instrument of social criticism.[16] Scholars influenced by

　　13. "On the English Novelists," in *Lectures on the English Comic Writers*
(1818; reprint, London: Oxford University Press, 1907), 152.
　　14. See F. W. Boege, *Smollett's Reputation as a Novelist* (Princeton: Princeton University Press, 1947).
　　15. *The History of Sexuality: An Introduction*, trans. Robert Hurley (1978;
reprint, New York: Vintage, 1990), 155.
　　16. While Nancy Fraser suspects that for Foucault the body is "not simply an
object-within-a-regime-of-practices but is, rather, a transcendental signified"
and faults Foucault's "body talk" for insufficiently thematizing "major social
and political issues" (*Unruly Practices: Power, Discourse, and Gender in Con-*

Foucault are struggling variously with the paradox that, though power is "immanent" in the human body, yet that body has a material existence which is not equivalent to "the techniques of knowledge and procedures of discourse" that invest it (98). Despite Foucault's cautions to the contrary, scholarship is still attracted to the notion that some aspect of the body and its experience may be "exterior" to the workings of power.[17] Work in the sociology of the body, in particular, hankers after this possibility. For example, Arthur W. Frank, reviewing work in this field, insists that bodies are "the foundation [of both discourses and institutions] as well as their product," and John O' Neill's polemical work *Five Bodies: The Human Shape of Modern Society* urges a radical anthropomorphism and posits that we can "rethink society with our bodies," that we are not "caught in categorical systems that think us."[18]

The discussion surrounding the status of the body in Foucault is similar to debates that have been going on among feminist scholars for some time. Within certain strands of feminist thought any notion that bodily experience might be somehow foundational is deeply distrusted: "'The body' is not, for all its corporeality, an originating point nor yet a terminus; it is a result or an effect."[19] The

---

temporary Social Theory [Minneapolis: University of Minnesota Press, 1989], 60, 62), Barry Smart claims that Foucault's demonstration of the ways ethics "have been embodied in quite different styles of existence and conduct" makes his work "positive, radical, and politically progressive" ("On the Subjects of Sexuality, Ethics, and Politics in the Work of Foucault," *Boundary 2* 18 [1991]: 225).

17. Foucault's major insistence, of course, is that the "perpetual spirals of power and pleasure" traced on bodies make a sexual pleasure exterior to power impossible (*History of Sexuality*, 45).

18. Arthur W. Frank, "For a Sociology of the Body: An Analytical Review," in *The Body*, ed. Mike Featherstone, Mike Hepworth, and Bryan S. Turner (London: Sage Publications, 1991), 91; John O'Neill, *Five Bodies: The Human Shape of Modern Society* (Ithaca: Cornell University Press, 1985), 63. I have taken the liberty of presenting O'Neill's questions as the statements they clearly are. O'Neill's work is highly political: "Our appeal to the logic of the body seeks to re-embed the now hegemonic technological and bureaucratic knowledge in the common-sense *bioknowledge* of persons and families whose lives are otherwise administered by the modern corporate economy and its therapeutic state" (68), and my incorporation of it here should not be read as implicit endorsement of a "bioknowledge" that has troubling gender implications.

19. Denise Riley, *"Am I That Name?": Feminism and the Category of "Women" in History* (Minneapolis: University of Minnesota Press, 1988), 102.

problem is, of course, that an emphasis on female physicality may veer dangerously close to an oppressive biological essentialism. Nonetheless, just as sociologists hope to rethink society through the body, some feminists feel the body's materiality needs to be reassessed. Rehearsing the hold that "essentialist/constructionist binarism has on feminist theory," and citing the body as the most vexed object of that binarism, Diana Fuss ponders how one might "begin the project of reintroducing biology, the body as *matter,* back into poststructuralist debate."[20] The materialism of Smollett's characters is neither simple nor totalizing. In his work, he accompanies the shock of physical contact, the immediacy of physical experience, with an awareness that the body becomes an object of knowledge
Χ through the discourses of law, medicine, and philosophy. Smollett's novels reveal the body as a synthetic, cultural product, but his works also emphasize that bodies are matter. If you prick a socially constructed body, it still bleeds.

Representations of materiality are crucial because the body is used to naturalize political and social systems. One of the body's most important functions is to serve as a "natural symbol" of social order.[21] The particular intensity with which eighteenth-century culture viewed the body is, in part, a response to philosophers like Locke and Descartes who increased the body's prominence only to undermine its usefulness as a symbol. Their mechanistic and monstrous versions of human physicality made the relationship between physical being and social order both vulnerable and intensely fraught. Consequently, one of the tasks assumed by various kinds of eighteenth-century writers is the repair of the body so that it can once more fulfill its symbolic uses. The philosophy of Francis Hutcheson and David Hume, the satire of the Scriblerians, and the physiology of Robert Whytt, to name but a few examples, are diverse kinds of cultural work, yet they all acknowledge the threat seventeenth-century philosophy poses to the social uses of the body, and they all refashion the body so that it can once more securely represent models of social and political order. The first chapter of this study presents these complex transactions concern-

20. *Essentially Speaking: Feminism, Nature, and Difference* (London: Routledge, 1989), 1, 52.
21. Mary Douglas, "The Two Bodies," in *Natural Symbols: Explorations in Cosmology* (London: Barrie and Jenkins, 1973).

ing the body as a context for the rise of the novel, and it closes by suggesting how Smollett's writing is influenced by his understanding of them.

Smollett's most notorious account of the body is his *Travels through France and Italy* (1766). According to Laurence Sterne, its author set out with "the spleen and jaundice," and the work that resulted was "nothing but the account of his miserable feelings."[22] The *Travels* is not only, as Sterne rightly asserts, written of the body, it is also consistently concerned with interpreting the physicality of others. Throughout, the narrator tries to explain what determines bodies in appearance and behavior, an attempt that involves him in a serious dilemma. He wants to note (often celebrate) differences between British and foreign bodies, but he does not want to abandon belief in a human materiality, or nature, which transcends national cultures. In the *Travels* Smollett is displaced, and he reads the body in the context of cultural differences. When we read eighteenth-century writing, we too cross boundaries, and often what we find makes us uneasy. The predicament of the twentieth-century reader is certainly not Smollett's, but there is a family resemblance. That is why I have chosen to orient my own reader, and to confront essential critical questions, by offering first a discussion of the *Travels*.

In a way, most of Smollett's novels share the same basic plot. In the closing pages, characters retire into rural felicity, but first they must subject their esteem and their physical selves to an uncertain and sometimes brutal world. The fiction derives its interest from the variety and increasing sophistication of that subjection. From first to last, characters are endangered by other bodies, chance blows, overturned carriages, and bad food. As his career progresses, however, Smollett's expansive consideration of the body in the world comes to include the body's definition under eighteenth-century English law, the body as the object of, and source of resistance to, political manipulation, and the inherent instability of the body as sign.

Smollett's first novel, *The Adventures of Roderick Random*, immerses its reader in a world of physical experience: the excite-

22. *A Sentimental Journey,* ed. Ian Jack (Oxford: Oxford University Press, 1991), 29.

ments offered by the early modern city, the physical hardships of eighteenth-century war, the energies of desire. To many early readers the vigor and detail of this novel, and the fact that the course of the hero's adventures so clearly mirrored Smollett's own, suggested that the work was autobiographical. All the more striking then, that the body to which all this experience is occurring, the body in which it is unfolding, is such an insecure object of knowledge. At several junctures in the novel, Roderick's life is endangered because those who surround him refuse to acknowledge that his body *is* a body. The episodes of *Roderick Random* are connected not only by the hero's search for prosperity and social standing, but also by his need to resolve the status of his own physical form. In Roderick, a hero who is paradoxically all body and no body, Smollett creates a disjunction between physical experience and the social significance of that experience, between sensation and sociability. Smollett begins his fictional career by suggesting the body's induction into society is traumatic and selective.

Female physicality was particularly crucial to eighteenth-century social constructions. Indeed, eighteenth-century writers often distinguish the power of the female body from the power of male law. So, the marquis of Halifax can advise his daughter that women have more strength in their Looks than men have in their Laws; Samuel Johnson can say that Nature has given women so much power the Law has very wisely given them little; and William Alexander, at century's end, can claim that female sensibility is a compensation for all the "disadvantages" women are laid under by law and custom.[23] Implicit in all these statements, of course, is the notion that female looks, nature, and sensibility can exist independent of the law, and that women's physicality is a self-regulating mechanism. It is often assumed that Smollett has nothing of interest to say about women. In a fairly representative remark, Jane Spencer speaks of how Smollett concentrates on his heroes and makes the

23. The marquis of Halifax, George Savile, *The Lady's New Year's Gift, or Advice to a Daughter* (1688; reprinted in *The Works of George Savile, Marquis of Halifax*, ed. Mark N. Brown (Oxford: Clarendon Press, 1988), 18; *The Letters of Samuel Johnson*, ed. Bruce Redford (Oxford: Clarendon Press, 1992), 1:228; William Alexander, *The History of Women, from the earliest antiquity, to the present time, giving some Account of almost every interesting Particular concerning that Sex, among all Nations, ancient and modern* (Dublin, 1779), 2:439.

heroine a "static image of goodness."[24] On encountering Emilia, the heroine in *The Adventures of Peregrine Pickle* (1751), most readers will endorse Spencer's observation. The story of Emilia and Peregrine is, however, only one strand of a fragmented novel that contains two lengthy and powerful interpolated tales: "Memoirs of a Lady of Quality," and the story of the Annesley claimant. Moreover, the several parts of *Peregrine Pickle* are connected not only by the hero but by variations upon the female experiences of pregnancy, childbirth, and mother/child relationships—precisely the experiences that eighteenth-century writers chose to represent as the unproblematic basis of female social power. The plot of *Peregrine Pickle* has more pregnancies, comic and tragic, than any other eighteenth-century novel, and none of them is straightforward. Difficulties arise because pregnancy is, of course, a vital moment in the transmission of property. Smollett's second novel foregrounds the female body, exposing the extent to which its experiences are determined (and in this novel perverted) by a male law. The materiality of the female body cannot compensate women for their legal disadvantages because even their most intimate physical experiences are enacted in the grip of the law.

Smollett's two subsequent novels, *The Adventures of Ferdinand Count Fathom* (1753) and *The Life and Adventures of Sir Launcelot Greaves* (1760–61), are works of crisis. Unpopular in their day, they are virtually unknown now. Despite their improbability, rank sentiment, and facile closure, both novels enable an important shift in Smollett's representation of physicality. In these novels Smollett tries to accommodate, for the first time, human subjectivity, particularly the passions of fear and terror and the threat of madness. In the dedication to his third novel, *The Adventures of Ferdinand Count Fathom,* Smollett self-consciously addresses the problem of representing the body in fiction. He informs the reader that he has two main intentions: to reform (that is, excise) the treatment of human physicality and to use the reader's terror for didactic purposes. His anomalous representation of Ferdinand's body, a variety of erasure that gives Ferdinand affinities with the sublime, results directly from these intentions and bears

24. *The Rise of the Woman Novelist: From Aphra Behn to Jane Austen* (Oxford: Blackwell, 1986), 141.

witness to their collapse. In *Fathom* Smollett discovers that the "false perspectives," the fears, and the superstitions he intended to expose are, in fact, an inevitable part of human experience. If fear and apprehension, rather than sensation and experience, govern our relation to the world, then even our sense of our own bodies is controlled by that apprehension. Roderick Random, a creature marked by the strength of his sensations, is most vulnerable to physical damage and brutality. The subjects of *Fathom* are prone to dread and fear, and as such they suggest the possibility of the political exploitation of such passions.

There is a seven-year interval between *Fathom* and *The Life and Adventures of Sir Launcelot Greaves*. In *Greaves* Smollett tries to argue against the discovery he made in *Fathom*. He extricates himself from the previous novel's subjectivity by insisting both on a reassuring physicality and on the apparently communal perspective provided by the law. But the discovery made in *Fathom* is finally not denied. Although the most overt oppositions in *Greaves* are between violence and the law, between the ungovernable body and the reason, the novel's most essential opposition is between rival forms of apprehension, or of terror—that of the judgment of the last day and that of the madhouse. In *Greaves* Smollett confronts a political system based not on reason but on the passions, and he intimates how such a system can be resisted.

After *Greaves* Smollett delineates with complete confidence the implication of the body into systems of social order. In *The History and Adventures of an Atom* (1769), a scatological satire of English politics mainly during the Seven Years' War, political power is exerted not only over the material body but also over images of the body. At its most successful the political system forces its subjects to inhabit images of their own vulnerability; it seeks to control not only the literal body, but the subject's conceptualization of that body. The satirist is at his most powerful when he counters with a fantasy of invulnerability. The atom who narrates this tale cannot be "annihilated, divided, nor impaired." It cannot be damaged and therefore it cannot be terrorized; because it is not susceptible to fear and dread, the atom is perfectly placed to expose the use of such passions by the political system, and to disrupt a narrative particular to eighteenth-century order.

Unquestionably, Smollett's last novel is also his most success-ful. The formal satisfactions this novel offers, particularly in its de-velopment of epistolary technique, go far beyond those afforded by his other novels and have caused *Humphry Clinker* to be the single Smollett fiction unreservedly accepted into the literary canon. *The Expedition of Humphry Clinker* is also Smollett's most sophisti-cated articulation of the body as sign. In this novel, signs—both physical and linguistic—slip. Petticoats, breeches, discourses, and carriages all slide off, split apart, and overturn. Various attempts are made at mastery, most noticeably in Matthew Bramble's efforts to control—through medical and social discourse—his body's trans-lation into linguistic and social sense. In the end, though, even the sign "Matthew Bramble" divides. No attempt to render the body in language can ever be completely stable or perfectly achieved. The novel is a comedy of gratified love, family bonds, and the instability of the sign.

This study emphasizes Smollett's use of a fragmentary, at-omistic account of individual physical experience to undermine so-cial complacency. His emphasis on sensation disrupts convenient accounts of how society works and gives his fiction a contentious, subversive cast. Smollett was an alien in English society, and this may explain his inability to take it entirely on its own terms. Forced to make his living in London, Smollett continued to feel uneasy there, and even after the capital had been his home for years, he still assuaged his discomfort with thoughts of Scotland: "I do not think I could enjoy Life with greater Relish in any part of the world than in Scotland among you and your Friends, and I often amuse my Imagination with schemes for attaining that Degree of Happi-ness, which, however, is altogether out of my Reach. I am heartily tired of this Land of Indifference and Phlegm where the finer Sensa-tions of the Soul are not felt, and Felicity is held to consist in stupe-fying Port and overgrown Buttocks of Beef" (*Letters,* 33). Even the most embattled and determined social critics amuse their imagina-tions with visions of Utopia. Here, Scotland serves that purpose. Similarly, in Smollett's fiction, the estates his heroes inevitably in-herit are important as images of what the world might be. Smollett was proud of being "a gentleman by birth, education, and profes-sion," and this study neither discovers nor would persuade otherwise.[25] Smollett's hopes, his endorsement of a social paternalism centered on the estates of landed gentlemen, are deeply conservative. That does not, however, compromise or vitiate his atomization of the land of injustice, corruption, "indifference and phlegm" he actually inhabits.

When eighteenth-century writers used the phrase "uneasy sensations," they intended hunger, thirst, lust. Such discomforts, an important element in the body's self-regulation, rouse it to obtain necessary satisfactions. This kind of uneasiness, although it may be unpleasant for a while, is ultimately beneficial. Within our daily lives we experience pangs of hunger and stabs of pain as interruptions of sophisticated activities—reading books, writing letters. In the structure of Smollett's novels the materiality of his characters functions in a similar way, interrupting the stories eighteenth-century society chose to tell about itself. The phrase "uneasy sensations," then, usefully encapsulates, and justifies, what I take to be the most pronounced feature of Smollett's writing.

At the same time, the locution acknowledges a more problematic aspect of reading Smollett. There are instances when Smollett's rendition of physicality makes his reader uneasy and uncomfortable. I am thinking here, in particular, of his representations of grotesque female bodies. There is, for example, the episode where Roderick is tricked into an assignation by "a wrinkled hag turned of seventy."

> One while, she ogled me with her dim eyes, quenched in rheum; then, as if she was ashamed of that freedom, she affected to look down, blush, and play with her fan, then toss her head that I might not perceive a palsy that shook it, ask some childish questions with a lisping accent, giggle and grin with her mouth shut, to conceal the ravages of time upon her teeth, leer upon me again, sigh piteously, fling herself about in her chair to shew

25. The phrase comes from an impassioned letter Smollett addressed to Alexander Hume Campbell. Smollett thought the latter had defamed him (*Letters*, 23). Donald Bruce's sympathetic assertion that Smollett was "classless" is untrue (*Radical Dr. Smollett* [Boston: Houghton Mifflin Co., 1965], 15). For a consideration of what gentle status meant to Smollett, see Ian Campbell Ross, "Tobias Smollett: Gentleman by Birth, Education, and Profession," *British Journal for Eighteenth-Century Studies* 5 (1982): 179–90.

her agility, and act a great many more absurdities that
youth and beauty can alone excuse. (304)

Roderick says it is the woman's "monstrous affectation" (303) that
occasions his disgust, but attempts to justify the passage as satire
will not convince. After this interview ends, we never see the
woman again. What we are looking at here is misogyny: the woman
is disgusting because she is old and still feels sexual desire. Through
her grotesque body the text excises fear of the flesh and its appetites. It would be appropriate to use here those terms in which
Carol Houlihan Flynn describes writing by Swift and Defoe: women
are creatures of "insatiable appetite," the body is "material in the
way," "material always ready to betray."[26] Smollett is not, however,
primarily a writer driven by his fear of appetites, or of bodily corruption, and his work, despite the evidence of passages like that
quoted above, interprets the problem of the body differently. In
Smollett the body is more often betrayed than betraying: he does
not fear the body will engulf patterns of social and political order so
much as he fears corporeality will be denied. The grotesque female
body does appear in Smollett, and any feminist critic who finds in
him a completely ideal author should make the reader very nervous
indeed. At the same time, and to use adjectives Flynn uses of Swift
and Defoe, Smollett is neither "unreflecting nor uncaring" in his
apprehensions of physicality. His novels think through issues of
bodily and social regulation crucial to feminism.

Terry Eagleton has recently denounced what he sees as a
"fashionable turn to the somatic": "[T]he new somatics is simply
the return in a more sophisticated register of the old organicism.
Instead of poems plump as an apple, we have texts as material as an
armpit . . . Bodies are ways of talking about human subjects without going all sloppily humanist, avoiding that messy interiority
which drove Michel Foucault up the wall."[27] Behind what Eagleton
says is the charge of critical sharp practice: literary critics with somatic interests are too fastidious to deal with the truly messy aspects of the job; denying they practice a version of humanism, they

26. *The Body in Swift and Defoe* (Cambridge: Cambridge University Press,
1990), 1, 56, 111.
27. Review of Peter Brooks, *Body Work,* in *London Review of Books,* 27 May
1993, 7.

avoid questions that an acknowledged and rigorous humanism
would force upon them. There is something in this charge, and the
book in hand is obviously yet another example of what he considers
a "suspect genre." It seems to me, however, that talking about
"human subjects" without going "all sloppily humanist" is a worth-
while activity. There are profound differences between eighteenth-
century versions of the physical and our own, differences sufficiently astringent to prevent easy blending, sloppy humanism.
Awareness of such differences should not cause us to ignore
Smollett's insistence that bodies matter. As physical creatures in a
complicated social and political world, feeling urgent sensations,
worrying that our bodies are not entirely our own, we can only be
helped by such insistence.

CHAPTER ONE

THE BODY IN EIGHTEENTH-CENTURY NARRATIVE

We are used to speaking of an early eighteenth-century reformation of manners. The phrase conjures up images of newly decorous bodies, behaving themselves in the theater and—in their coffee-shop visits—politely contributing to the growth of the public sphere. The phrase and image have undoubted validity, and, as Peter Stallybrass and Allon White have pointed out, the emergence of polite, informed, critical opinion was "marked out by a number of changes in the interrelationship of place, body, and discourse."[1] Inhabiting new forms of social space, bodies changed their behavior. But at this very time, notions of the body itself were in crisis. Elaine Scarry states that "at particular moments when there is within a society a crisis of belief—that is, when some central idea or ideology or cultural construct has ceased to elicit a population's belief . . . the sheer material factualness of the human body will be borrowed to lend that cultural construct the aura of 'realness' and 'certainty.'"[2] Seventeenth-century philosophy, however, severely shook concepts of the body, thereby seriously impairing its ability to ground complex social and cultural systems. Challenged by Locke's denial that bodies can be perfectly defined, and by Descartes's mechanistic version of human physicality, eighteenth-century writers responded by representing the body as both know-

---

1. *The Politics and Poetics of Transgression* (London: Methuen, 1986), 83.
2. *The Body in Pain: The Making and Unmaking of the World* (Oxford and New York: Oxford University Press, 1985), 14.

able and, by virtue of its social significance, distinguishable from other animate forms. These acts of reclamation, some characterized by delighted vigor, others by exhausted resignation, occur in many forms of intellectual endeavor—medicine, philosophy, satire—and are a central feature of eighteenth-century culture. This chapter looks at some of these narrations of the body and ends by considering their place in Tobias Smollett's writing.

Seventeenth-century philosophy brought the body newly and dramatically into focus, but texts like Locke's *Essay concerning Human Understanding* and Descartes's *Passions of the Soul* also generate uncertainty about what the body is. Discussing the names of substances in his *Essay,* Locke demonstrates that "man" is what we agree to call a complex idea derived from sensation. Ignorant of "man's," or any other, "real Essence," we get by with "nominal Essences, which we make our selves" (454). The bodies through which we know the world are an act of intellectual, as well as physical, creation. To exemplify the uncertainties and problems of such intellectual acts, Locke offers the case of the abbot of St. Martin who

> was very near being excluded out the *Species* of *Man,* barely by his Shape . . . 'tis certain a Figure a little more oddly turn'd had cast him, and he had been executed as a thing not to be allowed to pass for a Man. And yet there can be no Reason given, why if the Lineaments of his Face had been a little alter'd, a rational Soul could have lodg'd in him; why a Visage somewhat longer, or a Nose flatter, or a wider Mouth could not have consisted, as well as the rest of his ill Figure, with such a Soul, such Parts, as made him, disfigured as he was, capable to be a Dignitary in the Church. (454)

Denying there are any "precise and unmovable Boundaries" for our species, and unable decisively to distinguish man and monster, Locke concludes by recording his "material Doubts": "none of the Definitions of the word *Man,* which we yet have, nor Descriptions of that sort of Animal, are so perfect and exact, as to satisfie a considerate inquisitive Person; much less to obtain a general Consent" (455). Locke's refusal to accept commonsense definitions of the body generates a profound unease that is felt not only in philosophical writings but also in the most popular forms of polite letters. Monstrous possibilities lurk even in the urbane pages of *The Spectator,* where Joseph Addison, engaged both in popularizing Locke and in defusing any uneasiness his arguments might cause, displaces problems of definition with an aesthetic solution. We find, Addison submits, "that there are several Modifications of Matter which the Mind, without any previous Consideration, pronounces at first sight beautiful or deformed." He further points out, "[T]is very remarkable that wherever Nature is crost in the Production of a Monster (the Result of any unnatural Mixture) the Breed is incapable of propagating its Likeness and of founding a new Order of Creatures, so that unless all Animals were allured by the Beauty of their own Species, Generation would be at an end, and the Earth unpeopled."[3] Addison, whose greatest talent is deriving comfort from the most frightening ideas, reassures his reader that monsters are sterile.

Locke's argument, that "man" and the body he inhabits are "nominal essences" that "we make ourselves," implies that naming is equivalent to creation and gives narration a critical importance. While naming and narrative are guided and limited by a general sense of fitness—Locke, at least, can draw a boundary between an "odly-shaped Foetus" (454) and "Chimaera's" which join, say, the voice of a sheep and the shape of a horse (455–56)—the *Essay* emphasizes the possibility of disagreement and contention between different definitions of the human body. The primary sense in the *Essay* is vision, and accordingly the test of the human frame Locke proposes is a visual one: how do we distinguish human shapes and forms from those of other species? There are, of course, additional grounds of discrimination that Locke ignores, for although he had a keen interest in medical matters and served as Shaftesbury's medical advisor, the physiology and workings of the human body do not concern him here; as he begins his *Essay,* he genially declines speculations about the physical details of sensation as "lying out of [his] way" (43). A generation before Locke, Descartes had undertaken such speculations, but the model of human physicality he proposed was even more disturbing than Locke's uncertainty. Locke, after

3. "Pleasures of the Imagination," nos. 412 and 413 in *The Spectator,* ed. Donald F. Bond (Oxford: Clarendon Press, 1965), 3:542, 546.

all, had only doubted that human forms could be definitively separated from monstrous ones, and he comfortably suggests that imperfect ideas of the human form suffice in the common affairs of life, but Descartes seemed to obliterate the boundaries between humans and the entire animal kingdom. At any rate, he made distinctions between human and animal physicality a "philosophical problem," one with which philosophers "felt it necessary to deal."[4]

Not that Cartesians themselves suffered any confusion in this matter. For Descartes the fact that humans could produce automata without cogitation made it reasonable to suppose that nature too could produce such works in animal form. In fact, as Descartes wrote to the English philosopher Henry More, it was "more astonishing that some mind may be discovered in every human body than that none may be found in any of the brutes."[5] If it were intended as a gloss on eighteenth-century satire, Descartes's comment could not be more appropriate. Certainly, the literary career of Jonathan Swift, devoted first to mechanical men and subsequently to rational horses, expresses a similar astonishment. In orthodox Cartesian thought, animal movement is purely corporeal and mechanical. In contrast, the workings of the human body combine with a soul to which "every kind of thought which exists in us" belongs.[6] In his *Passions of the Soul* Descartes quickly establishes and subsequently complicates this human dualism. He distinguishes first between the "passions of the soul," which are a species of thought, and the purely physical actions of the body (which cause the soul to perceive a given passion), and then he goes on to discriminate between passion as a mode of thought—which the close alliance between body and soul renders "confused and

4. Albert G. A. Balz, *Cartesian Studies* (New York: Columbia University Press, 1951), 106.

5. Letter to Henry More, in L. D. Cohen, "Descartes and Henry More on the Beast-Machine: A Translation of Their Correspondence Pertaining to Animal Automatism," *Annals of Science* 1 (1936): 53.

6. *The Philosophical Works of Descartes*, trans. E. S. Haldane and G. R. T. Ross (1911; reprint, Cambridge: Cambridge University Press, 1978), 1:332. The argument against the animal soul was an important part of the Cartesian argument for human immortality. The human ability to think implied a substance distinct from the corporeal and thereby immortal. By this reasoning, animal thought implied animal immortality—not an acceptable theological conclusion.

obscure"—and "clear cognition" (344). The union of body and soul is one of the major concerns of this treatise, and it is within the context of this union that the body is examined. Nonetheless, the range and complexity of actions Descartes attributes entirely to the bodily machine exclude the soul from participation in much of daily life. Indeed, *Passions* is explicitly written against the "very considerable error" by which the movements of the body were thought to "depend on the soul" (333), and Descartes's avowed aim is to show that "all movements of our members which accompany our passions spring from, not the soul, as I see it, but simply the bodily machine."[7] Without the aid of the soul, the bodily machine can "breathe, walk, eat, and . . . perform all those actions which are common to us and the brutes . . . just as the movements of a watch are produced simply by the strength of the springs and the form of the wheels" (339–40). In fact, the purpose of the passions is to "incite the soul to consent and contribute to the actions which may serve to maintain the body," and the bodily actions that result are similar to those through which "all the animals devoid of reason direct their lives" (392). By attributing more and more complex powers to the animal machine, to purely physical passions, Cartesians made it easier to dispense with the animal soul; but designing, through argument, a more satisfactory model of the beast machine increased the danger that the argument would also be applied to humans, thereby dissolving the distinction between human and animal constitutions. If one accepts that man does possess "a spiritual substance" added to his bodily machine, then "it is extraordinary that this bodily machine should so greatly resemble these other machines, called animals, which do not possess any soul whatsoever."[8] For Descartes, language satisfies the need for a decisive difference between men and beasts: "all men use it, even the most stupid and mentally deranged, and those deprived of their tongue and vocal organs, whereas on the other hand not a single brute speaks, and consequently this we may take for the true difference between man and beast."[9] Locke, however, is not convinced: "yet should there a Creature be found, that had Language and Reason,

7. Letter to Henry More, 55.
8. Balz, *Cartesian Studies*, 122.
9. Letter to Henry More, 53.

but partaked not of the usual shape of a Man, I believe it would hardly pass for a *Man,* how much soever it were *Animal Ratio-nale.*[10] Tobias Smollett's first novel dramatizes a version of the puzzle Locke here describes. Roderick Random has language and reason, he even has the "usual shape of a Man," yet for much of the novel he struggles to have his human form recognized.

Both Locke and Descartes concentrate on the experience, technicalities, and results of sensation; their work represents mere physical being as a source of significant exhilaration—the impression of objects on the eye, the distinctive taste of a pineapple, the pressure and force of other objects on human skin, are not only sensations but also matters of philosophical moment. Nonetheless, when the glories and excitements of sensation fade, an intractable problem remains: if the body, newly privileged as the instrument of sensation, cannot be isolated satisfactorily from a multiplicity of animate and inanimate forms, if it is lost within a confused heap of shapes both quick and mechanical, then it cannot be used to assuage societal crises: its "sheer material factualness" provides no comfort.

We know contemporaries felt this loss because we see the various attempts they made to provide more reassuring, comfortable, and stable models of human physicality, thereby recovering the body for the purposes of social definition. In some cases, indeed, writers explicitly tell their readers that they aim to realign the human body with patterns of political and social order. Ronald Paulson has argued that the acts of "breaking" and "remaking" are paradigmatic for eighteenth-century aesthetic experience.[11] The assertions and suggestions explored above all iconoclastically "break" conceptions of the human body. Confronting Locke and Descartes, eighteenth-century writers undertake the repair of the body with ingenuity, alacrity, and the sheer bluster of common sense. They "remake" the body not only through intellectual innovations but also through the intensification and redirection of established arts and sciences. Their work can be seen not only in the emergence of sensibility, a discourse particular to the late seven-

10. *Essay concerning Human Understanding,* 456.
11. *Breaking and Remaking: Aesthetic Practice in England, 1700–1820* (New Brunswick: Rutgers University Press, 1989).

teenth and eighteenth centuries, but also in the revival of the ancient art of physiognomy and in the particular direction taken by Augustan satire. Sensibility, physiognomy, and satire are disparate and individually complicated phenomena, but all three have a material basis and share an emphasis on the body as an object of social significance. At the peak of Tobias Smollett's literary career, the cultural task of separating the human body from the monstrous and the mechanical was still ongoing.

Of literary genres, satire is the most self-consciously physical. The very language in which Augustan satirists present their relationship to subject and reader is that of physical effect. As the narrator of *A Tale of a Tub* informs us, satirists "use the Publick much at the Rate that Pedants do a naughty Boy ready Hors'd for Discipline: First expostulate the Case, then plead the Necessity of the Rod, from great Provocations, and conclude every Period with a Lash."[12] Even Pope, more given to Horatian conversation, occasionally slashed the bodies of his readers with the whip of Juvenal and the Elizabethan verse satirists. True, as we read Augustan satire, we are aware that all this talk of posteriors and lashing has more to do with generic predictability than it has with the body, but it is also obvious that the relentless, extreme, and ingenious treatment of the body in Augustan satire indicates some sort of anxiety. Bakhtin attributes this anxiety to Augustan awareness of the unruly, grotesque body—which is "unfinished, outgrows itself, transgresses its own limits"—and he claims that eighteenth-century satire works to replace this subversive body with one that is "completed, self-sufficient" and therefore amenable to moral controls.[13] Building on the Bakhtinian model, but with a fuller recognition of the ways in which writers like Swift and Pope blur and distort the human shape, Peter Stallybrass and Allon White argue that "Augustan satire was the generic form which enabled writers to express and negate the grotesque simultaneously."[14] The tropes of Augustan satire spring not so much from the desire to control an unruly, grotesque popular body (in Bakhtin's terms) but from the fact

12. Jonathan Swift, *A Tale of a Tub*, ed. Herbert Davis (Oxford: Blackwell, 1957), 29.

13. *Rabelais and His World*, trans. Hélène Iswolsky (Bloomington: Indiana University Press, 1984), 26, 29, 62.

14. *Politics and Poetics of Transgression*, 106.

that seventeenth-century philosophy forced intellectual consideration of the human form. Along with philosophical respondents to Descartes, Augustan satirists see that the differences between human and animal physicality are a problem with which it is "necessary to deal."

That this necessity becomes a source of anxious fascination is obvious in central Augustan texts, like *Gulliver's Travels, The Dunciad,* and *The Memoirs of Martinus Scriblerus.*[15] *The Memoirs* is an episodic satire that charts the involvement of its hero in various arts and sciences, and it makes sense that, as part of an ambitious (and never completed) project dedicated to exposing abuses in learning, it is also the Augustan text that most explicitly attempts to contain the deleterious effects of seventeenth-century philosophy on conceptualizations of the human body. Significantly, the satiric rout of this particular "abuse" of learning requires a visit to the fair. The fairground episode of *The Memoirs,* one of the most adroitly hilarious passages in eighteenth-century literature, begins when the polymathic Martin, unbending his mind after the "long and severe Studies of the day," goes for a stroll. Suddenly, his attention is arrested by a large piece of canvas on which "was display'd the pourtrait of two Bohemian Damsels, whom Nature had as closely united as the ancient Hermaphroditus and Salmacis; and whom it was as impossible to divide, as the mingled waters of the gentle Thames and amorous Isis."[16] In 1708 a pair of seven-year-old Hungarian twins, joined at the back, were put on public exhibition in London, and Swift wrote that the sight, "in the newsmonger's phrase, causes a great many speculations; and raises abundance of questions in divinity, law, and physic."[17] Swift insinuates that speculations about the twins' form are driven by commercial interest—the object of *The Memoirs* is to contain such

15. For the argument that *Gulliver's Travels* satirizes Locke's epistemology, see W. B. Carnochan's *Lemuel Gulliver's Mirror for Man* (Berkeley: University of California Press, 1968), 116–65; Christopher Fox delineates the importance of Locke to *The Memoirs* (*Locke and the Scriblerians* [Berkeley: University of California Press, 1990]).

16. *The Memoirs of the Extraordinary Life, Works, and Discoveries of Martinus Scriblerus,* ed. Charles Kerby-Miller (Oxford: Oxford University Press, 1988), 143.

17. Quoted by Kerby-Miller in ibid., 295.

speculations. Martin pays his entrance fee and, on seeing the damsels themselves, falls deeply in love. The satire unites Martin's philosophical curiosity and amorous inclinations and can then present the nonsense of love and the nonsense of philosophy as indistinguishable. In his own person, Swift admits that man, not nature, sets the boundaries of the species; as a satirist, he discredits this view, associating it with the imperatives of youthful lust.

> How great is the power of Love in human breasts! In vain has the Wise man recourse to his Reason, when the insinuating Arrow touches his heart, and the pleasing Poison is diffused through his veins. But then how violent, how transporting must that passion prove, where not only the Fire of Youth, but the unquenchable Curiosity of a Philosopher, pitch'd upon the same object! For how much soever our Martin was enamour'd on her as a beautiful Woman, he was infinitely more ravish'd with her as a charming Monster. What wonder then, if his gentle Spirit, already humaniz'd by a polite Education to receive all soft impressions, and fired by the sight of those beauties so lavishly expos'd to his view, should prove unable to resist at once so pleasing a Passion, and so amiable a Phaenomenon? (146–47)

This passage denies the problem of discrimination that so troubled Locke. For a start, this monster is unquestionably a monster, albeit a "charming" one safely exhibited as "other." More importantly, in the entire episode the physical construction of the twins is subordinate to the objects of the satire—pedantry and muddle-headed abuses of language. The satirist is not made uneasy by monsters; he deploys them. The dominant monstrosity is Martin himself, a callow youth who confuses lust and philosophy and whose "polite education" has left him unable to discriminate between poison and pleasure.

A similar strategy of containment works when Martin is approached by a group of Free-Thinkers who propose to construct a sort of "Hydraulic Engine"

> in which a chemical liquor resembling Blood, is driven through elastic chanels resembling arteries and veins, by the force of an Embolus like the heart, and wrought

> by a pneumatic Machine of the nature of the lungs, with
> ropes and pullies, like the nerves, tendons and muscles:
> And we are persuaded that this our artificial Man will
> not only walk, and speak, and perform most of the out-
> ward actions of the animal life, but (being wound up
> once a week) will perhaps reason as well as most of your
> Country Parsons. (141)

The fear at the heart of this Scriblerian sketch is that all men are, in
some sense, "artificial" men, complicated machines formed and
operated, like inanimate objects, by rules of physics and motion.
Such a fear is, however, exorcised even as it is expressed, by comparing the "hydraulic engine" to the country parson. The satirists
contain the threat posed by modern mechanistic notions of the
body by appropriating these images for their own purposes. The peculiarities of the "artificial" man's interior are given in some detail
but become unimportant when the reader is returned to the familiar shortcomings of the English clergy. Implicitly, the passage argues that speculations about the body's workings, no matter how
disturbing, are insignificant because the most important questions
are moral, not physiological. The "hydraulic engine" appears only
to remind us that "our intercourse with intellectual nature is necessary; our speculations upon matter are voluntary and at leisure."[18]
Humans and animals may share, as Descartes argues, certain characteristics with a watch, but in contrast to both watches and animals, humans exist in a sophisticated society. The proper study of
mankind is the differences among men and the social roles they
play. We may choose to conceive of ourselves as mechanisms with
nerves and tendons instead of ropes and pulleys; but unlike other
mechanisms, human bodies are "wound up" by the demands and
expectations of society. Even as *The Memoirs* incorporates, and is

18. Samuel Johnson, "Milton," in *The Lives of the English Poets,* ed. George
Birkbeck Hill (1905; reprint, Hildesheim: Georg Olms Verlagsbuchhandlung,
1968), 1:100. Johnson continues: "[P]hysiological learning is of such rare emergence that one man may know another half his life without being able to esti-
mate his skill in hydrostaticks or astronomy, but his moral and prudential
character immediately appears." While Johnson's observation is true in a certain sense, one of the major arguments of this study is that "physiological learning" is, during this period, closely connected to understandings of "moral and
prudential character."

animated by, monsters and machines, it refuses to see such models as important in and of themselves; the eye and attention of the reader are always directed onward and elsewhere, away from mechanical and monstrous forms and towards a social problem that can be addressed and solved. Our inability to provide a "perfect and exact" description of the human body does not interfere with the functioning of that uncertain form in a community amenable to description, clarification, and improvement.

Even by the end of the eighteenth century no one had provided the "perfect and exact" definition of "man" that Locke had required a hundred years before. Instead, like all students at an impasse, his respondents rewrote the question. Ludmilla Jordanova has argued that, during the eighteenth and nineteenth centuries, "it was taken for granted that the human body was legible, even if there was no consensus on exactly how it could and should be 'read.'"[19] This statement should, I think, be even more heavily qualified: during the eighteenth century it was very much wished that the human body were legible, even though there was uncertainty about whether it actually was. Certainly, interest in physiognomy, a science that had for centuries claimed access to invisible human passions and motivations through exterior, physical, visible signs, intensified during this period.[20] Given that physiognomy had, during the Renaissance, become associated with astrology and black magic, its revival in the "Enlightenment" seems, initially, a little odd. Yet, as Douglas Lane Patey remarks, the science gained a good deal of notice and respect in the eighteenth century, attention he attributes to "new scientific grounding" (91). In this opinion other historians of physiognomy concur, telling us that physiognomy benefited from "the growth of empiricism in science and phi-

19. *Sexual Visions: Images of Gender in Science and Medicine between the Eighteenth and Twentieth Centuries* (Hemel Hempstead, Herts. Harvester Wheatsheaf, 1989), 51.
20. See Douglas Lane Patey, *Probability and Literary Form: Philosophic Theory and Literary Practice in the Augustan Age* (Cambridge: Cambridge University Press, 1984); Alan T. McKenzie, *Certain, Lively Episodes: The Articulation of Passion in Eighteenth-Century Prose* (Athens: University of Georgia Press, 1990); Michael Ketcham, *Transparent Designs: Reading, Performance, and Form in the* Spectator *Papers* (Athens: University of Georgia Press, 1987). See also Thomas R. Preston, "The 'Stage Passions' and Smollett's Characterization," *Studies in Philology* 71 (1974): 105–25.

losophy" and that "for the eighteenth-century man of taste and understanding, the pathetic style was a serious and satisfying means of painting the whole range of human passions in their general truth."[21] Given that we have just discussed how Descartes's *Passions of the Soul,* by amplifying the powers of the body machine, impaired the usefulness of the body in explanations of society, it is initially surprising to realize that this same work is a key text in the revival of physiognomy, a science that uses its interpretation of physical signs as the basis of social coherence.[22] Descartes's list of passions (astonishment, grief, anger, and so on) and their exterior signs—"actions of the eye and face, changing of colour, tremors, languor, laughter, tears, groans and sighs"—does not contain anything that had been ignored by ancient rhetoricians. What Descartes could offer, however, was greater interpretive assurance, and this by virtue of the very mechanism that, in another context, caused such problems. Even Henry More, whose early admiration of Descartes later soured, agreed that Descartes proved the value of the passions as "a most certain and solid Treasure of the Soul" because "there is not room for Deception in them."[23] Looked at in one way, Descartes brought the very existence of the soul into question; but looked at from a different perspective his work made it easier to connect the disposition of this (doubtful) soul to exterior, physical signs. Descartes validated the epistemology of spectatorship and increased the social significance of the human body. When his French students, men like Charles Le Brun, translated *The Passions of the Soul* into a series of aesthetic principles, the human body became methodized in a representational system which in turn became an important element in a wide range of cultural forms. In England, one might number among such forms the *Spectator* papers of Steele and Addison, the acting of David Garrick, and novels of Fielding and Smollett. In general, however,

21. Graeme Tytler, "Letters of Recommendation and False Vizors: Physiognomy in the Novels of Henry Fielding," *Eighteenth-Century Fiction* 2 (1990): 97; Brewster Rogerson, "The Art of Painting the Passions," *Journal of the History of Ideas* 14 (1953): 94.
22. As Richard W. F. Kroll points out, there is also an important seventeenth-century English tradition of physiognomy, independent of Descartes. See *The Material World* (Baltimore: Johns Hopkins University Press, 1991), 183–225.
23. *An Account of Virtue* (New York: Facsimile Text Society, 1930), 39.

novelists represent physiognomy as an unreliable science. Scenes in which rogues and villains simulate the signs of emotion, turning their bodies into living lies, are a regular occurrence in the eighteenth-century novel. Neither satire, which registers but dismisses the problem, nor physiognomy, which only seems to solve it, adequately brings together the physical form and social meaning of the human body.

During this period, the most innovative and ambitious rethinking of the human body is found in ideas of sensibility. Notions of sensibility dissolve the distinction between the physical form and the social meaning of the body. I would argue that doctrines of sensibility as they emerge in the late seventeenth and the first half of the eighteenth century are a concerted attempt both to acknowledge and supersede uncomfortable models of human physicality. The germ of sensibility is to be found in the intense desire of philosophers and men of letters to gain for moral feeling and passion the same epistemological centrality that empiricists had assigned to raw, physical sensation. The key tenets of sensibility—that the individual is a naturally sympathetic creature primed with social instinct, and that such sympathy is natural because it is a function of the human constitution, the human nervous system—elaborate a particular kind of response to empiricism and mechanism, one that understands and represents empirical philosophy as an essentially accurate but incomplete account of human sensation.[24] Propo-

24. R. S. Crane isolates "benevolence as feeling" as one of the major teachings of "numerous Anglican divines of the Latitudinarian tradition" in whose combined influence he sees "the key to the popular triumph of 'sentimentalism' toward 1750" ("Suggestions toward a Genealogy of the 'Man of Feeling,'" *English Literary History* 1 [1934]: 214, 207). Donald Greene argues that three of the four elements of sensibility isolated by Crane "were far from novel in the eighteenth century." Greene's focus is what he takes to be Crane's misunderstanding of eighteenth-century religion, and he does not offer an alternative genealogy for sensibility ("Latitudinarianism and Sensibility: The Genealogy of the 'Man of Feeling' Reconsidered," *Modern Philology* 75 [1977]: 160). G. S. Rousseau finds sensibility at the "very heart" of an eighteenth-century revolution in thought that owes a "superlative debt" to John Locke. He also ascribes critical importance to physiological texts, such as those by Thomas Willis, which attempted "to answer Cartesian science." Locating the soul in the brain, Willis allowed not only scientists but also philosophers to assume man's essentially nervous nature and develop an "integrated physiology of man" ("Nerves, Spirits, and Fibres: Towards Defining the Origins of Sensibility," in *Studies in*

nents of sensibility do see physical experience as foundational, but they refuse any attempt to interpret that experience in strictly physical terms. For them, physical experience is also social and moral experience. Bodies can never be mere bodies because what they feel, and the ways in which they react, always bear testimony to their implication in social and moral life. Those who thought out this particular version of human physicality instructed their readers in how to value it. They were, as we shall see, explicit about its social expediency, its usefulness in rendering the body both legible and controllable.

The filiation between empiricism and sensibility sketched out above can be translated into biographical terms. One of the first attempts to exploit the vocabulary and prestige of empiricism, while at the same time transmuting the physical sensation central to that philosophy into moral and social sense, was undertaken by a man whose early education had been supervised by John Locke: Anthony, third earl of Shaftesbury. In fact, it is to Shaftesbury that we owe the term "moral sense." His *Characteristicks* (1711), particularly that work's "Inquiry concerning Virtue and Merit," posits that our perception of moral qualities, the right and wrong of actions and dispositions, is as immediate as our perception of color or form. The work begun by Shaftesbury was carried on by his

the Eighteenth Century, vol. 3, ed. R. F. Brissenden and J. C. Eade [Toronto: University of Toronto Press, 1973], 141, 144, 150). From the mid-1740s on, the most advanced work on "integrated physiology" was carried out in Edinburgh by physiologists such as Robert Whytt. Christopher Lawrence has persuasively argued that "integration through feeling" is a common concept in "the Edinburgh theory of the body and the Edinburgh theory of social order" and that "physiological conceptions were sustained by social interests" ("The Nervous System and Society in the Scottish Enlightenment," in *Natural Order: Historical Studies of Scientific Culture,* ed. Barry Barnes and Steven Shapin [Beverly Hills: Sage Publications, 1978], 35). G. J. Barker-Benfield sees sensibility as the defining feature of eighteenth-century culture and attributes its rise to the advent of consumerism (*The Culture of Sensibility: Sex and Society in Eighteenth-Century Britain* [Chicago: University of Chicago Press, 1992]). Terry Eagleton ponders the "ambivalent" political implications of sensibility in *The Ideology of the Aesthetic* ([Oxford: Blackwell, 1990], 31–69). In thinking through Smollett's representations of the body I have been much helped by John Mullan's study of sensibility's ideological contradictions (*Sentiment and Sociability: The Language of Feeling in the Eighteenth Century* [Oxford: Clarendon Press, 1988]).

follower, Francis Hutcheson, professor of moral philosophy at Glasgow. Like Shaftesbury, Hutcheson assumes the validity of empirical philosophy, particularly the importance of physical sensation and the life of the body, but he clearly sees these as preliminary to a more complete understanding of how the body works. His *Essay on the Nature and Conduct of the Passions and Affections* (1728) takes empiricists to task and wishes "they had as carefully examin'd into the several kinds of *internal Perceptions,* as they have done into the *external Sensations:* that we might have seen whether the former be not as *natural* and *necessary* as the latter" (xi). Hutcheson accepts that external sensations are "natural and necessary." He has no wish to deny their importance, but, in fact, he uses the language of the senses and the authority of that language—its natural necessity—both to displace raw physicality and generate an idea of a virtuous, social body. According to Hutcheson, our senses and desires are fixed for us by the "Author of our Nature," and they are "subservient to the Interest of the System: so that each Individual is made, previously to his own choice, a Member of a *great body,* and affected with the Fortunes of the whole" (117). As Hutcheson defensively suggests, he sacrifices the physical to the metaphysical.

> It may perhaps seem too *metaphysical* to alledge on this Subject, that other *Sensations* are all dependent upon, or related by the Constitution of our Nature, to something different from our *selves;* to a *Body* which we do not call *Self,* but something belonging to this *Self.* That other *Perceptions* of *Joy* or *Pleasure* carry with them Relations to *Objects,* and *Spaces* distinct from this *Self;* whereas the Pleasures of Virtue are the very Perfection of this self and are immediately perceived as such, independent of external Objects. (159–60)

Locke says that all born into the world are "perpetually and diversly" affected by the bodies that surround them. This Hutcheson acknowledges when he speaks of our sensations as being dependent on "something different from our *selves.*" Overcoming our vulnerability to sensation, and limiting its importance, however, is explicitly part of Hutcheson's philosophic enterprise. That is how he comes to conceptualize the pleasures of "Virtue" as a respite from sensation, a "perfection" of the self that renders one "independent" of the external world.

Both Shaftesbury and Hutcheson use the physical experience of the body to sustain a particular view of society. Both acknowledge and supersede the importance of sensation. Nonetheless, while neither Hutcheson nor Shaftesbury would admit it, their arguments come perilously close to mere analogy. Their writings can seem merely to be using physicality to explain moral views, rather than demonstrating that the "moral" is just as natural and necessary as the other senses. From the 1740s on, however, followers of Shaftesbury and Hutcheson, eager to prove that the animal economy transcends mere matter, and that the body is inevitably motivated by moral principles, could rely on the impeccable support offered by experimental science. Surveying English physiology between 1730 and 1770, Theodore M. Brown has explained the "precipitous decline of varieties of mechanism and the rapid rise to preeminence of alternate varieties of vitalism" in terms both of changes in the social context of medical institutions and of a shift in the general intellectual climate.[25] Certainly, individual scientists were very much aware of the social implications of each theory.

One does not immediately perceive that the effect of opium on dismembered frogs has social ramifications, but in the hands of Robert Whytt, professor of medicine at the University of Edinburgh, such studies led to new perspectives on human physiology which in turn rehabilitated the body as a pattern of social order and coherence. Whytt's *Essay on the Vital and Other Involuntary Motions in Animals* was begun in 1744, but not published until 1751. Monsters, Whytt briskly reassures his reader, have no place in science: "No reasoning drawn from a few monstrous cases, can be sufficient to overthrow a doctrine founded upon the plainest phaenomena observed in perfect animals, and confirmed by almost numberless experiments made upon them" (8). Nor is Whytt perturbed by mechanism. He hesitates to call involuntary motions (for example, the beatings of the heart) "automatic" because the name might suggest "a mere inanimate machine," a notion of the animal frame "too low and absurd to be embraced" (2). Whytt's tone to-

25. "From Mechanism to Vitalism in Eighteenth-Century English Physiology," *Journal of the History of Biology* 7 (Fall 1974): 179.

wards his intellectual adversaries is one of condescending pity: he thinks it "really wonderful" to find Descartes and his disciples "so far imposing upon themselves, as seriously to believe [animals] were machines formed entirely of matter, and, as it were, so many curious pieces of clock-work warmed up and set a-going" (291). Whytt may patronize Descartes's peculiar notions, but he also knows exactly where those notions lead: "after once admitting all the actions of the most perfect brutes to result from mere mechanism, the ascribing everything in man to no higher a principle, would be a natural and easy consequence" (291). Several observations are to be made here: the first, that one hundred years after Descartes first adumbrates his understanding of human passions and physicality, his model is still current; the second, that to one of the major figures of the Scottish Enlightenment, that model is still subversive and provocative in the ways I have been describing. Whytt's answer to that provocation helps develop, and lend credence to, the emergent discourse of sensibility.

Ultimately, and this is where the dismembered frogs come in, Whytt concluded that "the vital, as well as the other involuntary motions of animals, are directly owing to the immediate energy of the mind or sentient principle" (268). Whytt's "sentient principle" unites the ancient "anima" and "animus," the faculty of sensation and that of reason. Immaterial as this principle is, it unites, enlivens, and actuates every fiber of the human frame. The attribution of the beatings of the heart, the lowering of the eyelids, the action of the diaphragm, to a single principle that animated and integrated the whole made it easier for thinkers who came after Whytt to argue that society, like the body, was united by a subtle, invisible force. Sympathy between body parts allowed the heart to affect the skin and the brain to affect the limbs, and, eventually, sympathy of exactly the same kind allowed individual bodies to affect one another, drawing isolated beings into a coherent, integrated society.

In traveling from John Locke to Robert Whytt, from the *Essay concerning Human Understanding* to *An Essay on the Vital and Other Involuntary Motions of Animals,* one moves through half a century in which the body is transformed from a monstrous to a social possibility. In the interval, philosophers not only shifted attention away from what the body is, to what it does, but they also

redefined the nature of physical experience, moving away from isolated discrete sensations—the relish of the pineapple and the
sound of the trumpet—and favoring instead the social integration
made possible by doctrines of sensibility. Once this shift was accomplished, the body was less likely to be a source of unease and
disruption, more likely to serve as the focus of a coherent, socially
constructive narrative.

One does not, however, have to examine texts scattered
across time to assess the breakage and remaking of the body in the
eighteenth century. In exemplary fashion David Hume's *Treatise of
Human Nature* unites both processes. The "breakage" of the body
first appears in Hume's work metaphorically, in an explanation of
his philosophical method. Significantly, Hume is explaining himself to Francis Hutcheson, who had favored Hume with remarks on
the latter's "Of Morals," the third, then unpublished, part of the
Treatise. Hutcheson's claim that the work lacked "Warmth in the
Cause of Virtue" stung Hume, who chose in his reply to represent
their differences through images of the body.

> There are different ways of examining the Mind as well
> as the Body. One may consider it either as an Anatomist
> or as a Painter; either to discover its most secret Springs
> & Principles or to describe the Grace & Beauty of its Ac-
> tions. I imagine it impossible to conjoin these two
> Views. Where you pull off the Skin, & display all the
> minute Parts, there appears something trivial, even in
> the noblest Attitudes & most vigorous Actions: Nor can
> you ever render the Object graceful or engaging but by
> cloathing the Parts again with Skin & Flesh, & present-
> ing only their bare Outside.[26]

Hume contests both the nature of metaphysics, and the nature of the metaphorical vehicle, the body, with the older philosopher. A metaphysician must either "pull off the Skin, & display all
the minute Parts," or "render the Object graceful or engaging."
What Hutcheson sees as "Warmth in the Cause of Virtue," Hume
suspects as a species of painterly pleasure, one that ignores fundamental physical truths to obtain aesthetic, and/or moral gratifica-

26. *The Letters of David Hume*, ed. J. Y. T. Greig (Oxford: Clarendon Press,
1932), 1:32–33.

tion. Hume's metaphors suggest that Hutcheson has "remade" the body, rendering it graceful and engaging, in order to support a particular understanding of virtue. As the letter continues, Hume tactfully indicates his unwillingness to follow that road and announces his divergence from the senior philosopher. The anatomist who unmakes the body to understand its "secret springs and actions" can never be united with the painter who remakes the body in a particular fashion and to a particular social end. Hume admits that "[a]n Anatomist . . . can give very good Advice to a Painter or Statuary: And in like manner, I am perswaded, that a Metaphysician may be very helpful to a Moralist; tho' I cannot easily conceive these two Characters united in the same Work" (33). The letter to Hutcheson echoes Hume's presentation throughout the *Treatise,* where he consistently uses metaphors of anatomy to describe his philosophical method. In "Of the Understanding," the first book of the *Treatise,* Hume performs an anatomy that separates and isolates the elements of consciousness. As anatomists undo the body, sacrificing a view of the whole so they can better understand a particular limb or muscle, so too does Hume's method, centered on individual perceptions, result in a loss of "self." "Of the Understanding" closes with the famous discussion of identity in which Hume denies any "simple and continu'd" principle that he can call "himself."[27]

In the first book of the *Treatise* the problematic status of the body is not a primary issue, and Hume invokes the deleterious effects of anatomy only to clarify a philosophical position. Whereas Locke, in his more skeptical moments, takes the body as his subject and speaks of humans as a "sort of Animal" that cannot be satisfactorily defined, Hume, although working in the same philosophical tradition, applies his skepticism to the concept of continuous consciousness, to human identity. The close of Book 1 is not, however, the final moment of the *Treatise.* Forced by his method to deny his own existence, Hume seeks more cheerful conclusions elsewhere. Book 3, "Of Morals," opens with the admission that, "[w]hen we leave our closet, and engage in the common affairs of life, its conclusions [those of abstruse reasoning] seem to vanish, like the phantoms of the night on the appearance of the morning" (455). In

27. *A Treatise of Human Nature,* ed. L. A. Selby-Bigge and revised by Peter H. Nidditch (Oxford: Clarendon Press, 1978), 252.

the remainder of the *Treatise*, ghouls and anatomies are banished as Hume, released from the night of abstruse reasoning, moves into the bright light of "common affairs." Having unmade "himself," Hume now puts a version of "himself" back together again. At this point he makes an important decision; his chosen act of repair requires that human bodies in society be certain objects: that is, that he replace his metaphorical breakage of the body with an act of making.

Hume resolves the problematic nature of the body by declaring that it is a social construction naturally constituted to a social end. The principles of necessity and sympathy ensure that the body is knowable. As we survey society, we see an "external performance" that has no merit. We spectators must be able to interpret the physical "signs and indications" of others if we are to reach the "springs and actions" of their minds. At this point Hume invokes the concept of necessity to facilitate the spectator in assigning motives to action. Even though necessity for Hume is not the "ultimate connexion" of cause and effect, the "constant union" provided by experience is efficient enough. Hume adamantly claims that "our actions have a constant union with our motives, tempers, and circumstances" (401). In fact, "[n]o union can be more constant and certain, than that of some actions with some motives and characters" (404). Hume can connect action and motive so decisively because he defines individuals by their social position: "Whether we consider mankind according to the difference of sexes, ages, governments, conditions, or methods of education; the same uniformity and regular operation of natural principles are discernible. Like causes still produce like effects; in the same manner as in the mutual action of the elements and powers of nature" (401). This determination is comprehensive; it extends even to the physical makeup and constitution of individuals. "The skin, pores, muscles, and nerves of a day-labourer are different from those of a man of quality: So are his sentiments, actions and manners. The different stations of life influence the whole fabric, external and internal; and these different stations arise necessarily, because uniformly, from the necessary and uniform principles of human nature" (402). Hume attributes to class position, "the different stations of life," the same type of power the twentieth century associates with genetic coding. No element of the body—skin, pores, muscles, or nerves—escapes the determinant of class. In Hume's view the body is literally a social construction; its very form and "fabric" is a product of social factors.

As the doctrine of "necessity" allowed Hume to insist on the knowability of internal motive from external action, so the doctrine of "sympathy," the ability of the mind to pass "easily from the idea of ourselves to that of any other object related to us" (340), transforms the flat surfaces of gestures and countenances into mirrored surfaces that "communicate meaning" to one another. Hume's sympathy, which has similarities with Whytt's "sentient principle," allows him to postulate that the relationship between people in society is one of physical response, even though, as in Whytt, the precise form of the stimulus may not be visible.

> [T]he minds of men are mirrors to one another, not only because they reflect each others emotions, but also because those rays of passions, sentiments and opinions may be often reverberated, and may decay away by insensible degrees. Thus the pleasure, which a rich man receives from his possessions, being thrown upon the beholder, causes a pleasure and esteem; which sentiments again, being perceiv'd and sympathiz'd with, encrease the pleasure of the possessor; and being once more reflected, become a new foundation for pleasure and esteem in the beholder. (365)

Once again, Hume's certainty about the body is derived from a certainty about class. His story of how bodies in society "perpetually and diversly" affect one another begins with the "pleasure, which a rich man receives from his possessions." This pleasure is "thrown upon" the beholder, who answers it by participation. The rich man can now sympathize with the beholder's passions (which are of course derived from the rich man himself), and so his own pleasure is increased. The beholder, in this scene, exists only to strengthen the rich man's self-esteem. Hume remakes the body, placing it in a series of tableaux where it serves particular class interests and maintains social cohesion and stability.

Hume's presentation of the body illuminates a major tension in the eighteenth-century novel. He chose to dissolve the problem of the body's epistemological status by arguing that class and social difference are the grounds on which we can sort and know the body. Our ability to tell bodies apart covers our inability to say what the body is. That social and physical difference are isomorphic is a position with which the early novel simultaneously flirted and quarreled. In fact, novelists such as Smollett and Burney often use explicit physicality to challenge forms of social distinction.

It might be argued that this chapter, in etching out thus broadly eighteenth-century representations of the body and physical experience, has collapsed distinctions between very different kinds of writing. Certainly, I do assume that medical and fictional writings shared, to at least some extent, the same audience. The validity of this assumption can be judged from a survey of eighteenth-century periodicals. Publications like the *Monthly Review*, begun by Ralph Griffith in 1749, or Smollett's *Critical Review*, begun in 1756, commonly abstracted technical scientific work, as well as providing assessments of, and extracts from, recent fiction. Writers like Whytt were seen as contributing to the same literary world that contained *Pamela* and *Joseph Andrews*. Such at least is the implication of the treatment Whytt's *Physiological Essays* received in the *Monthly Review* in 1756. Whytt had written the *Essays* in response to attacks on his earlier work by the German physiologist Albrecht von Haller. Whytt and Haller disagreed about which parts of the body were irritable and sensible and to what extent. The disagreement had important implications, for Haller's views supported confining "the soul" to the brain, whereas Whytt's ideas (as we have seen) allowed him to hold that the entire body was animated by an "immaterial principle." The rival physiologists fought over the body, organ by organ, Whytt taking exception to Haller's having allowed irritability to "the lacteal veins, mucous glands, and sinuses, and yet denied it wholly to the kidneys and ureters, and almost wholly to the arteries, veins and excretory ducts of the glands." The reader of the *Monthly Review* would know all this because the volume contained a fourteen-page abstract from Whytt's work, which concluded: "Should we have been thought to have allowed the subject too much room, we have only this apology to make, that as we are expected to give an account of whatever is most remarkable in the literary world, many of our readers may, possibly, think this controversy of no little importance."[28] Admittedly, the "possibly" is a shade defensive, and suggests that even the reviewer is daunted by the technicalities of the controversy on hand. The debate between the two doctors is, however, firmly represented as a remarkable event in the "literary world," exactly the kind of thing that the *Monthly Review* is "expected to give an account of." The evidence of the periodicals suggests that even readers who did not have a professional interest in medicine or philosophy might follow esoteric debates about the body and its interpretation.

Intellectually, we acknowledge that our sense of our bodies is modified by the categories through which we know them. The need to control how individuals understand their own physicality is a powerful, and surprisingly transparent, motive in eighteenth-century thought. By this I mean that the process is not a sinister operation of "power" in the Foucauldian sense, but one that writers will discuss matter-of-factly with their readers, explicitly drawing attention to the fact that some models of human physicality are more conducive to social order than others. Consider the conclusion of Robert Whytt's *Essay on the Vital and Other Involuntary Motions in Animals,* in which he explains the broad implications of his work to his readers:

> From what has been offered, then, in the preceding pages, it may appear, how unjustly the study of Medicine has been accused of leading men into Scepticism and irreligion. A little Philosophy may dispose some men to Atheism; but a more extensive knowledge of nature, will surely have the contrary effect. If the human frame is considered as a mere Corporeal system, which derives all its power and energy from matter and motion; it may, perhaps, be concluded, that the immense universe itself is destitute of any higher principle: but if, as we have endeavoured to show, the motions and actions of our small and inconsiderable bodies, are all to be referred to the active power of an immaterial principle, how much more necessary must it be, to acknowledge, as the Author, Sustainer, and Sovereign Ruler of the universal sys-

28. *Monthly Review* 14 (1756): 140.

tem, an incorporeal Nature everywhere and always present, of infinite power, wisdom, and goodness; who conducts the motions of the whole, by the most consummate and unerring reason, without being prompted to it by any other impulse, than the original and eternal benevolence of his nature. (391–92)

Whytt freely acknowledges that his version of our "small and inconsiderable" bodies is intended to sustain belief in the "active power of an immaterial principle." Through his experiments and scientific writing he has "endeavoured to show" that our physical experience is to be referred to the "Author, Sustainer, and Sovereign Ruler of the universal system." Both Whytt's "justly favourite method of experiment" and the piety of his final paragraph are applauded by the reviewer of the *Monthly*—who quotes the conclusion in full.[29]

A number of years later, Tobias Smollett came to review similar experimental work by Whytt, this time presented in a collection, *Essays and Observations, Physical and Literary* (Edinburgh, 1756).[30] Although Smollett found the collection as a whole "valuable" and praised the authors for exerting their talents "in those pursuits which tend to the ease, convenience, and real advantage of their fellow creatures," he excoriates Whytt's contribution.

> The twentieth article is filled with the account of such barbarities, as must fill every humane reader with horror. Such as opening animals alive, plucking out their hearts, pinching and burning their spinal marrow, poisoning them with glysters, injections, etc. in order to ascertain the *modus operandi* of opium; and what benefit has mankind reaped from all this cruelty and torture inflicted upon our fellow creatures? We knew the effects of opium before, and now we guess how opium produces these effects. We find that the heart of an animal torn or cut from its situation in the thorax, and im-

29. *Monthly Review* 6 (1752): 466.
30. My attention was drawn to this review by James Basker's discussion of it in his *Tobias Smollett: Critic and Journalist* (Newark: University of Delaware Press, 1988), 121. My discussion of the *Critical Review* is generally indebted to James Basker's scholarship, in particular to his attributions (229–78).

mersed in a solution of opium, does not continue to beat so long, as the heart of an animal plucked from its bosom and laid upon a plate, without immersion in a solution of opium . . . From these and other experiments Dr. Whytt infers, that the effects of opium are not owing as some have thought to its producing sleep; on the contrary, the sleep which it occasions, seems to be only a consequence of its impairing the sensibility of the whole nervous system. Is this really a discovery? Or, supposing it to be a discovery is it of consequence enough to justify such a series of cruel executions, as one would be apt to imagine, must destroy the humanity and tenderness of heart by which every physician ought to be distinguished?[31]

Others might praise Whytt for replacing theoretical speculation on monsters and machines with experiments whose results supported social cohesion. Smollett considers the situation differently. What good is establishing the "original and eternal benevolence" of God, if the proof injures the "humanity and tenderness" of the scientist? This review is also instructive because it reminds us that the savagery of Smollett's prose is intimately connected to its humanity. He tells us about the plucking, pinching, and burning because he wants us to understand that the process of "discovery" is also one of "cruelty and torture."

Smollett's review of Whytt's experimental work exemplifies an important aspect of his writing, the way in which his appeals to the "humane reader" are often cast in horrendous prose. For Smollett, to be humane is to respect the physical experience of one's "fellow creatures"; it requires that one recognize and reject cruel, barbarous, and savage practices. Only the demonstration of cruelty will cause this recognition and rejection to occur, because the reader has to be convinced by Smollett's judgment. I am thinking here, in particular, of Smollett's denunciation of the execution of Robert Damiens, the French regicide, as "shameful to humanity,"[32] and his condemnation of the "circumstances of barbarity" under which the rebels of the Forty-five were executed.[33] Smollett

31. *Critical Review* 1 (1756): 414–15.
32. *A Continuation of the Complete History of England,* 1:248.
33. *Present State,* 2:175.

makes these judgments at a time when such "barbarity" was regarded by many as a legitimate exercise of state power. He writes in
the knowledge that not only the definition of human bodies, but the
definition of what is owing to bodies—humanity—is uncertain and
contested.

Locke's statement that "these Boundaries of *Species,* are as
Men, and not as Nature makes them" introduces the possibility that
human bodies are cultural constructs. What passes as a body is a
matter of common consent, not a natural fact. The apprehension
and representation of bodies depends upon social and political de-
terminants. These, of course, vary according to time and place. The
boundaries shift. Our sense of what bodies are, and what is owing to
them, is not identical with Smollett's, although it may coincide with
his. Reading the body in Smollett, we identify and withdraw, we
recognize and reject.

We find this same process embedded in Smollett's *Travels
through France and Italy.* This text's reading of foreign bodies involves familiarity and estrangement. As a sturdy, independent-
minded Briton traveling in Europe soon after the cessation of the
Seven Years' War, the narrator wants to emphasize the differences
between British deportment and Continental manners. To this end,
he emphasizes the importance of national customs. The danger
here is that belief in the determining power of custom, if pushed far
enough, undermines the idea of a natural physicality that, existing
across cultures, transcends social differences, making foreign
bodies legible to one another and allowing moral claims on behalf of
human materiality. One of Smollett's major preoccupations in the
Travels is to explicate the cultural differences between bodies
without sacrificing some notion of their fundamental uniformity,
their humanity. Smollett's desire to understand human materiality
as independent of national culture leads not only to some of the dis-
missive, prescriptive writing in the *Travels* but also to some of its
most impressive and passionate interludes. To consider the
eighteenth-century body is to enter another cultural context. We
cross a boundary. Our predicament, as readers of Smollett, resembles that of the *Travels'* narrator: we want to understand what we
find, but we do not always like it. The *Travels* allows us to read
Smollett reading the body. It is an ideal place to begin.

CHAPTER TWO

"MATTER OUT OF PLACE":
TRAVELS THROUGH FRANCE AND ITALY

We are left with the old definition of dirt as matter out of place. This is a very suggestive approach. It implies two conditions: a set of ordered relations and a contravention of that order. Dirt then, is never a unique, isolated event.

Mary Douglas, Purity and Danger

In Tobias Smollett's *Travels through France and Italy* dirt is the most regular of events. The narrator's intense awareness of dirt suggests, if we adopt the definition above by Mary Douglas, that the *Travels* is also a text concerned with the contravention of ordered relations. The narrator who cannot sleep at night for the filth of his surroundings is uneasy because his sense of order has been violated. He talks so much about dirt because he is concerned about how matter is regulated. Of course, as a stranger in a foreign land the "matter" most obviously "out of place" is the narrator himself. Dirt, in the *Travels,* is the manifestation through which the narrator confronts his own sense of dislocation and bewilderment. The narrator's sensitivity to dirt signals his awareness of bodies organized in a different system and governed by a different decorum, and his inability to accept this bodily difference fully. Dirt is also, as the history of criticism testifies, a problem for Smollett's readers. As the dirtiest, and most rebarbative, of his texts, the *Travels* allows us to explore cultural variations—between Smollett and the bodies he reads, between the twentieth-century reader and Smollett —in the ordered relations that govern the body.

At one particularly "dismal and dirty" inn near Arezzo, the
narrator of the *Travels,* having confronted "bed-cloaths filthy
enough to turn the stomach of a muleteer" and "victuals cooked in
such a manner, that even a Hottentot could not have beheld them
without loathing," takes elaborate precautions when the time
comes for sleep: "We had sheets of our own, which were spread
upon a mattrass, and here I took my repose wrapped in a great-coat,
if that could be called repose which was interrupted by the innumerable stings of vermin" (298). The narrator's elaborate—and
futile—attempts to shield himself from his nauseating surroundings, the careful placement of the sheets, the dogged effort to sleep
in his overcoat, only make the cause of his disgust more potent in
his reader's mind. So we too experience repugnance, not from some
long-harmless Italian vermin, but from the text. The more layers
the narrator places between his own body and the sordid cause of
offense, the more often he hops out of bed to escape insects, the
more intensely the reader associates him with the causes of his distress, and the more powerfully his abhorrence redounds upon him.

Bodily discomfort and unease are major themes in the
Travels, but literary representations of distress do not elicit predictable responses. Will we, like some nineteenth-century readers
of the *Travels,* be disgusted?[1] Do we castigate the narrator for his
casual assumptions about muleteers and Hottentots and deny the
sympathy for which he is angling? What name do we attach to this
body? Laurence Sterne says the body is Smollett's own, but that
such monstrous, diseased physicality requires a more suggestive
name: Smelfungus.[2] John F. Sena and R. D. Spector defend Smollett
by removing him from the scene; the body in question is not his but
that of a persona.[3]

Scenes like that in Arezzo call forth multiple interpretations
because in them the narrator is goaded not only by insects but by

1. Leigh Hunt said that the *Travels* "disgusted me, as they have some
others" (quoted by Felsenstein, *Travels,* lxiii).

2. *A Sentimental Journey,* ed. Ian Jack (Oxford: Oxford University Press,
1991), 29.

3. John F. Sena, "Smollett's Persona and the Melancholic Traveler: An Hy-
pothesis," *Eighteenth-Century Studies* 1 (1969): 353–69; R. D. Spector,
"Smollett's Traveler," in *Tobias Smollett: Bicentennial Essays Presented to
Lewis M. Knapp,* ed. P.-G. Boucé and G. S. Rousseau (New York: Oxford University Press, 1971), 231–46.

cultural difference. That is why he understands dirt, matter out of place, through the concepts of nature and custom.

> If there is no cleanliness among these people, much less shall we find delicacy, which is the cleanliness of the mind. Indeed they are utter strangers to what we call common decency; and I could give you some high-flavoured instances, at which even a native of Edinburgh would stop his nose. There are certain mortifying views of human nature, which undoubtedly ought to be concealed as much as possible, in order to prevent giving offence: and nothing can be more absurd, than to plead the difference of custom in different countries, in defence of those usages which cannot fail giving disgust to the organs and senses of all mankind . . . There is nothing so vile or repugnant to nature, but you may plead prescription for it, in the customs of some nation or other. (33–34)

Smollett's *Travels* concealed nothing, repeatedly offered mortifying views, gave disgust to many readers, and so dramatically offended the residents of Nice that it was said "[t]he People would rise upon him and stone him in the Streets on his first Appearance."[4] A fine instance of a writer digging a pit to bury himself in, passages like the above also reveal Smollett's belief that one can, despite differences, make some statements about the body with certainty; there are some usages that "cannot fail giving disgust to the organs and senses of all mankind." Nor does it take the reader long to register that this is a belief on Smollett's part, rather than a clearly argued position, for no sooner has he asserted that the senses operate in the same way across cultures than he has to concede that custom modifies nature; in fact, custom can so alter sensory experience that the natural being is lost. Organs and senses can be so perverted that individuals experience as natural sensations that are "vile or repugnant."[5] Nonetheless, having run through some of the off-

4. *New Letters of David Hume,* ed. R. Klibansky and E. C. Mossner (Oxford: Oxford University Press, 1954), 173. Hume had assisted Smollett's effort to gain a consulship in a warm climate.
5. In *Humphry Clinker* Matthew Bramble expresses the same view, saying of those who prefer the "adulterate enjoyments of the town," "their very organs of

putting practices enjoyed by a variety of the world's inhabitants,
Smollett does not retract his belief that certain things are univer-
sally disgusting. This stubbornly confused passage is a salutary one
for a critic absorbed by Smollett's recognition of human materiality. How can one do justice to Smollett's insights and moral passion without holding—along with him and despite all the evidence
—to some transcendent, universal truth of the body? We can only
proceed with determined caution, constantly refreshing our awareness that bodies are never independent of the contexts in which
they are found, be those contexts temporal or spatial.

     Its first reviewers welcomed the *Travels* as a book that "grati-
fied rational curiosity" and was structured according to "an ethic-
plan" "tending to introduce and improve our acquaintance with
men and things; to display a comparative sketch of human nature,
and to establish true notions of life and living."[6] In short, the
Travels was an Enlightenment text that digested and made available information, introduced British readers to scenes and lands
they had not directly experienced, and by dint of comparing nations enriched the reader's understanding of human nature. There
was also a general sense in early reviews that comparative sketches
achieved their proper end in this book by proffering such views "as
must endear England to Englishmen."[7] Even the first reviewers of
the *Travels* realized, however, that Smollett's approach to "true notions of life and living" concerned itself with particulars others left
unremarked. At one point, the reviewer for the *Critical,* no longer
calmly benefiting from Smollett's "ethic-plan," begins to feel no
little concern "lest he [the narrator] should either be assassinated,
or starved by the unwholesomeness of the provision he meets with;
but above all, lest his neck should be broken by the awkwardness
and insufficiency of his carriages."[8] The reviewer's mock sympathy
gently suggests that, while this intelligent book gratifies curiosity,
it also articulates much that, revealing vulnerability and improp-

---

sense are perverted, and they become habitually lost to every relish of what is
genuine and excellent in its own nature" (118).
     6. *Critical Review* 21 (1766): 322. While Smollett's own journal might be
expected to praise his work, the rival *Monthly* also admired the *Travels* as the
"work of a man of genius and learning" (34 [1766]: 429).
     7. *Critical Review* 22 (1766): 406.
     8. Ibid., 403.

erly soliciting concern, could have gone unsaid. The *Travels* is Smollett's most notorious account of the body abroad in the world, and its insistent materiality caused it to be parodied, mocked, and dismissed by influential contemporaries. It is true that the narrator of the *Travels* is very attentive to his own needs, and that the circumstantial details of his physical state are sometimes oppressive; but it is also true that this obsession with physical detail is simultaneously the narrator's way out of self-involvement.

In June 1763 Smollett, who had recently suffered the loss of his only child and was upset by the failure of the *Briton* (a periodical he had run in defense of the Bute ministry), left England in search of health. On his return, two years later, he recast his travel notes and letters into the epistolary *Travels* (1766). During the time he spent abroad, Smollett was a sick man. The first paragraph of the work mentions its author's "distemper and disquiet" (2). The third letter begins by thanking his correspondent for enquiring after his health and then offers a list of his present symptoms: violent cough, fever, stitches in the breast, discharge by expectoration, lowness of spirits (13). The Italian expedition is summarized as one in which the narrator was exposed to "a great number of hardships," which served to "brace up the relaxed constitution, and promote a more vigorous circulation of the juices" (309). In the final letter, he confides he had thought his health restored, "but betwixt Fontainbleau and Paris, we were overtaken by a black storm of rain, sleet, and hail . . . there was no resisting this attack. I caught cold immediately" (345).

It is the suffering body of the narrator that caused the *Travels,* initially well received, to be discredited. Once Laurence Sterne published *A Sentimental Journey,* the materiality of the *Travels* appeared merely self-regarding and solipsistic.

> The learned Smelfungus travelled from Boulogne to Paris—from Paris to Rome—and so on—but he set out with the spleen and jaundice, and every object he pass'd by was discoloured or distorted—He wrote an account of them, but 'twas nothing but the account of his miserable feelings.
>
> I met Smelfungus in the grand portico of the Pantheon—he was just coming out of it—*'Tis nothing but a huge cock-pit,* said he—I wish you had said noth-

ing worse of the Venus of Medicis, replied I—for in pass-
ing through Florence, I had heard he had fallen foul
upon the goddess, and used her worse than a common
strumpet, without the least provocation in nature.[9]
I popp'd upon Smelfungus again at Turin, in his return home; and a sad tale of sorrowful adventures had
he to tell, "wherein he spoke of moving accidents by
flood and field, and of the cannibals which each other
eat: the Anthropophagi"—he had been flea'd alive, and
bedevil'd, and used worse than St. Bartholomew, at every stage he had come at—
—I'll tell it, cried Smelfungus, to the world. You had
better tell it, said I, to your physician. (28–29)

It is a brilliant stroke of parody for Sterne to put Othello's words in
Smollett's mouth, for the latter does indeed seem to consider
French and Italian innkeepers as cannibals and anthropophagi who
intend to first starve and then fleece him. In a typical episode
Smollett, not inclined to eat the meatless fare offered on a day of
abstinence, is "obliged to quarrel with the landlady"; rejecting eggs
and vegetables, he insists "upon a leg of mutton, and a brace of fine
partridges, which I found in the larder" (109). So regular are
Smollett's altercations with innkeepers that Philip Thicknesse re-
named his book *Quarrels through France and Italy.*

In Sterne's view, Smollett's *Travels* are literally, and at every
level, pathological. They are the fruit of a diseased body, concerned
only with itself. Smollett may travel through France and Italy, but
his true subject is his own, miserable body. This book requires not
so much a reading, as a diagnosis. Sterne's parody is made all the
more pointed by the fact that Smollett's *Travels* do contain an epis-

9. "I cannot help thinking that there is no beauty in the features of Venus;
and that the attitude is aukward and out of character . . . Without all doubt, the
limbs and proportions of this stature are elegantly formed, and accurately designed, according to the nicest rules of symmetry and proportion; and the back
parts especially are executed so happily, as to excite the admiration of the most
indifferent spectator" (*Travels,* 236). It is worth remarking, given our earlier
consideration of custom and nature in the *Travels,* that Smollett, in his discussion of the Venus, rejects as "a bad plea" the notion that "the antients and we
differ in the ideas of beauty."

tolary medical consultation. While at Montpellier, Smollett indited an account of his health (in Latin) and sent it to Antoine Fizes, professor of medicine. So disgusted was Smollett by Fizes's negligent reply (in French) that he wrote back, pointing out the "passages in my case which he had overlooked" (100). Telling it to his physician was the least of what Smollett was prepared to do.

Subsequent criticism shows that Sterne's view of *Travels* was decisive and long-lived.[10] In response, twentieth-century admirers of the work have tended to minimize its immediacy, its direct account of bodily experience, in order to discover and elaborate some "artistry" on Smollett's part. Rather than accept the "seemingly personal letters" that constitute the *Travels* as Smollett's own view of the Continent, and conclude that the author "is indeed a confirmed misanthrope and an insufferable hypochondriac," John F. Sena suggests that the narrator of the letters is a "splenetic or melancholic" persona deliberately adopted by Smollett so as to employ "contemporary medicine for artistic purposes" (354, 369). R. D. Spector takes these ideas further, saying that the persona serves the overall didactic purpose of the book: to teach Britons how to travel abroad, warning them "not to be taken in by foreign practices and foreign affectation" (238).[11] So Smollett's modern admirers protect him from Sterne's criticism, arguing that the materiality of the *Travels* serves artistic and didactic purposes. Despite their opposition, Sterne and his modern critics agree in their definitions of the narrator's materiality. All of them criticize or explain the body in terms of illness, discomfort, dirt, and stomach-churning adventures at inns. While these are obvious elements in the *Travels*,

10. "Smollett never manages to see beyond the reality he abhorred . . . he treats France with the attitude of the surgeon he was, as if he were in front of a gangrenous limb" (Frédéric Ogée, "Channelling Emotions: Travel and Literary Creation in Smollett and Sterne," *Studies on Voltaire and the Eighteenth Century* 292 [1991]: 38).

11. Both of these readings have some validity, but they are overly schematic and require the reader to overlook significant elements of the *Travels*. Sena's argument is weakened by the fact that large chunks of the work—the account of silkworms or the register or the weather at Nice—are not narrated by the kind of persona he describes. Similarly, while many of the comparisons within the *Travels* do favor British institutions and achievements, the *Travels* is also alive, in ways Spector does not recognize, to the sensual delights of life abroad.

other no less obvious elements of the narrator's physicality have
been excluded from discussion. The literary history of the *Travels*
shows how selective and partial readings of the body are.

The *Travels* is a sensual book that attempts to anatomize sensation and to describe the narrator's delight in the scents and color
of an unfamiliar landscape.

> When I stand upon the rampart, and look round me, I
> can scarce help thinking myself inchanted. The small
> extent of country which I see, is all cultivated like a gar-
> den. Indeed, the plain presents nothing but gardens, full
> of green trees, loaded with oranges, lemons, citrons, and
> bergamots, which make a delightful appearance. If you
> examine them more nearly, you will find plantations of
> green pease ready to gather; all sorts of sallading, and
> pot-herbs, in perfection; and plats of roses, carnations,
> ranunculas, anemonies, and daffodils, blowing in full
> glory, with such beauty, vigour, and perfume, as no
> flower in England ever exhibited. (121)

Reading the *Travels,* one feels Smollett's desire to convey the pleasures of bodily experience in a new and different climate. For example, some of the most enjoyable passages of the book occur when he
tries to impart the taste of exotic foods like eggplant or watermelon
to his English readers: "From Antibes and Sardinia, we have another fruit called a water-melon, which is well known in Jamaica,
and some of our other colonies. Those from Antibes are about the
size of an ordinary bomb-shell: but the Sardinian and Jamaica
water-melons are four times as large. The skin is green, smooth, and
thin. The inside is a purple pulp, studded with broad, flat, black
seeds, and impregnated with a juice the most cool, delicate, and refreshing, that can well be conceived" (167). A good deal has been
written about the unpalatable descriptions in the *Travels,* but little
recognition has been paid to this closely related feature of the work:
its attempt to do the impossible, to translate pleasurable sensation
into language, so that the experience can be shared.

The optimistic writings of moral-sense philosophers like
Hutcheson emphasize the immediacy of sensation and base a social
theory upon it. Commentators, even as they critique such notions,
enjoy choosing explanatory relishes: moral-sense philosophy holds

that the values that govern social life are "as self-evident as the taste of peaches," or "the taste of sherry," and have as little to do with reason as "the smell of thyme or the taste of potatoes."[12] Immediacy is not, however, all. Sensation entails isolation, and brings on "solipsistic unease":[13] "*Light,* and *Colours,* are busie at hand every where, when the Eye is but open; *Sounds,* and some *tangible Qualities* fail not to solicite their proper Senses, and force an entrance to the Mind; but yet, I think, it will be granted easily, That if a Child were kept in a place, where he never saw any other but Black and White, till he were a Man, he would have no more *Ideas* of Scarlet or Green, than he that from his Childhood never tasted an Oyster, or a Pine-Apple, has of those particular Relishes."[14] That Locke's little puzzle has a spatial dimension—his hypothetical child is "kept in a place, where he never saw any other but Black and White"—is in keeping with the *Essay*'s recurring images of enclosure and containment. The understanding is "not much unlike a Closet wholly shut from light" (163); it is as a "worm shut up in one drawer of a Cabinet" (120). Locke's localization of sensation is revealing, because it demonstrates how the immediacy of sensation is linked to limitation. Smollett's accretion of physical detail attempts to overcome limitation, to breach the barriers between individual understandings. At such moments, he treats his reader, not as a complacent and hygienic Briton, but as a version of Locke's child, ignorant of watermelons and flowers with "such beauty, vigour, and perfume, as no flower in England ever exhibited" (121). Smollett, in Arezzo, wrapping his body again and again so as to escape insect bites and contamination, provides a graphic image of his desire to maintain his insularity, but the *Travels* consists of more than confrontations with the French or Italian "other" against whose inferiority the Briton defines himself. It also involves the more subtle feat of recreating that moment when the body itself becomes other and foreign, when it incorporates through sight and taste elements previously unknown.

12. This attractive, and nutritious, selection is made by Terry Eagleton, *Ideology of the Aesthetic,* 34, 38, 14.

13. The phrase is that of A. D. Nuttall, who considers this aspect of seventeenth- and eighteenth-century thought in his *Common Sky: Philosophy and the Literary Imagination* (London: Chatto and Windus, 1974).

14. Locke, *Essay concerning Human Understanding,* 106–7.

In the *Travels* Smollett is concerned not only to give account
of his own physical experiences, but to read the bodies of others. In
this respect the *Travels* resembles Smollett's fiction, where the
notion that bodies can be sorted according to class is regularly dis-
proved. Smollett's views on how bodies are determined are superficially similar to those of his contemporary David Hume, and at
several junctures in the *Travels* one is reminded of Hume's assertion that "the different stations of life influence the whole fabric,
external and internal."[15] When one considers the issues involved
more precisely, however, there are distinct differences in emphasis
between the two writers. In 1748 Hume's "Of National Characters"
categorized the moral and physical factors that accounted for national differences.

> By *moral* causes, I mean all circumstances, which are
> fitted to work on the mind as motives or reasons, and
> which render a peculiar set of manners habitual to us.
> Of this kind are, the nature of the government, the revo-
> lutions of public affairs, the plenty or penury in which
> the people live, the situation of the nation with regard
> to its neighbours, and such like circumstances. By
> *physical* causes I mean those qualities of the air and cli-
> mate, which are supposed to work insensibly on the
> temper, by altering the tone and habit of the body, and
> giving a particular complexion, which, though reflec-
> tion and reason may sometimes overcome it, will yet
> prevail among the generality of mankind, and have an
> influence on their manners.[16]

What is striking, when one looks at the *Travels* with this list in
mind, is the amount of attention Smollett pays to one of Hume's
moral causes: "the plenty or penury in which the people live." The
Travels is remarkable for the detail and attention with which it regards the bodies of working people, bodies that are often simply
edited out of eighteenth-century accounts of society.

> The common people here, as in all countries where
> they live poorly and dirtily, are hard-featured, and of

15. *Treatise of Human Nature,* 402.
16. "Of National Characters," in *Essays Moral, Political, and Literary,* ed.
Eugene F. Miller (Indianapolis: Liberty Classics, 1987), 198.

very brown, or rather tawny complexions. As they seldom eat meat, their juices are destitute of that animal
oil which gives a plumpness and smoothness to the
skin, and defends those fine capillaries from the injuries of the weather, which would otherwise coalesce, or
be shrunk up, so as to impede the circulation on the external surface of the body. As for the dirt, it undoubt-
edly blocks up the pores of the skin, and disorders the
perspiration; consequently must contribute to the
scurvy, itch, and other cutaneous distempers. (40)

At times, Smollett's deterministic view of human physicality leads
to reckless, reductive (and often uncomplimentary) generaliza-
tions about the bodies he encounters: "I have likewise observed,
that most of the females are pot-bellied; a circumstance owing, I believe, to the great quantity of vegetable trash which they eat. All the
horses, mules, asses, and cattle, which feed upon grass, have the
same distension" (154). When Smollett compares women's bodies
to those of horses, mules, and asses, few readers are likely to be impressed by either his scientific acumen or his decorum. Nonetheless, the kind of thinking that here seems faintly comic can appear a
good deal more sympathetic in other formulations. Smollett asserts
that the laboring people of Nice are "diminutive, meagre, withered,
dirty and half naked," but he reads these characteristics as "the
outward signs of extreme misery." Like the pot-bellied women,
these individuals are determined by what they eat, and Smollett is
as circumstantial about the details of their material existence as he
is elsewhere: "The nourishment of those poor creatures consists of
the refuse of the garden, very coarse bread, a kind of meal called
polenta, made of Indian corn, which is very nourishing and agreeable, and a little oil: but even in these particulars, they seem to be
stinted to very scanty meals" (173).

Despite the Enlightenment confidence with which Smollett
ranges bodies into classes, explaining the factors that determine
their physical appearance, episodes on the road suggest that the
body is not so easily legible as all that. In Champagne, Smollett,
provoked by the information that a traveler who arrived later at the
post is being provided first with horses, goes up to the man he takes
to be postmaster and reads him articles from the postbook with
"great vociferation" (69). The narrative continues at the next inn

on the road, where Smollett first upbraids and then rebuffs the stranger whom he still takes for an innkeeper, only to discover subsequently that he is a nobleman. Acknowledging that the incident will only "confirm the national reproach of bluntness, and ill breeding" under which the English lie in France, Smollett continues defensively: "The truth is, I was that day more than usually peevish, from the bad weather, as well as from the dread of a fit of the asthma, with which I was threatened: and I dare say my appearance seemed as uncouth to him, as his travelling dress appeared to me. I had a grey mourning frock under a wide great coat, a bob wig without powder, a very large laced hat, and a meagre, wrinkled, discontented countenance" (70). The signifiers of class position are not universal, nor are they foolproof. Bodies are determined by so many factors that the end result may be illegible: English and French gentlemen do not necessarily recognize each other as such. Then, as Smollett's self-deprecatory description also recognizes, sometimes individual features are more remarkable than those of class. When the gentleman of Auxerre confronted Tobias Smollett, what did he make of his "meagre, wrinkled, discontented countenance"?

Not all bodies, however, were bundles of signs to be interpreted. In his *Commentaries on the Laws of England,* Blackstone tells us that, as a master is in some cases answerable for his servant's misbehavior, he is legally justified in using, within reasonable bounds, the power of correction.[17] Such a legitimization (which also applied to the correction of wives) makes us see the domestic realm as one that mediates between the individual and the state. The master assumes responsibility for another body and is therefore entitled to exercise restraint upon it. Smollett, in the *Travels,* physically chastises servants. When a guide gave him advice he didn't like, "I collared him with one hand, and shook my cane over his head with the other. It was the only weapon I had, either offensive or defensive; for I had left my sword, and musquetoon in the coach" (300). E. P. Thompson has made us familiar with the notion that social structures in England in the eighteenth century were kept in place by a continuing theatrical style comprising "gestures

17. William Blackstone, *Commentaries on the Laws of England* (Oxford, 1765), 1:432.

and posture."[18] Our initial reaction to Smollett's action is that we are witnessing farce. Had he been better supplied, would Smollett have shaken both sword and musquetoon over the servant's head? That the servant understands the action to be purely symbolic is shown by his continuing, despite the threats, to crack "severe jokes" at the narrator's expense. Smollett's attempts at chastising servants always seem slightly ridiculous or belated in the *Travels,* but he never expresses any abhorrence of the custom. Indeed, in one passage he seems surprised that a servant might take it amiss: "An English gentleman at Florence told me, that one of those fellows [a postilion], whom he had struck for his impertinence, flew at him with a long knife, and he could hardly keep him at sword's point. All of them wear such knives, and are very apt to use them on the slightest provocation" (243). Implicit in this little bit of hearsay is the understanding that striking a servant for impertinence is entirely natural; having a servant fight back is not. Such, of course, was the understanding sanctioned by English law. What is owing to bodies varies according to their class; not every person enjoys precisely the same rights. I dwell on these incidents from the *Travels* because they help refute a possible misinterpretation of my major argument. When I say that apprehension of bodily materiality and feeling is the root of Smollett's social and political criticism, I do not mean that his respect for the body can be ahistorically identified with our own. Smollett's sense of what is allowable will occasionally make his readers uneasy, but that does not alter the fact that much of his writing is shaped, and given point, by his moral sense of what is owing to bodies.

In the *Travels,* for the most part, Smollett describes bodies out and about, working at inns or in the fields, promenading in the towns; or he considers representations of the human form in various collections of art. Yet other forms of spectatorship described in the *Travels* remind us how historically specific are the ways bodies occupy space. Smollett's visit to a Parisian orphanage and his boarding of a Sardinian galley manned by prisoners involve a dynamic of exposure and spectatorship that is also important within eighteenth-century fiction. We think of Mackenzie's man of feeling

18. "Patrician Society, Plebeian Culture," *Journal of Social History* 7 (1974): 390.

visiting Bedlam, one of the "Sights in London, which every stranger
is supposed desirous to see," or of Richardson's Clarissa, recalling a
visit to Bedlam, and begging Lovelace that in her own distress and
insanity she not "be made a show of."[19] The details of Smollett's
visit to the galley reveal the distinct economy and degree of ritual of
such "shows": "When you enter by the stern, you are welcomed by
a band of musick selected from the slaves; and these expect a gratification" (130). The visit also becomes a contemplation on the legitimacy of different modes of physical punishment.

> I went on board one of these vessels, and saw about two
> hundred miserable wretches, chained to the banks on
> which they sit and row, when the galley is at sea. This is
> a sight which a British subject, sensible of the blessing
> he enjoys, cannot behold without horror and compas-
> sion. Not but that if we consider the nature of the case,
> with coolness and deliberation, we must acknowledge
> the justice, and even sagacity, of employing for the ser-
> vice of the public, those malefactors who have forfeited
> their title to the privileges of the community . . . It is a
> great pity, however, and a manifest outrage against the
> law of nations, as well as of humanity, to mix with those
> banditti, the Moorish and Turkish prisoners who are
> taken in the prosecution of open war. It is certainly no
> justification of this barbarous practice, that the Chris-
> tian prisoners are treated as cruelly at Tunis and Al-
> giers. (128–29)

The passage continues with Smollett describing in detail the physical conditions on the galleys: where the men sleep, what they eat,
how they wash. The accretion of disgusting physical detail here
serves to support Smollett's social criticism; he wants his reader to
know the severities that must "shock humanity" (130).

The passage demands a complexity of response from the
modern reader. We note quickly enough that Smollett uses the
physical experiences of the galley slaves as the basis of a moral argument, in which he denounces the cruelty of their treatment as

19. Henry Mackenzie, *The Man of Feeling,* ed. Kenneth C. Slagle (New York:
Norton, 1958), 19; Samuel Richardson, *Clarissa, or The History of a Young
Lady,* ed. Angus Ross (Harmondsworth: Penguin, 1985), 895.

being against the "law of humanity." Even as we respond to Smollett's anger, however, we are aware that the "law of humanity" takes different forms at different moments. To many twentieth-century readers the exposure of the slaves to the eye of the tourist (however compassionate and humane) is an infringement of the same law of humanity to which Smollett appeals. There is, then, no simple identity between eighteenth- and twentieth-century understandings of what is owing to bodies, but our awareness of this difference does not invalidate either Smollett's argument on behalf of the galley slaves or our attempt to understand it.

The *Travels* negotiates between routine Enlightenment tropes (comparing societies, generalizing about groups of individuals) and a lively apprehension of individual physical experience. When Smollett begins a paragraph "I believe the moderns retain more of the customs of the antient Romans, than is generally imagined," the reader fears some inert scholarly detail. But the passage does not take quite the direction one might expect: "When I first saw the infants at the *enfans trouvés* in Paris, so swathed with bandages, that the very sight of them made my eyes water, I little dreamed, that the prescription of the antients could be pleaded for this custom, equally shocking and absurd: but in the Capitol at Rome, I met with the antique statue of a child swaddled exactly in the same manner; rolled up like an Aegyptian mummy from the feet" (255–56). The evidence for Smollett's belief in the persistence of Roman influence is not compelling, but the passage is arresting for other reasons. Confronted with an "antique statue," Smollett's mind moves back to the living children in the Parisian orphanage, whose plight "made [his] eyes water." Caught by this memory and impassioned by it, Smollett begins a characteristic onslaught: "What are the consequences of this cruel swaddling? the limbs are wasted; the joints grow rickety; the brain is compressed, and a hydrocephalus, with a great head and sore eyes, ensues. I take this abominable practice to be one great cause of the bandy legs, diminutive bodies, and large heads, so frequent in the south of France, and in Italy" (256). This is a representative Smollettian passage. Here we have distasteful physical detail, and careless insult presented as scientific observation. The passage rudely states that misshapen bodies are more frequent in France and Italy than in England, but Smollett is not writing to be rude. He graphically represents gro-

tesque deformity because he hopes to eliminate it. The whole rant-
ing farrago is driven by his detestation of cruel and abominable
practices.

We began with an image of the self-protective narrator, carefully placing his own sheets between himself and his Italian bed,
and wrapping his body tightly in his own overcoat. We end with an
antique statue, brought to life in the shape of a French infant—
whose "cruel swaddling" Smollett itches to unbind. One image reverses the other, but both represent crucial aspects of the *Travels*.
When Smollett received the diagnosis from Antoine Fizes, he felt
obliged, "in justice to [him]self," to point out the passages in the
case that Fizes had overlooked. Such moments in the *Travels* provided Sterne with a good joke. Ultimately, though, it is a joke the
Travels turns to good account. In telling it to the physician,
Smollett considers more than his case alone.

CHAPTER THREE

"SURROUNDED WITH BODIES":
SOCIAL EXPERIENCE IN
RODERICK RANDOM

Eighteenth-century writers, as we have seen, countered Locke's argument that there is no "perfect and exact" description of the "sort of Animal" man, by claiming that man is a distinctively social animal whose body is rendered both stable and knowable by social position and station. The novel is the literary form in which this argument receives its most detailed exposition, for the eighteenth-century novel describes social life, to a remarkable extent, in physical terms. The social world is a series of physical acts and responses: the throbbing heart with which a lover approaches his mistress; the tears that fall when a parent rediscovers a long-lost child; the blush with which a young lady recognizes impropriety. Yet noteworthy also is that novels often abandon this language, insistent and weighted with significance as it is, to estrange us from the comfortable notion that we know what bodies are and how they behave. Even novels most caught up in promulgating the idea that human physicality is instinct with social meaning include, every so often, a scene in which human bodies are treated as strange, exotic life-forms, as phenomena outside the spectator's range of experience. In Smollett's *Roderick Random,* for example, the hero's body is regularly treated as an object of suspicion to be reconnoitered from a distance rather than approached directly. Roderick knows exactly who he is. He is a gentleman by birth and education who has been dispossessed by his sadistic grandfather. Forced by poverty to leave Scotland, Roderick's fruitless attempts to gain patronage in

London are interrupted by the press-gang. Through sea battles, shipwreck, and servitude, Roderick never loses his sense of self, but his certainty contrasts poignantly with the bewilderment and disdain his physical form occasions. The predicament of the body whose humanity is denied or questioned fascinated the eighteenth century. Locke dramatizes it in the story of the abbot of St. Martin; Swift inflicts it on Gulliver in Brobdingnag. Smollett involves Roderick in it several times. Commanded to appear before the captain of the *Thunder* (the vessel on which he is an involuntary sailor), Roderick discovers what it is like to have one's body treated as an offensive, and possibly dangerous, object: "When I entered the room, I was ordered to stand by the door, until captain Whiffle had reconnoitred me at a distance, with a spy-glass, who having consulted one sense in this manner, bid me advance gradually, that his nose might have intelligence, before it could be much offended: I therefore approached with great caution and success, and he was pleased to say, 'Ay, this creature is tolerable'" (197). In a parody of empirical method, Smollett has the captain slowly create an "abstract" idea of Roderick from the discrete sensations of sight and smell. The height of Roderick's "success," however, is to be judged only a "tolerable" creature. Later in the novel, responses to the hero's body deteriorate even further. Having survived the *Thunder,* Roderick is shipwrecked, robbed of his clothing, beaten, and left to die. In a novel dedicated to exposing the "selfishness, envy, malice, and base indifference of mankind" (xxxv), we might expect the hero to sustain physical damage and suffer from cruelty and abuse. Less predictable, however, is the failure of those he encounters to recognize or act upon the bond of a shared physical form. As Roderick lies near death, his body is "reconnoitred" by a pair of rustics. The man who finds him,

> discovering a body all besmeared with blood, stood trembling, with the pitch-fork extended before him, his hair erect, his eyes staring, his nostrils dilated, and his mouth wide open . . . At length an old man arrived, who seeing the other in such a posture, cried, "Mercy upon en! the leaad's bewitch'd!—why Dick, beest thou besayd thyself?"—Dick, without moving his eyes from the object that terrified him, replied, "O vather! vather!

here be either the devil or a dead mon: I doan't know
which o'en, but a groans woundily."—The father,
whose eyesight was none of the best, pulled out his
spectacles, and having applied them to his nose, reconnoitred me over his son's shoulder. (212)

Although the half-naked, half-dead Roderick has, for very near "a
quarter of an hour," implored compassion and assistance, his body
remains an epistemological problem.[1] Neither the passage of time,
nor the application of spectacles, ascertains whether his form is
that of "a devil or a dead mon." There is no scene of spontaneous
recognition, no hand extended instinctively in human sympathy.
Finally, an old woman arrives who correctly identifies Roderick as
"a poor miserable wretch" (213) and orders that he should be
placed in a wheelbarrow and deposited at the door of someone who
can afford to minister to him. Before he faints away completely,
Roderick is "tumbled out like a heap of dung" (213) at the door of a
wealthy farmer. His body is treated as noxious, offensive matter,
and his fellow beings want only to dispose of it.

The uncertain, confused, and ultimately brutal responses
that Roderick's body elicits are, of course, part of Smollett's satiric
project, but it is nonetheless significant that his satire should foreground the body in this way. Indeed, much of what happens to the
hero's body in *Roderick Random* inverts the treatment of the body
in Augustan satires like *The Memoirs of Martinus Scriblerus:*
whereas the Scriblerians contend that society and social roles create a distinctive difference between humans and monsters, the satire of *Roderick Random* suggests that society functions by making
monsters of some men. Poor in Scotland, Roderick finds himself
avoided as a "creature of a different species, or rather as a solitary
being, no ways comprehended within the scheme or protection of
providence" (25–26). Poor in London, his monstrosity becomes
more specific, and he is greeted as "a cousin-german of Ouran
Outang" (67). Roderick's physical form becomes a test, and its dismissal, both by the privileged Whiffle and the ignorant rustics, ne-
gates the possibility that society is unified through sympathetic,

1. This scene exactly inverts the phenomenon with which David Marshall is
concerned in *The Surprising Effects of Sympathy: Marivaux, Diderot, Rousseau, and Mary Shelley* (Chicago: University of Chicago Press, 1988).

intensely physical response. Unprotected by wealth and social standing, the human body becomes monstrous, an orangutan, a mere "creature," and a "devil."[2] Not only is "society" a closed space into which the hero cannot enter, but those inside justify his exclusion by denying his humanity, his human form and shape. As the press-ganging episode illustrates, Roderick's society does, of course, recognize his body as matter capable of work, decisively not the kind of recognition our gentlemanly hero seeks. Demonstrating how society excludes the natural form of the human body, or incorporates it only as forced labor, Roderick's experience undermines the related assertions that the body is known because it is social, and that social experience is identical to physical experience. Smollett, subjecting Roderick to Whiffle's spyglass, satirizes the captain's inhumanity, but he also pointedly asserts that the body is not necessarily a social entity. The way in which physical form and experience acquires, or is denied, social meaning is the major concern of Smollett's first novel.

The shape of Roderick's adventures is proleptically rendered by a dream his mother has while pregnant: "She dreamed, she was delivered of a tennis-ball, which the devil (who to her great surprize, acted the part of a midwife) struck so forcibly with a racket, that it disappeared in an instant; and she was for some time inconsolable for the loss of her off-spring; when all of a sudden, she beheld it return with equal violence, and earth itself beneath her feet, whence immediately sprung up a goodly tree covered with blossoms, the scent of which operated so strongly on her nerves that she awoke" (1). The interpretation offered of this dream is that her child will be a great traveler who will eventually return to prosperity in his native land. The adventures Roderick undergoes are similar, in many respects, to those of his author: both laid claim to gentle status; both left Scotland to pursue medical careers in London; both served as naval surgeons and participated in the siege of

2. Of course, in satirizing social evils Smollett also creates some monsters of his own. As Jerry C. Beasley rightly points out, "A majority of the characters in the fictional world are grotesques, and Smollett frequently represents them as bestial figures, so that Roderick's environment is rather like a zoo with no cages, where the animals look remotely like people, but are animals after all, deficient in the human qualities of thought and compassion" (*Novels of the 1740s* [Athens: University of Georgia Press, 1982], 119).

Cartagena. From the first, however, Smollett insisted that the story of Roderick Random was not autobiographical: "the *whole* is not so much a Representation of my Life as of that of many other needy Scotch Surgeons whom I have known either personaly or by Report" (*Letters*, 8). In fact, as critics have recognized, the novel is not so much an account of "needy Scotch Surgeons" as it is of any individual's entrance into society.

One of the most appealing aspects of Smollett's novel to its first readers was the range of experiences through which the author propelled his protagonist, even though such variety included the novel's notorious descriptions of low life. Roderick sees and mingles in it all. He takes passage south to London on a crowded wagon, physically pressed against perfect strangers; he stumbles into the dense, murky atmosphere of a London ordinary; he catches venereal disease and recovers only to suffer the confines of an English ship at war; he ventures to South America on a trading mission and enjoys the sensations offered by an exotic climate. At a particularly desperate point in his adventures, Roderick signs up with a French regiment and gives the reader an especially vivid image of the body in eighteenth-century war.

> It is impossible to describe the hunger and thirst I sustained, and the fatigue I underwent in a march of so many hundred miles; during which, I was so much chased with the heat and motion of my limbs, that in a very short time the inside of my thighs and legs were deprived of skin, and I proceeded in the utmost torture.—This misfortune I owed to the plumpness of my constitution, which I cursed, and envied the withered condition of my comrades, whose bodies could not spare juice enough to supply a common issue, and were indeed proof against all manner of friction. (245)

Roderick does not tell us where the soldiers are marching, or why. The story focuses on his inconvenient plumpness, and his daily experience of "heat and motion."

Brisk and vigorous, Roderick's adventures give an individual, physical, everyday version of major eighteenth-century developments, such as the growth of the city and the extension of English domain. The novel generates excitement because it recognizes that social change does alter the ways in which bodies surround one another, the pace and force of their mutual effects. For example, the growth of London—a great topic for moral excoriation—multiplied the "perpetual and diverse" effects of anonymous bodies upon one another; in the environment of the city, bodily movement has a frenetic quality and is fraught with both possibility and danger. The multiplicity of sensations the city offers is a recurrent theme in Smollett's fiction. He gives it psychological dimension in the extraordinary susceptibility of his characters, particularly Matthew Bramble in *Humphry Clinker,* to claustrophobia. Bramble is, of course, well able to articulate the nature of the social change he observes. In his letters he speaks of the "immense wilderness" of London and opines that "the capital is become an overgrown monster; which, like a dropsical head, will in time leave the body and extremities without nourishment and support. The absurdity will appear in its full force, when we consider, that one sixth part of the natives of this whole extensive kingdom is crowded within the bills of mortality" (87). In the late satire *The History and Adventures of an Atom,* the sheer density of bodies in the city, and their ability to coagulate into a mob, is given political importance and effect. Novelists like Smollett, already encouraged by philosophy to reconceptualize the body, added to that challenge the realization that, at least for the huge number of people drifting towards the city and swelling its population, physical experience simply *was* different now. The novel's ability to evoke and confront the nature of that difference made it extremely valuable, both to readers who had experienced it and those who had not.

If the main part of *Roderick Random* encourages the above speculations, the conclusion of the novel forces us to take them a step farther. Eventually, having exposed himself to most of the sensations that the capital city, the British navy, and the colonies have to offer, Roderick rediscovers his long-lost father (in South America), establishes himself on a country estate, and observes the "unity and coherence of society."[3] The estate is a symbol of status and prosperity; it is also a place where the hero's body is safe from overwhelming sensation. Undeniably, the society Roderick surveys

---

3. John Barrell, *English Literature in History, 1730–1780: An Equal, Wide Survey* (London: Hutchinson, 1983), 177.

at the end of the novel makes a good deal more sense to him than
the fragmented social world in which he begins his adventures. It
would be a mistake, however, to express this development simply in
terms of the hero's growth and his newfound ability to perceive
what had previously gone unnoticed, because such a vocabulary
obscures the way in which the novel achieves social coherence by
replacing a disruptive, fragmentary, violent model of human physicality with one in which each bodily detail resonates with social significance. Social unity, as Smollett represents it at the novel's end,
is, literally, a matter of mirroring and matched body parts. The
novel's crisis resembles those passages in Hume where the ever-
increasing, never-abating pleasures of wealth lock the bodies of
both possessors and beholders in appreciative regard. In Roderick's
discovery of his father the two bodies mirror each other: "'O bounteous heaven! (exclaimed Don Rodriguez, springing across the table, and clasping me in his arms) my son! my son! have I found thee
again? do I hold thee in my embrace, after having lost and de-
spaired of seeing thee, so long?' So saying, he fell upon my neck and
wept aloud with joy; while the power of nature operating strongly in
my breast, I was lost in rapture, and while he pressed me to his
heart, let fall a shower of tears into his bosom" (413). The arm of the
father finds the neck of the son, and the breast of one presses the
bosom of the other. This physical symmetry constitutes, rather
than merely symbolizes, a society unified through sympathetic response. Yet, even if the reader were disposed to accept this identity
of the physical and the social, the rest of the novel has tutored her
to understand it not as "the power of nature" but as the culmination
of a process whereby the purely physical acquires social resonance.
In *Roderick Random* the entrance of the hero into society requires
the transmutation of his physical experience.

The fluidity and symmetry of Roderick's reunion with his father contrasts dramatically with the jangling, abrasive physicality
of most of the novel's events. Roderick's mother dreamed not only
the shape of her unborn child's life, but also something of its force
and violence. In *Roderick Random* the body is not naturally
equipped to function in society; it only learns to do so after shocks
and pains. At first the social world causes astonishment, wonder,
sensory failure, and motor incapacity. The moments of astonishment and wonder that Roderick experiences on the journey from

Scotland to London, for example, dramatize the predicament of characters so besieged by the sensation of being in the world that they are unable to impress themselves upon their environment. Journeying to London, Roderick and his faithful friend Strap are first cheated by an innkeeper and then stopped by a highwayman. This introduction to society as it really is freezes Roderick completely, leaving him astonished: "My comrade's fate, and my own situation, rivetted me to the place where I stood, deprived of all sense and reflection; so that I did not make the least attempt either to run away, or deprecate the wrath of this barbarian, who snapped a second pistol at me; but before he had time to prime again, perceived a company of horse-men coming up; whereupon he rode off, and left me standing motionless as a statue, in which posture I was found by those whose appearance had saved my life" (38). One by one, each of Roderick's faculties suspends operation. First, he cannot hear; then he is mute; then he is "rivetted" to the spot, and finally he is "deprived of all sense and reflection." In representing Roderick's entrance into society, Smollett draws heavily on Cartesian notions of the passions. For Descartes the body's confrontation with the unknown is the most intriguing moment of passion, and the anatomical explanation he gives for wonder is more detailed and complete than those he gives other passions.

> And this surprise has so much power in causing the spirits which are in the cavities of the brain to take their way from thence to the place where is the impression of the object which we wonder at, that it sometimes thrusts them all there, and causes them to be so much occupied in preserving this impression that there are none which pass from thence into the muscles, nor even which in any way turn themselves away from the tracks which they originally pursued in the brain: and this causes the whole body to remain as immobile as a statue, and prevents our perceiving more of the object than the first face which is presented, or consequently of acquiring a more particular knowledge of it.[4]

The subject is invaded, possessed entirely by images of the external world. The spirits in the cavity of the brain are so much occupied in

4. *Philosophical Works of Descartes,* 1:363–64.

"preserving this impression" that they do not pass into the muscles, and the entire body temporarily shuts down. Standing like a statue, the wonder-struck subject is completely disabled. Immobility and the inability to process sensory data are primary symptoms of "wonder," and insofar as Smollett uses such symptoms this scene is formulaic, but Smollett protracts the moment of breakdown and suspension. Each advance in the narrative makes the hero less present. Our perspective as readers is that of spectators who come upon Roderick after the highwayman has left: we see him "standing motionless as a statue, in which posture I was found by those whose appearance had saved my life." In the main, as Alan McKenzie writes, eighteenth-century writers used the passions to generate social stability in ways that were "fairly conservative."[5] Typical of the conservatism McKenzie has in mind is the practice of David Hume, whose *Treatise of Human Nature* quickly passes from raw physical sensation to social passions of various kinds. Significantly, Hume's lack of interest in sensation is paralleled by his dismissal of the concept of the state of nature, which he regards as a "mere philosophical fiction, which never had, and never cou'd have any reality" (493). This statement does more than debunk a theory of society's origins; it also excludes a variety of perspectives on present social arrangements. Dismissing both the state of nature and the possibility of asocial sensation, Hume obliterates, for cultures generally and for the individual in particular, a perspective that is before or outside the social. The body's feelings and expressions are, for Hume, matters of social orientation. The passions he discusses at greatest length are pride, humility, and "our esteem for the rich and powerful." Those passions that bespeak isolation or separation—fear, for example, or astonishment—he passes over silently or quickly. In contrast, Smollett pays conspicuous attention to the physically traumatic passions of wonder and astonishment, thereby forcing the reader to imagine the human animal machine confronting society. Smollett's representations of physicality have radical potential because they deny that sociability is inherent in the human body.

This perception underlies Smollett's divergence from his French model, Lesage's *Gil Blas,* a novel that he translated into En-

5. *Certain, Lively Episodes,* 21.

glish and that he explicitly acknowledges in the preface to *Roderick Random*.[6]

> The following sheets I have modelled on his plan, taking the liberty, however, to differ from him in the execution, where I thought his particular situations were uncommon, extravagant, or peculiar to the country in which the scene is laid.—The disgraces of Gil Blas, are for the most part, such as rather excite mirth than compassion; he himself laughs at them; and his transitions from distress to happiness, or at least ease, are so sudden, that neither the reader has time to pity him, nor himself to be acquainted with affliction. (xliv–xlv)

The sudden transitions in *Gil Blas* that Smollett most resolutely and explicitly rejects occur because Gil Blas is a hero wrapped in discourses. No matter where he goes, he meets with a spate of orienting, onward-guiding narrations. None of the social structures or characters he encounters is ever completely unfamiliar to Lesage's hero. He is a picaro with an ever-loquacious, if constantly changing, courier by his side. The son of a retired soldier, Gil Blas leaves his

6. P.-G. Boucé discusses Smollett's divergence from Lesage in detail in *The Novels of Tobias Smollett*, trans. Antonia White in collaboration with the author (London and New York: Longman, 1976), 71–89. Smollett's relationship to Lesage raises the question of his relationship to the picaresque generally. G. S. Rousseau argues against the "age-old claptrap" that Smollett is a picaresque novelist ("Smollett and the Picaresque: Some Questions about a Label," *Studies in Burke and His Time* 12 [1970–71]: 1903), an argument to which P.-G. Boucé responds ("Smollett's Pseudo-picaresque: A Response to Rousseau's 'Smollett and the Picaresque,'" *Studies in Burke and His Time* 14 [1972–73]: 73–79). Those who read Smollett as a degenerate example of the picaresque include Robert Alter ("The Picaroon as Fortune's Plaything," in *Essays on the Eighteenth-Century Novel*, ed. R. D. Spector [Bloomington and London: Indiana University Press, 1965], 131–53); and A. G. Fredman ("The Picaresque in Decline: Smollett's First Novel," in *English Writers of the Eighteenth Century*, ed. John H. Middendorf [New York: Columbia University Press, 1971], 189–208). I agree with J. V. Price that "Smollett's departures from the tradition are more numerous and more interesting than his very few adherences to it" (*The Expedition of Humphry Clinker* [London: Edward Arnold, 1973], 18) and, this study not being essentially concerned with literary classification, shall limit my discussion to those "departures" of Smollett from Lesage that bear on my general argument.

native village and sets off on a peregrination round Spain. In the course of his adventures he is imprisoned by robbers, works as a physician, serves as a valet, spends time with a troop of actors, acts as a scribe for the archbishop, and gains a position as secretary for the prime minister of Spain. Of course, Gil Blas also suffers some reversals, during one of which he ponders: "I had, while I served my last masters, conceived too great an affection for the conveniences of life, and could no longer, as formerly, look upon indigence with the eye of a cynic philosopher. I will own, however, that I was very much in the wrong to let myself fall prey to melancholy. After having so often experienced that Fortune no sooner overthrew than she raised me up again, I ought to have regarded the troublesome situation in which I was, as an introduction to prosperity."[7] The "introduction" of which Gil Blas speaks is often given by an audible human voice. Throughout the novel, Gil Blas is inducted and initiated into each set of circumstances he confronts, and he brings to those circumstances considerable powers of ingratiation. Wayfarers, stewards, actors, and employers, all cue, prompt, and instruct the hero; he makes his way on the breath of others. The ability of the hero to understand and reproduce the behavior a given situation requires is matched and facilitated by the willingness of other characters to open up, through speech, the particular society in which Gil Blas must find a niche. Gil Blas does not need to interpret his society; it is constantly explained to him. Like the theater, which plays such an important part in the novel, society becomes a collaborative effort in which any notion of difference is vitiated by constant, prolix communication. In *Gil Blas* all the important acts are linguistic. The mock-heroic allusions that pepper the novel deliberately draw attention to the work as a verbal construct that plays a part in a complex literary system. We are more conscious of our narrator's skill than we are of his predicaments, and hence his disgraces excite mirth. Characters in *Gil Blas* are the stories they narrate, and story merges with story until the novel becomes a swollen river of loquacity. Such universal linguistic competence provides a simulacrum of social coherence. Everyone

7. *The Adventures of Gil Blas of Santillane,* trans. Tobias Smollett (London: Willoghby and Co., 1841), 475.

speaks the same language; no narration is markedly different from any other; and the energy of such general and human utterance carries the hero from place to place, from situation to situation.

Smollett, like Lesage, explores the social implications of linguistic competence, but offers very different conclusions. Roderick has verbal talent and can make his case, but unlike Gil Blas, Roderick does not benefit from his ability to articulate. Voice offers specious power. In fact, the hero's attempts to improve his lot through language only involve him further in an unameliorated life of the body. As an adolescent, Roderick tries to gain his grandfather's respect and affection by writing him Latin epistles. This initiative causes Roderick's teacher to construct a board with five holes in it, "through which he thrust the fingers and thumb of my right hand, and fastened it by whip-cord to my wrist, in such a manner, that I was effectually debarr'd the use of my pen" (5). Later, the Greek journal Roderick keeps upon the *Thunder* leads to his being fastened to the mast as a spy. Latin and Greek are the languages of gentlemen, but any attempt on Roderick's part to use them, either to gain the respect of others or to maintain his own self-respect, invariably brings trouble. Each time he tries to assert his body's gentlemanly status, he is rudely reminded that his society is not willing to entertain his claims and punished—as his society punished malefactors—with physical constraint and exposure.

One might object at this point that "society" in Smollett's novel cannot be restricted to corrupt institutions, sadistic schoolmasters, and the press-gang. There is a good deal of warmth and affection in *Roderick Random,* and the bonds between Roderick and his seafaring uncle, Tom Bowling, or between Roderick and his school friend Hugh Strap, must be included in any definition of the social. These are, after all, the relationships Hazlitt had in mind when he praised Smollett for the "generosity" of his characters. Attractive as these relationships are, however, they too are jeopardized by the inconstant nature of human physicality; which is to say that, in the chaotic world of *Roderick Random,* even the closest friends can have trouble recognizing one another. While bodily signs can be easily read, any given body remains mysterious and unknown.[8] Although Smollett fills his fiction with concrete physi-

---

8. To some extent this difficulty is inherent in representations of the pas-

cal detail and graphic description, his characters assimilate and retain this material only with difficulty. Bodies in motion, once Smollett's characters go their separate ways they hardly remember the form and shape of the other. Their fleeting impressions of each other's bodies do not augur well for the possibilities of knowable, social identity. These difficulties are exemplified by Roderick's reunion with his old school friend Strap.

> [T]he young man, while he lathered my face, accosted me thus: "Sir, I presume you are a Scotchman." To which I answered in the affirmative.—"Pray (continued he) of what part of Scotland?"—I no sooner told him, than he discovered great emotion, and not confining his operation to my chin and upper lip, besmeared my whole face with great agitation.—At which I was so offended, that starting up, I asked him what the d—l he meant by using me so?—He begged pardon, telling me his joy in meeting with a countryman, had occasioned some confusion in him; and craved my name.—But when I declared my name was Random he exclaimed in a rapture, "How! Rory Random?" The same, I replied, looking at him with astonishment; "What, cried he, don't you know your old school-fellow, Hugh Strap?" At that instant recollecting his face, I flew into his arms, and in the transport of my joy, gave him back one half of the suds he had so lavishly bestowed on my countenance; so that we made a very ludicrous appearance, and furnished a great deal of mirth to his master and shop-mates, who were witnesses of this scene. (32)

Roderick's meeting with Strap is represented in intensely visual terms. When Strap hears the part of Scotland from which Roderick comes, he "discover[s] great emotion," and Strap's signs of confusion and agitation cause Roderick to look at the latter "with astonishment." Yet, even though Roderick and Strap do nothing but look

---

sions. Patey reminds us that the passions "lend themselves to piecemeal rather than connected portrayals of character" (*Probability and Literary Form*, 98), and McKenzie warns that movement away from the "self-contained episodes" the passions govern ought to be made, if at all, "with great caution" (*Certain, Lively Episodes*, 19).

at one another throughout the passage, they do not succeed in recognizing one another until names are exchanged. Their exchange
of names shows that "recognition" is made possible not by a memory of shapes and gestures but by the elements of the social narrative through which we approach experience. Strap gives his
name, and "at that instant" Roderick recollects his face. The scene
emphasizes the body as the object of vision—discovery, "ludicrous
appearance," and "witnesses of this scene"—but it offers no reassurance about the success of such operations. We see individuals
slowly reconstitute the idea of the familiar. The visible world, so
palpably present, is still astonishingly opaque. Characters' bodies,
always shifting into new, unrecognizable forms, do not provide social knowledge—they have to be fixed by elements (for example,
names) in a preexisting social narrative. When Roderick is press-
ganged onto the *Thunder,* he meets up with his friend Thomson.

> If I knew him at first sight, it was not so easy for him to
> recognize me, disfigured with blood and dirt, and al-
> tered by the misery I had undergone.—Unknown as I
> was to him, he surveyed me with looks of compassion,
> and handled my sores with great tenderness. When he
> had applied what he thought proper, and was about to
> leave me, I asked him if my misfortunes had disguised
> me so much, that he could not recollect my face? Upon
> this he observed me with great earnestness for some
> time, and at length, protested he could not recollect one
> feature of my countenance. (143)

Thomson has both "surveyed [Roderick] with looks of compassion" and "observed [him] with great earnestness," and still he does
not "recollect one feature." In Smollett's writing, sudden agitation
and passion can be read in the faces of characters, but the faces
themselves cannot easily be remembered. Social knowledge does
not accumulate. Familiarity is evanescent. *Roderick Random*
makes the definition of the human body an issue, insists that the
body is not naturally social, and says that even strong relationships
are often impaired by our unstable physicality. Taken together,
these features of the novel rob the body of the certainty and reassurance it normally carries. This effect is in complete keeping with
Smollett's intentions, because if we cannot take the body for

granted, then we have to look twice at accounts of society that use the body to establish credibility and force.

Smollett does represent the body as legible in certain circumstances, and this provides some local stability. When, in the preface, he distinguishes Roderick from the cast of characters through whom he must move and with whom he is at various times identified, he promises that the "judicious" will "find entertainment in viewing those parts of life, where the humours and passions are undisguised by affectation, ceremony, or education; and the whimsical peculiarities of disposition appear as nature has implanted them" (xlv). These lines describe many of the secondary characters of the novel: Strap, Roderick's school friend; his uncle Tom Bowling; and Morgan, the eccentric surgeon on the *Thunder*. All of these characters are Cartesian mechanisms, and all express their passions in external signs.[9] Repositories of social virtue, these characters are also, for reason of education or race, marginal figures in society.[10] It is conventional enough to posit that only those outside a corrupt society can behave in natural ways, but Smollett shows members of society adept in natural language but unable to express themselves through the conventional language of speech. *Roderick Random* is full of characters who cannot textualize themselves. Their inability or reluctance to express themselves pointedly in the terms of common speech makes these characters vulnerable to the indolent interpretation of others. Tom Bowling, whistling "with great vehemence, . . . his visage being contracted all the while into a most formidable frown" (15), is registering his fury at Roderick's grandfather's last will and testament—a piece of injustice Bowling is powerless to change. On board the *Thunder* Morgan bursts forth "into a Welch song, which he accompanied with a thousand contortions of face and violent gestures of body" (176). He sings in Welsh because he is afraid he will be overheard and reported if he expresses his opinions in English. The languages Bowling and Morgan command are expressive, but they are also in-

9. See page 253, where, in a description of Strap listening to Roderick's adventures, Strap runs through some of the best-known conventions.

10. For references to Bowling's lack of education and worldliness, see pages 11 and 19.

consequential.[11] These characters can vent their frustration, pain, and anger, but they cannot alter the circumstances that produced these passions in the first place. Smollett's expansive style makes the predicament of these characters sharply present to the reader. Through an appreciation of their extremity we realize that human expression is rarely economical and only occasionally effective in the external world. Smollett's protracted accounts of the events of sensation interrupt the flow of his own narrative. Through these characters he demonstrates that the pressure of the external world, to which we are all vulnerable, has a highly mediated relationship to social significance. His fiction suggests that society limits the field of social knowledge and furthers its claim to coherence by labeling certain forms of human behavior "extravagant," and unworthy of consideration in the social economy.

While *Roderick Random* directs the reader's attention to the problems of defining and reading the human body, the novel's most memorable sections impress upon us the ways in which political systems silently exploit it. Those parts of the novel set on the *Thunder* dramatize the extent to which the body is written out of political accounts. In pursuing their ends, governments use, but do not acknowledge, the body. That way, the costs of both failure and success are minimized. While it is entirely fitting to examine how eighteenth-century society justifies itself through particular ways of narrating bodily experience, it is also important to acknowledge when such kind of representation is beside the point. Social economy and coherence require that some bodies simply be used and excluded from the social narrative while the bodies within resonate with meaning. Much of the impact of the shipboard scenes in *Roderick Random* comes from discrepancies between what Roderick tells us and the official story of events. Roderick's narration is concerned with the feelings of bodies that become, in the official version, both invisible and inaudible.

Roderick's very presence on the ship indicates that his society sees his body as nothing more than animate matter without vo-

---

11. In 1762 Thomas Sheridan lamented that the English disposition was not attracted to the social purposes of sensation: "of all nations in the world, the English seem to have the least use of this language of signs" (*A Course of Lectures on Elocution* [New York: Benjamin Blom, 1968], 118).

lition: "good enough to toss; food for powder." Prostrated, after he
has been press-ganged, Roderick ineffectually complains to the
midshipman that his wound may be fatal: "compassion was a weakness of which no man could justly accuse this person, who squirting
a mouthful of dissolved tobacco upon me, through the gratings, told
me, 'I was a mutinous dog, and that I might die and be damned'"
(140). Roderick survives to be thrust into the hold "among a parcel
of miserable wretches, the sight of whom well nigh distracted me."
Later, as a surgeon, he is introduced to the sick berth.

> Here I saw about fifty miserable distempered wretches,
> suspended in rows, so huddled one upon another, that
> not more than fourteen inches of space was allotted for
> each with his bed and bedding; and deprived of the light
> of the day, as well as of fresh air; breathing nothing but a
> noisome atmosphere of the morbid steams exhaling
> from their own excrements and diseased bodies, de-
> voured with vermin hatched in the filth that sur-
> rounded them, and destitute of every convenience
> necessary for people in that helpless condition. (149)

When the *Thunder* receives sailing orders, Roderick and his fellows
are dramatically instructed in the negligible importance of the human body. The captain, Oakhum, coming aboard, Morgan the doctor visits him with a list of the sick. Morgan's list honors the physical
state of the men and represents his own knowledge of actual conditions on ship. The list, however, is dismissed by the captain, who
asserts, "[T]here shall be no sick in this ship while I have the command of her" (157). An altercation ensues in which the captain
throws the list at Morgan, damning it and the doctor. Morgan's response, that "his indignation ought to be directed to Got Almighty,
who visited his people with distempers, and not to him, who con-
tributed all in his power towards their cure" (157), points, as he
thinks, to the limits of the captain's control and is further emphasized by Morgan's announcement to his fellows that the captain,
"by his sole word and power and command, had driven sickness a
pegging to the tevil, and there was no more malady on poard" (157).
Morgan's satire is directed against what he sees as the captain's
hubris; no command can erase the signs of illness with which the
Almighty has been pleased to visit his people. In the dystopia the

Thunder represents, however, power and command can obliterate the experiences and sensations of others. Oakhum eradicates sickness by the simple expedient of doing away with the sick: commanded to appear on deck and ordered to return to work, many of them die. One of Oakhum's victims, a man "loaded with a monstrous ascites or dropsy," is ordered to climb the mast: "but when the enormous weight of his body had nothing else to support it than his weakened arms, . . . he quitted his hold, and plumped into the sea" (159). By such measures "the number of sick was reduced to less than a dozen; and the authors of this reduction [applauded] themselves for the service they had done to their king and country" (159). No sign of illness or distress can defeat the captain's assertion that the sick men are "lazy, lubberly sons of bitches, who were good for nothing on board, but to eat the king's provision, and encourage idleness in the skulkers" (158). Oakhum's brutality reads illness as an incitement to idleness, and it is his reading that proves decisive.

Those in positions of power on board ship completely deny the reality of the crew's sensations, and succeed in supplanting the reality of their experience by a false narration of events. Social knowledge here is the result of an arbitrary decision. Roderick does succeed in giving us an account of his "capricious fate" (166) at sea, but he knows that any connections he may make between the motives and conduct of those who control his fate will be disregarded, and that his own actions will be subject to willful misinterpretation. Roderick himself suffers from the captain's authoritative misinterpretations when he is accused of being a spy on board. The decisive piece of evidence against him is a book in "cyphers" found among his papers. The book is nothing other than a diary, which Roderick has kept in Greek, "of every thing remarkable" that has occurred on the voyage. Roderick's claim to authority, his ability to relate the events of his own life in "the true original tongue, in which Homer, Pindar, the evangelists and other Great men of antiquity wrote" (176), is turned against him, and he is carried to the poop where he is "loaded with irons, and stapled to the deck" (166). While he is in this unfortunate position, the *Thunder* engages another ship in battle.

> I concealed my agitation as well as I could, till the head
> of the officer of Marines, who stood near me, being shot

off, bounced from the deck athwart my face, leaving me
well-nigh blinded with brains.—I could contain myself
no longer, but began to bellow with all the strength of
my lungs; when a drummer coming towards me, asked
if I was wounded; and before I could answer, received a
great shot in his belly which tore out his intrails, and he
fell flat on my breast.—This accident entirely bereft me
of all discretion; I redoubled my cries, which were
drowned in the noise of the battle; and finding myself
disregarded, lost all patience and became frantick; ven-
ted my rage in oaths and execrations, till my spirits being quite exhausted, I remained quiet and insensible of
the load that oppressed me. (167–68)

In this passage Roderick is a figure of powerless witness. He attempts to absent himself from the scene through reason and self-
control. He "endeavours to compose" himself; he reflects; he "con-
ceal[s] his agitation," but despite all his efforts he is "entirely bereft
. . . of all discretion." Failing to maintain a sense of his own integrity, he also fails to draw attention to his condition. Bellows, cries,
oaths, and execrations are all in vain. At last, he is nothing but the
sum of his sensations; his faculties fail him and he remains "quiet
and insensible" under his oppressive load. Roderick's extremity is
one of complete isolation in overwhelming sensation. Although he
does survive the ordeal, his elaborate and detailed account weighs
for nothing in the official version of the episode. He may have been
"blinded with brains" and covered with entrails, but his shocking
intimacy with the details of the battle does not give him any interpretive power. His entire sequence of sensation is canceled out by
the captain's simple, economical explanation of the naval operation: "The engagement lasted till broad day, when captain Oakhum,
finding he was like to gain neither honour nor advantage by the affair, pretended to be undeceived by seeing their colours; and hailing
the ship with whom he had fought all night, protested he believed
them Spaniards, and the guns being silenced on each side, ordered
the barge to be hoisted out, and went on board of the French com-
modore" (168). The captain's "pretense" and "protestations"—both
words that draw attention to the duplicity of narrative—outweigh
every single one of the sensations Roderick has experienced.
Smollett's satire points out that the protests and pretenses of those

in power, and their ability to manipulate language for their own purposes, cancel out even the most plain and veracious account of sensation that the powerless can offer. Subsequently, of course, Roderick exploits his own sensations for ironic effect. As he lays down detail after detail of mismanagement and misjudgment, he assumes ironically that there is a master narrative, to which he does not yet have access, which will explain his observations away.

> At last, however, we weighed, and anchored again somewhat nearer the harbour's mouth, where we made shift to land our marines, who encamped on the beach, in despite of the enemy's shot, which knocked a good many of them on the head.—This piece of conduct in chusing a camp under the walls of an enemy's fortification, which I believe never happened before, was practised, I presume, with a view of accustoming the soldiers to stand fire, who were not as yet much used to discipline, most of them having been taken from the plough-tail a few months before.—This again has furnished matter for censure against the Ministry, for sending a few raw recruits on such an important enterprize, while so many veteran regiments lay inactive at home: But surely our governours had their reasons for so doing, which possibly may be disclosed with other secrets of the deep. (179–80)

Roderick provides the reader with ironic explanations for the conduct of the siege, but his certainty that the "governours" had reasons that will be "disclosed with other secrets of the deep" insinuates that those in power are not bound to give account of their actions. Roderick may "presume" ironically because those who led the expedition have not been properly held to account.

Roderick's account of his time on ship is a record of sensation. For the men in the sick berth, as for Roderick himself, the experience of the ship is oppressive. There is no possibility of escaping the environment that impresses itself upon them; such good fortune is enjoyed by others. That social position mediates sensation is clearly seen in the exchange between Roderick and Captain Whiffle at which we have already looked. The privileged position of the captain allows him to keep sensory experience at a distance. Roderick has been thrust into all the sensations of ship-board life, but the captain, who is theoretically in charge, exists at many removes from the scenes that Roderick endures. The captain is determined to have no more "intelligence" of shipboard life than suits his own needs. Roderick, and the story he might tell, are set at nothing. During this episode, Roderick, the narrator, is nothing other than the series of effects he has on the nerves of the captain, whom he approaches with "caution" and therefore with "success." Luxury, normally defined as a surfeit of pleasurable sensations, be-comes here the ability to protect oneself from sensations likely to cause pain. One of the functions of power in this novel is that it per-mits withdrawal from sensation. "All that are born into the world" may, as Locke asserts, be "surrounded with Bodies," but one of the functions of power and affluence is that it permits the individual to ignore most of them.

Smollett's detailed, elaborate, and sensational account of Cartagena has been noted by critics.[12] A historian of the Georgian navy, speaking of Smollett as a writer whose "works have perhaps been drawn on rather more than they deserve," explains his deci-sion to avoid using Smollett's fiction: "As he had served one voyage as a surgeon's mate he was not wholly unacquainted with the Navy, but he remains a poor, or rather an over-rich, substitute for docu-mentary evidence."[13] The naval passages of *Roderick Random* are "over-rich" because they are grotesque: the narrative attends to in-dividual bodies distorted and rendered fantastic by mutilation and injury. Roderick's own body has been constantly under threat, but on the *Thunder* he confronts wounded bodies undergoing obscene transformations: "Their wounds and stumps being neglected, con-

12. Of this section of *Roderick Random* Louis L. Martz has written: "[H]is style is . . . expansive; he makes little effort to maintain economy and concen-tration, and frequently prefers to write loosely constructed and deliberately di-gressive sentences. Such a style is often extremely effective: ironical overtones are achieved by inclusion of ridiculously digressive material, or by use of a pur-posely inflated style which forms a ludicrous contrast with the triviality of the matter." Martz contrasts this style with the "precise and regular" style of the *Compendium of Voyages,* in which Smollett later gave another account of the expedition (*The Later Career of Tobias Smollett* [New Haven: Yale University Press, 1942], 183–84).

13. N. A. M. Rodger, *The Wooden World: An Anatomy of the Georgian Navy* (London: Collins, 1986), 14.

tracted filth and putrefaction, and millions of maggots were hatched amid the corruption of their sores" (187). As David McNeil points out in his study of grotesque depictions of war, Roderick cannot see that this kind of detail, this insistent recording of individual degradation, is beside the point: "nations go to war to win, not to treat those who fall."[14]

For the greater part of the novel Roderick's sensations are denied any significance or validity, and at certain moments in the text the very humanity of his shape is openly challenged. How then is this questionable shape suddenly vouchsafed social significance? How is the body of the hero metamorphosed? The answer is both crude and powerful. Roderick's body acquires meaning, and becomes the beneficiary of sympathy, whenever it is close to money. Even before Roderick discovers his patrimony, scenes of sympathy do punctuate the novel, but they are frequently accompanied by the flow of money. The connection is very clear in an early passage when Strap offers his purse to Roderick: "I was so touched with the generous passion of this poor creature, that I could not refrain from weeping also, and we mingled our tears together for some time.— Upon examining the purse, I found in it two half guineas and half a crown, which I would have returned to him, saying, he knew better than I how to manage it; but he absolutely refused my proposal, and told me, it was more reasonable and decent that he should depend upon me who was a gentleman, than that I should be controuled by him" (73). Sentimental tears and money go together; Roderick can mingle his tears with those of Strap because he is about to examine the contents of the purse. All that distinguishes this sentimental expression from the "extravagant" body language of Strap, Bowling, and so on is the imminence of some financial transaction. Where emotional exchanges are not accompanied by financial exchange, then the expression of emotion is diverting and entertaining. Strap bails Roderick out often enough, but he is only a barber, and so his resources are limited. For the constant exchange of much emotion a more solid financial base is required. Marriage, of course, establishes both emotional and financial economy. On his return from Cartagena, and after suffering shipwreck, Roderick can only sur-

---

14. *The Grotesque Depiction of War and the Military in Eighteenth-Century English Fiction* (Newark: University of Delaware Press, 1990), 91.

vive by entering service. At this point he meets Narcissa, the niece of his employer, and becomes her passionate, if often distant and occasionally forgetful, lover. For the remainder of the novel Narcissa will be the image that connects Roderick to the hope of social position. When Roderick is imprisoned, he would have "blessed the occasion that secluded me from such a perfidious world, had not the remembrance of the amiable Narcissa, preserved my attachment to that society of which she constituted a part" (397). The image of Narcissa is, as her name suggests, also an image of Roderick himself. Partly through their relationship, and partly through the rediscovery of his father, Roderick's body is transformed, and he satisfactorily completes the social constitution of self, becoming implicated in a sympathetic, and completely coherent, account of society.[15]

Prior to his departure on the voyage that will make his fortune, Roderick plays a stolen visit to his Narcissa, who is undergoing house imprisonment at the hands of her boorish brother. He climbs over the garden wall and conceals himself in a thicket: "Here I absconded from five a-clock in the morning to six in the evening, without seeing a human creature; at last I perceived two women approaching, whom by my throbbing heart I soon recogniz'd to be the adorable Narcissa and Miss Williams" (405). The happy conjunction of sympathy and money allows Roderick to acknowledge the signs of his passion. He recognizes Narcissa with complete ease and economy by his "throbbing heart." Then Roderick, guessing that Narcissa and Miss Williams will sit in the alcove, "stept into it unperceiv'd, and laid upon the stone-table a picture of myself in miniature, for which I had sat in London, purposing to leave it with Narcissa before I should go abroad" (405). The beautiful Narcissa takes up the miniature: "No sooner did she cast her eye upon the features, than she startled, crying, 'Gracious God!' and the roses instantly vanished from her cheeks." After declaring her acceptance of the picture, Narcissa "kissed it with surprising ardour, shed

15. Speaking of Narcissa's role in the novel, Raymond Stephanson persuasively argues that "the positive metamorphosis and entry into paradise" she promises is undercut by the novel's "play of allusion." The negative perspective that dominates the novel "refuses to be contained by the ending" ("The [Non]Sense of an Ending: Subversive Allusion and Thematic Discontent in *Roderick Random*," *Eighteenth-Century Fiction* 1 [1989]: 107).

a flood of tears, and then deposited the lifeless image in her lovely bosom" (406). Roderick's possession of the miniature and his gift of it to Narcissa are deeply symbolic. It is entirely fitting that a hero whose body has been consistently ignored or maltreated should choose as his first luxury a becoming representation of himself, one that will cancel out all the images of his form that have accumulated throughout the novel. After his multiple exposures at home and abroad, Roderick is now able to dictate, to artists and to others, the way in which he will be perceived. Moreover, Narcissa's care of the "lifeless image," which she deposits in her "lovely bosom," prefigures the way in which Roderick himself will soon be cherished and protected.

Roderick's brief meeting with Narcissa literally sets the stage for his second voyage. Within a paragraph he is "clear of the Channel," and off to Guinea for "slaves and gold dust." This journey invites comparison with Roderick's time on the *Thunder*. Throughout, Roderick implicitly contrasts this enterprise with his earlier voyage. The precautions he takes for the health of the crew are so successful that "we lost but one sailor during our whole passage to the coast" (407). Once again the ship encounters what they take to be an enemy ship, but this time the crew are promised by Bowling that any man injured in the encounter will receive "recompence according to his loss" (409). Finally, more than adequate care is taken of provisions so that "not only we, but the whole ships company, fared sumptuously during the voyage" (419). In some ways, then, Roderick's voyage is the corrected version of his own experiences at sea.

Despite Roderick's care and the sumptuous supplies, the ship is not a Utopia, and in the complacency of Roderick's narrative we can still discern a more disturbing, sensational account. After all, this ship also has its plague, and it has its quota of involuntary passengers. When Roderick, as ship's surgeon, remarks that he had been a "miserable slave" to the "disagreeable lading" of negro slaves, we remember the illnesses and suffering of which he earlier gave us such a detailed account. Then, the casual care with which Roderick tells us his adventure was "laid out chiefly in gold dust" seems an attempt to distance himself from the questionable basis of his wealth. Finally, Roderick offhandedly tells us that when the ship returned to England it was obliged to put in at Spithead to the "great mortification of the crew, thirty of whom were immediately pressed on board of a man of war" (420). In one sentence Roderick sends thirty men off to precisely the same experience that forms the central, and most detailed, part of his adventures. Smollett makes us aware of the persistence of conditions from which Roderick is now retiring. As our hero hurries off to the consummation of his love affair, thirty of his crew involuntarily go to war. The body of the hero may be exempted, but the brutality of his society is unchanged.

Roderick's return to England and his happy reunion with his adored Narcissa is described by Smollett in a grand orchestration of sexual and monetary terms. The "forced contrivance" of the ending, especially in its use of the body, is extraordinarily deliberate.[16] Every touch, every sigh, is matched by a token of wealth and self-sufficiency. Narcissa herself, the image Roderick has pursued for so long, is now realized. The "dear object" of Roderick's hope is now his: "fortune hath at length recompenced me for all my sufferings" (425). Roderick, eager for the marriage, becomes "giddy with standing on the brink of bliss" (425), but the formalities prior to the wedding ceremony allow us to see clearly how the social vision of the novel's close is articulated. Body parts are matched with signs of wealth. Roderick stills Narcissa's bosom by "applying with my own hands a valuable necklace, composed of diamonds and amethysts set alternately" (425). When Roderick returns to his father, the latter not only inquires "very affectionately" about Narcissa, he also "put into [Roderick's] hand" a deed by which Roderick finds himself in possession of fifteen thousand pounds. The Randoms embrace tenderly and let fall "precious drops of sympathy" (426); bodies respond sympathetically to each other but are, at the same time, confused with, meld with, tokens of wealth and sufficiency. The valuable necklace allows the lover to touch his mistress's bosom. Hands touch as they transfer deeds.

The close of *Roderick Random* defines social knowledge as a particular kind of physical experience. What Roderick discovers at the end of the novel is a society in which bodies mirror each other,

16. The phrase belongs to James H. Bunn, who is skeptical of the novel's conclusion ("Signs of Randomness in *Roderick Random*," *Eighteenth-Century Studies* 14 [1980–81]: 469).

in which agitations, tears, and sighs find an immediate and equivalent response. Significantly, David Hume delineated exactly this
circularity in a description of the pleasures of wealth: "the pleasure,
which a rich man receives from his possessions, being thrown upon
the beholder, causes a pleasure and esteem; which sentiments
again, being perceiv'd and sympathiz'd with, encrease the pleasure
of the possessor; and being once more reflected, become a new
foundation for pleasure and esteem in the beholder."[17] Wealth is,
according to Hume, innocently and productively narcissistic. It
turns the bodies we encounter in the world into unthreatening versions of the self (that the beholders of wealth do not actually experience "pleasure and esteem" is a lesson we learn elsewhere in
Roderick Random). The closed circles formed by the reverbera-
tions of pleasure between wealthy man and beholder, Roderick and
the bride he adorns, Random Senior and the son he has discovered,
unite the participants in a tremulous social unity.

Roderick's body, previously ignored or invisible, when not the
object of abuse, is now reproduced symbolically in the portrait he
has painted for Narcissa, sympathetically by those who surround
him in his prosperity, and literally when Narcissa becomes pregnant with their child. *Roderick Random* ends with Narcissa's swelling form, and with the promise that their child, now sheltered in
the womb, will subsequently be shielded by the estate it will in-
herit. Roderick's body is no longer a mere instrument of sensation,
a mechanism that at times was denied even its humanity.

In denying that his first novel was autobiographical, Smollett
claimed that it was "representative" of a number of Scotch surgeons he had known. In fact, what the novel represents is the process whereby the hero's body, at first an object of suspicion,
acquires social meaning. Moreover, when Smollett engages our
sympathy on Roderick's behalf, he interests us in a whole class of
mute, sentient figures: the man with dropsy who falls from the mast
in the *Thunder;* the negro slaves to whom Roderick ministers in his
affluence. Roderick gives us a long account of the first, but barely
mentions the latter. In itself, this indicates his move to a social position from which certain kinds of physical experience become invisible and socially inconsequential. Over the course of his career

17. *Treatise of Human Nature,* 365.

Smollett continued to revise the social meanings of the body. In fact, his very next novel, *The Adventures of Peregrine Pickle,* offers disturbing versions of the bodily state invoked for symbolic purposes in the closing words of *Roderick Random.* I mean the "interesting situation" of Roderick's Narcissa, the pregnancy that the hero hopes will "produce something to crown [his] felicity."

CHAPTER FOUR

THE TROUBLED FEMALE BODY: *THE ADVENTURES OF PEREGRINE PICKLE*

Smollett's fiction often teases us because its strengths and real power seldom come from adroit use of novelistic convention, and the novels therefore tend to impress the reader in ways difficult to articulate economically. Particularly striking in this respect is his second novel, *The Adventures of Peregrine Pickle in which Are included the Memoirs of a Lady of Quality*. An uneven sprawl of a book, whose episodic nature is intensified by its inclusion of two lengthy interpolated tales, *Peregrine Pickle* is not easily represented as a whole. Most critical writing on the book, therefore, has centered on particular parts, either the story of the hero himself and the question of his moral growth, or the interpolated "Memoirs of a Lady of Quality," a sensational story of marital discord and adultery that eighteenth-century readers recognized as that of Lady Vane, born Frances Anne Hawes (c. 1715–88). While one would not want to force a spurious integrity upon the work, it is nonetheless true that its fragmentary nature does make those features its disparate sections share particularly provocative— especially when they are unexpected. A surprising aspect of *Peregrine Pickle* is that it houses so many varied images of the female body in trouble. In *Roderick Random* the heroine, as the name Narcissa suggests, simply represents a stage in the hero's own story, and that novel's treatment of women is fairly perfunctory. The one exception, of course, is that section of the novel narrated by Miss

Williams, the well-born young woman who reads too much, embarks on a love affair fatal to her happiness, is abandoned, and sinks into prostitution. Confronted with her sad tale, Roderick—who is not the most reflective of heroes—considers the gendered nature of experience.

> If one scheme of life should not succeed, I could have recourse to another, and so to a third, veering about to a thousand different shifts, according to the emergencies of my fate, without forfeiting the dignity of my character, beyond a power of retrieving it, or subjecting myself wholly to the caprice and barbarity of the world. On the other hand, she had known and relished the sweets of prosperity, she had been brought up under the wings of an indulgent parent, in all the delicacies to which her sex and rank entitled her; and without any extravagance of hope, entertained herself with the view of uninterrupted happiness thro' the whole scene of life— How fatal then, how tormenting, how intolerable must her reverse of fortune be! a reverse, that not only robbs her of these external comforts, and plunges her into all the miseries of want, but also murthers her peace of mind, and entails upon her the curse of eternal infamy!—Of all professions I pronounced that of a courtezan the most deplorable, and her of all courtezans the most unhappy. (136–37)

Male character can always be retrieved; once a woman sacrifices her bodily integrity, she suffers "eternal infamy." Roderick's stray reflection is powerfully dramatized in *Peregrine Pickle,* a novel that understands that within eighteenth-century society a woman's scheme of life is necessarily and intimately determined by her body, particularly her ability to bear children. In his *Commentaries on the Laws of England* Blackstone concluded that even the "disabilities" under which a wife lay were "for the most part intended for protection and benefit. So great a favourite is the female sex of the laws of England" (1:433). The attention *Peregrine Pickle* gives to the female experiences of pregnancy and motherhood is notable in itself. Even more striking, however, is that *Peregrine*

Pickle represents female physicality as endangered and threatened by the very social structures that are supposed to protect women's bodies: the family and the law.

Eighteenth-century England regulated the female role in the reproduction of the young and the transmission of property by a series of laws. Locke asserts that "every Man has a Property in his own Person. This no body has any right to but himself."[1] In practice, as the press-ganging in *Roderick Random* serves to remind us, bodily ownership in eighteenth-century England was often contested. Moreover, a woman's property in her person changed when she married. Marriage, Blackstone tells us, makes the husband and wife one person in law: "the very being or legal existence of the woman is suspended" (1:430).[2]

This suspension of the female person, this negation of her actual existence, is paradoxically supported and accompanied by a narrative in which female physicality is represented as both unproblematic in itself and serenely beyond and outside the political. We have already seen how doctrines of sensibility make the body pivotal in explanations of society. That the individual is innately virtuous, that such virtue manifests itself in physical response to those in need or distress, and that what bodies feel is socially significant, are all attractive doctrines—although they do have their limitations. Throughout the eighteenth century, female physicality in particular was constructed in terms of sensibility. Women, because their bodies are softer, their fibers laxer, than those of men, are also more sensible. The instinctive bond between mother and child, and the exquisite nature of maternal sensibility, also encouraged the notion that women are both consummately sociable and self-regulating in their sociability. It is the latter clause, of course, that needs to be emphasized, because representing female participation in society as immediate, natural response displaces the social real-

1. John Locke, *Two Treatises of Government,* ed. Peter Laslett (Cambridge: Cambridge University Press, 1966), 305.
2. Janelle Greenberg, although she argues against the misunderstanding that women in early-eighteenth-century England were "chattels and legal nonentities," concludes that upon marriage a woman was "subjected . . . to the disabilities implicit in the doctrine of a unity of person" ("The Legal Status of the English Woman in Early Eighteenth-Century Common Law and Equity," *Studies in Eighteenth-Century Culture* 4 [1975]: 171, 179).

ity of laws that control women. If one can summon up a well-regulated social world by representing the bonds between mother and child, then one need not advert to the fact that their relationship is also subject to a legal structure.

Discussion of the female body could create the illusion that women were somehow before and free of, rather than under and oppressed by, the law. Although the end results are unfortunate, such misapprehension of the female position could spring from poignant circumstance. In his *Treatise of Human Nature,* for example, David Hume considers the "union of male and female for the education of the young." Contemplating the considerable duration of this union in humans, Hume submits that for men

> to impose on themselves this restraint, and undergo chearfully all the fatigues and expences, to which it subjects them, they must believe, that the children are their own, and that their natural instinct is not directed to a wrong object, when they give a loose to love and tenderness. Now if we examine the structure of the human body, we shall find, that this security is very difficult to be attain'd on our part; and that since, in the copulation of the sexes, the principle of generation goes from the man to the woman, an error may easily take place on the side of the former, tho' it be utterly impossible with regard to the latter. From this trivial and anatomical observation is deriv'd that vast difference betwixt the education and duties of the two sexes. (570–71)

The fact that Hume himself never married or had children makes his acknowledgment of the "fatigues and expences" of bringing up the young, and of the psychological risks of giving "a loose to love and tenderness," particularly warm and human. His empathy is exhausted, however, and his tone turns matter of fact, once his focus shifts to the role of women in marriage. Hume flatly justifies the "vast difference betwixt the education and duties of the two sexes" by a man's need to know his own progeny, and does not voice the possibility that this "difference" may also be responsible for female unhappiness of various kinds. Nor does it seem unreasonable to him that female experience should be wholly determined by the peculiarities of male anatomy. While one would prefer Hume to be alert to these implications, most remarkable is his sense that the social construction of gender is a way of artificially creating for men the kind of security that women already enjoy. Hume thinks it "utterly impossible" for a woman to be mistaken about her child, and therefore she simply cannot direct her "natural instinct . . . to a wrong object." Men require the intervention of society if they are to enjoy their "natural instincts" in peace, but the structures of the human body make the exercise of female sensibility unproblematic; women can love their children without fear.

Celebrations of female sensibility and physicality encouraged the tendency to treat women's legal disabilities with sangfroid. Representative here is William Alexander, a Scotsman who published *The History of Women* in 1779. An enlightenment text, *The History* urges a "rational education" for women that will allow them to "assert the rights of nature" (1:iv), but it views their legal situation with complete equanimity. Rephrasing Blackstone, Alexander describes how the "political existence" of a woman is, in marriage, "annihilated, or incorporated into that of her husband." Women do not, however, lose through marriage, because the "little mortification" of political annihilation is made good by an "extensive list of privileges" (2:422). For example, a married woman cannot be imprisoned for any debts she contracts. Alexander's further elucidation of the bargain a married woman makes with her society employs two different understandings of the body. Married women, denied proprietorship of their own bodies, "excluded almost from every thing which can give them consequence," derive power from their charms, and these "when joined to sensibility, often fully compensate . . . for all disadvantages they are laid under by law and custom" (2:439). Their own self-regulating sensibility gives women a power equal to that they are denied by the law and political structures. As explicitly as Mary Wollstonecraft, though with a very different emphasis and attitude, Alexander links female sensibility to legal disadvantage: sensibility is what women have instead of a political identity.

Superficially convincing as it may be, Alexander's opposition misstates the relationship between female sensibility and political identity. Sensibility is treacherous not because it supplies women with an alternative to political existence, but because it occludes the ground of their political being. In his influential analysis of eighteenth-century sensibility, John Mullan succinctly explains that sensibility elides the difference between society as "a fellowship of feeling" and "political society, in which property is secured by 'Justice.'"[3] If society is defined as a system of charitable and benevolent impulses, then women are full participants in that society; but if society is defined in terms of property, then the position of women is severely compromised. If sensibility in general covers up the "potential disparity between the immediate experience of sociability . . . and the implication of belonging to a political society,"[4] then female sensibility is particularly hard worked. Female sensibility, far from being the ground of political exclusion, is in fact a particularly insidious adjunct of the law.

While it is relatively easy to theorize a relationship between the material power of the law and the ideological power invested in notions of sensibility, documenting manifestations of that relationship (especially outside fiction) proves more difficult. One instance is provided by the debates surrounding the passage of Hardwicke's Marriage Act in 1753. In these debates, lawmakers addressed the nature of marriage, the importance of passion and love, and the requirements of property. The primary aim of this legislation was to prevent clandestine marriage. Such marriages, performed by unscrupulous clergymen on unwitting or nonconsenting parties, or on minors acting without parental consent, were an acknowledged social problem. Not only did clandestine marriages remove marriage from parental control, they also facilitated bigamy and led to expensive law cases about the legitimacy of children. Proponents of the bill held that, if all marriages were public and accurately recorded, these problems could be eliminated. The bill required the reading of banns, the acquisition of a special license if the marriage was not solemnized in a church or chapel, the presence of two witnesses at the ceremony, and the entry of the marriage into a register. Eventually, after heated debates both within and outside the Houses of Parliament, the legislation passed.[5]

Opponents of the bill disputed Parliament's right to nullify

3. *Sentiment and Sociability,* 33–34.
4. Ibid., 34.
5. The Lords passed it by 100 to 11, the Commons (after amendments) by 125 to 56, and the Lords accepted the amended bill without a vote (Lawrence Stone, *Road to Divorce: England, 1530–1987* [Oxford: Oxford University Press, 1990], 127).

marriages recognized by canon law. They also argued that the de-
lays and deliberation it required before a couple could marry were
unsuited to the nature and sensibilities of the English people, "naturally sanguine, impatient, and as apt to change as the air they
breathe."[6] They suggested that the bill was an aristocratic conspir-
acy, designed to prevent wealth from circulating, and opined that
love was "an ungovernable and irresistible passion" (17) that could
not be regulated by law. Historians agree that the 1753 debates are
enormously significant, but disagree fundamentally in their interpretations. Christopher Lasch says it is "tempting" to see opponents of the bill as "advocates of a distinctively modern concept of
marriage," pitted against aristocrats merely interested in marriage
as "a means of arranging alliances," but that, in fact, the opponents'
emphasis on sexual attraction adheres to "a very old-fashioned
conception of marriage."[7] Lawrence Stone finds few of the arguments against the bill "convincing," although he does regard as
serious the allegation that "the real purpose of the bill was to give
parents of rank and fortune a veto power over the marriage of their
children."[8] Certainly, the class interests of the proponents were
very obvious in debate, and one of the main arguments made in the
bill's favor was that it would help do away with the distress some of
the "best families" had been brought into by heirs' marrying "common strumpets" and heiresses' being carried off by men "of low
birth" or "infamous sharper[s]" (3). Noting that historians have
tended to overlook the "interested" motives of the bill's opponents
and to emphasize their talk of passion and feeling, Erica Harth argues that the real subject of the parliamentary debate was "the
spoils of an industrious nation with a developing capitalist economy."[9] Speakers against the bill employed a limited view of equality in which "'love' stays within the ranks of the propertied."

6. William Cobbett, *The Parliamentary History of England from the Earliest Period to the Year 1803* (London, 1813), 57. Unless otherwise indicated, all
further references to the debate are from this account and will be given parenthetically in the text.
7. "The Suppression of Clandestine Marriage in England," *Salmagundi* 26
(1974): 90.
8. *Road to Divorce,* 126–27.
9. "The Virtue of Love: Lord Hardwicke's Marriage Act," *Cultural Critique* 9
(spring 1988): 139.

According to Harth, "Eighteenth-century virtue converted the property value of chastity into a sentiment that could resolve the contradictions of economic transformation" (151), and members of the House of Commons (irrespective of their stand on the bill) subscribed to the "ideology of a virtuous love that would preserve both the social and the sexual order" (154).[10] Harth's central point is both relatively simple and extremely important: parliamentarians are considering, not whether, but how money and property shall circulate in marriage. Once this point has been acknowledged, we are able to see that what unites these speakers is more fundamental than what divides them, for they all depend upon a version of female physicality marked by sentiment and sensibility.

Assessing Hardwicke's act in *A Continuation of the Complete History of England*, Smollett says that the evils foreseen by its opponents had not materialized, but that "the abuse of clandestine marriage might have been removed upon much easier terms than those imposed upon the subject by this bill" (67).[11] Smollett's measured dislike of the bill may have to do with the extreme punishments for which it allowed: anyone who celebrated a marriage without publishing the banns or obtaining a license was liable for seven years' transportation, and those who tampered with either licenses or registers committed a felony punishable by death. Alternatively, he may be expressing a more generalized suspicion of unnecessary state regulation. Smollett's nonfiction does not draw attention to, or dissent from, his culture's nonproblematic alignment of female virtue and property. Such a view, however, is complicated by the way his second novel insistently tries to narrate the physical experience, at once troubled and elusive, of female sensibility at odds with the law.

Work on issues of representation and gender in the eighteenth century has been enabled by Julia Kristeva's theorization of

10. Charlotte Sussman comments that one of the strengths of Harth's use of legal history is that it allows discussion of the formation of female identity "through both ideological pressures and material sanctions" ("'I Wonder Whether Poor Miss Sally Godfrey Be Living or Dead': The Married Woman and the Rise of the Novel," *Diacritics* 20 [1990]: 99).

11. In the *Atom* Smollett satirizes Hardwicke as one who "thought he had procured a new law for clapping padlocks upon the chastity of all the females in Japan under twenty, of which padlocks he himself kept the keys" (31).

the semiotic, a dimension associated particularly with the maternal body and opposed to the signifying order of the symbolic. Laurie Langbauer, for example, uses Kristeva to illuminate how in Mary Wollstonecraft the "maternal space remains curiously vacant" and the mother is "not completely represented, because her place is outside the signifying order, unrepresentable."[12] Wollstonecraft consciously set out to exhibit "the misery and oppression, peculiar to women, that arise out of the partial laws and customs of society."[13] Tobias Smollett never expresses any such intention; nonetheless, his fractured second novel is given strange coherence by its representation of female misery under the law.

The notion that *Peregrine Pickle* sympathetically renders bodies in trouble is not, however, likely to be the reader's first response to the novel. In certain ways *Peregrine Pickle* repeats the successful formula of *Roderick Random*. The hero, whom we accompany from birth to marriage, is a hot-blooded individual who travels a good deal, enjoys and suffers from various excesses, and is eventually reformed by the virtuous heroine. Peregrine, being more fortunate than Roderick, sees the world through a university education and the grand tour. The first impression created by this work is that Smollett's interest in what bodies feel and experience has become driven and obsessive, and, as manifested by the hero's "practical satire," distinctly unpleasant. Peregrine's "satire" involves disguise, cross-dressing, imposture, and mimicry, and in some instances, as when he passes himself off as a fortune-teller in London, he does expose and correct the vices of society in orthodox satiric fashion.[14] For much of the time, however, he just seems to enjoy inflicting physical pain on others. After one such adventure, the narrator comments that the passion that prompts persons "oth-

12. *Women and Romance: The Consolations of Gender in the English Novel* (Ithaca: Cornell University Press, 1990), 103.
13. *Maria, or The Wrongs of Woman* (New York: Norton, 1975), 21.
14. Estimates of Peregrine as satirist differ. According to David Evans, "Peregrine is the satirist of formal verse satire made flesh and sent to dwell among us . . . the satirist imagined as arbitrary victimizer, self-appointed nemesis of the concealed weakness, immorality, or foolishness in every man" ("Peregrine Pickle: The Complete Satirist," *Studies in the Novel* 3 [1971]: 260). Ronald Paulson, on the other hand, doubts that "the themes of Peregrine's satire and of his moral decline ever come together" (*Satire and the Novel in Eighteenth-Century England* [New Haven: Yale University Press, 1967], 185).

erwise generous and sympathising, to afflict and perplex their fellow-creatures" is both "preposterous and unaccountable" (72). There is certainly something mysterious and inexplicable in Peregrine's treatment of the bodies he encounters. The narrative aside quoted above suggests that the hero's moral education may consist in a growing respect for the physical experience of others, in his becoming accountable for what he does to other bodies. Much of what happens in *Peregrine Pickle* pivots on the hero's ability to protect his own body from exposure, while he subjects those of his satiric victims to discomfort and pain. Arguments that *Peregrine Pickle* is unified by the hero's moral rehabilitation center on his changed attitude towards the human body: we see his proclivity to satire corrected by his susceptibility to sensibility, his tendency to exploit the physical fragility of others tempered by a discovery of his own physical vulnerability.[15]

In this discovery the gendered nature of sensibility plays an important role. Smollett represents Peregrine's ability to right his own attitudes towards the body as being dependent on the sensibility of the heroine, Emilia Gauntlet. The crucial event in their story, one of the strands that most obviously holds the novel together, is Peregrine's attempt first to seduce, then to rape, the woman he supposedly loves. Significant, both in Peregrine's attempt and Emilia's ability to withstand it, are the versions of human physicality on which each relies. The scene is not only an attempt upon Emilia's body, but, because both characters articulate as well as occupy a particular position, a debate about the body. Having lured the unsuspecting Emilia to a brothel, Peregrine announces that he can "no longer live upon the unsubstantial food of expectation" (407). His assertion that passion has him "wound up" to an unbearable pitch is supported by the symptoms of intense feeling: his address is "abrupt," accompanied with "symptoms of frantic agitation," and tears gush from his eyes. Confronted with this display of physical intensity, Emilia is undaunted. She points out that she is not at liberty to lay her "reserve" aside until he has made his passion public. Her vocabulary ("avow," "form," "sanction," and

15. Susan Bourgeois gives a version of this argument in her *Nervous Juyces and the Feeling Heart: The Growth of Sensibility in the Novels of Tobias Smollett* (New York: Peter Lang, 1986).

"duty") is that of public discourse. Implicit in Emilia's response is
the notion that the institution of marriage can assuage Peregrine's
desires and bring the natural and social happily together. This harmony can be achieved, at least in part, because Emilia's sensibility,
unlike Peregrine's, is informed by social norms. Smollett's metony-
mic use of Emilia's heart (the center of sensibility), and the adjectives he uses to describe it ("virtuous," "sensible," "delicate,"
"tender" [407]), naturalizes Emilia's public vocabulary and associates it with her physical being. The conflict between the two inten-
sifies; Emilia continues to resist and Peregrine attempts to rape her,
only to be rebuffed by Emilia's eloquent scorn. Confidence in her
own innocence and "the authority of the law" protect her from
the horror of the situation (408). Then she walks resolutely out the
door. Emilia exemplifies the harmony of female sensibility and the
law that protects it.

Submerged in this scene is a narrative of class difference. Peregrine, at this point in the novel, seeks to ingratiate himself with the
nobility through marriage, and, out of pride, he aspires to the hand
of a "duchess dowager" (397). Emilia, however, is in the care of her
merchant uncle. Peregrine may gratify the uncle with "praise of
commerce, and the promoters thereof" and draw "ludicrous pictures of the manners and education of what is called high life"
(400), but he does not intend to ally himself with the merchant
class. Given these facts, Peregrine's attempt on Emilia uninten-
tionally vindicates marriage laws, including male property in
women's bodies, which are designed to protect women from "aristocratic or libertine conduct."[16]

The rape episode in *Peregrine Pickle* would seem to justify
the kind of thinking that led to the successful passage of Hardwicke's act: bodily feeling is as much a matter of the law as anything
else. Emilia's internalization of the law not only protects her own
body, but also leads to the rehabilitation of her would-be ravisher.
When she walks resolutely out the door, Peregrine's "keen re-

16. Keith Thomas, "The Double Standard," *Journal of the History of Ideas*
20 (1959): 204. For the view that a major concern in the novel is Peregrine's
coming to a proper understanding of his class position, see Ian Campbell Ross,
"'With Dignity and Importance': Peregrine Pickle as Country Gentleman," in
Smollett: Author of the First Distinction, ed. Alan Bold (Totowa, N.J.: Barnes
and Noble, 1982), 148–69.

morse" leads to "a violent fit of distraction" that makes him physically incapable (409). Ultimately, Peregrine is forced to undergo
the symptoms he had previously mimicked. No longer transcendent, his body now records his turbulence of spirit. Intermittently,
for the rest of the novel, his failure to make peace with Emilia
causes "an apoplexy of disappointment and despair" (419) or
forces him to retire from her presence "into another room, where
he threw himself upon a couch, and fainted" (589). Peregrine's
physical vulnerability is a prelude to his moral rehabilitation by
Emilia. Finally, their relationship is institutionalized by her assumption of "household affairs" (781) in marriage. The conflict between Emilia and Peregrine suggests that considerations of
property and law can inform sensibility in benign, beneficial ways.
Peregrine's identification of sensibility with pure physical passion
is rejected by Emilia, whose own sensibility incorporates the social
norms for a woman of her class. Shocked and frightened as she is by
Peregrine's conduct, Emilia is not overcome by her passions. Her
confidence in the "authority of the law" (408) gives her physical
strength. Peregrine, on the other hand, is physically overcome by
consciousness of his guilt. Emilia, the middle-class heroine, not
only successfully protects herself by placing sexuality within the legal contract of marriage; she also brings about a physical and moral
(the two cannot be distinguished here) reformation of the quasi-
aristocratic hero. The marriage plot of *Peregrine Pickle* shows how
an awareness of property rights influences and modifies sensibility.
    The most obvious objection to this reading of the novel is its
implausibility. Even after Peregrine is stricken by remorse over his
treatment of Emilia, he salves his self-esteem by buying a young
beggar woman from her mother: "The girl was about the age of sixteen, and notwithstanding the wretched equipage in which she appeared, exhibited to his view a set of agreeable features, enlivened
with the complexion of health and chearfulness" (596). This crude
affirmation of male purchasing power does not contrast as much as
one would wish with its more routine, refined form: marriage. Two
years later on the floor of the House of Commons, Charles Towns-
end would note that "the highest bloom of a woman's beauty, is
from sixteen to twenty-one: it is then that a young woman of little or
no fortune has the best chance of disposing herself to advantage in
marriage; shall we make it impossible for her to do so, without the

82 CHAPTER FOUR

consent of an indigent and mercenary father?" (28). One of the arguments against clandestine marriage was that "by this means women may be married against their wills and so lose the property of their own persons: which is the most valuable of all properties."[17] While Peregrine's roadside transaction and the bargain he makes with Emilia in marriage are both technically voluntary, both women "lose the property of their own persons." They differ because Emilia's loss is disguised through the rhetoric of sensibility.

One might also point out here the extent to which eighteenth-century understandings of female sensibility are class-bound. Peregrine metamorphoses his purchase into a fine lady and uses her to demonstrate (successfully for a time) that the only "essential difference" between polite company and the lower classes "is the form of an education" (599). Having passed her off in high society as his cousin, Peregrine begins "to be tired of his acquisition" and is just as pleased that she and his valet elope and are "buckled at the fleet" (602). In debating Hardwicke's bill the attorney general regretted that there could not be one form of marriage for the rich and one for the poor. Legally that was an impossibility, but ideologically it was achieved. Beggar girls circulate through roadside transactions and Fleet bucklings. Middle-class women only circulate through marriages involving sensibility and virtuous love.

Peregrine's rehabilitation is premised on an ultimately beneficial congruence of bodily feeling and social regulation, but nowhere else in the novel is this congruence established. In fact, one of the most haunting features of *Peregrine Pickle* is its representation of the female body and the way in which its experiences are troubled, rendered elusive and difficult by the law. In *Peregrine Pickle* the female body is as important a subject as the titular hero. The novel's episodes are united as much by an interest in pregnancy, birth, and mother/child relationships as they are by Peregrine's adventures. Each of the novel's three distinct parts—the story of Peregrine, "The Memoirs of a Lady of Quality," and the story of the Annesley claimant—foreground, in either a comic or a

17. Henry Gally, *Some Considerations upon Clandestine Marriages,* quoted in Randolph Trumbach, *The Rise of the Egalitarian Family: Aristocratic Kinship and Domestic Relations in Eighteenth-Century England* (New York: Academic Press, 1978), 151.

tragic way, the female body. In each of the three stories a woman's natural instincts, in particular her experience of sexuality and maternity, are seen to be perverted or rendered monstrous by her implication in property relations. As the stories are otherwise very different, the reader is led to understand that the conflict they portray is one common to diverse women. The implication, then, is that the structures of society, and not the choices of individual women, are to blame for the unhappy situations all the stories represent. I say "implication" advisedly, because *Peregrine Pickle* is not at all a schematic work, and atomization of female experience is not an avowed aim of the text. Yet Smollett's second novel, like his first, establishes a gap between bodily experience and the social meaning of that experience, and in *Peregrine Pickle* the body is often female. Simply including the female body would not, of course, make *Peregrine Pickle* significant, and Smollett does not tell *Peregrine Pickle* through the female body as Richardson does *Pamela* or *Clarissa.* Yet, when Smollett draws our attention to female bodies in *Peregrine Pickle,* he emphasizes their pain and uneasiness in ways that make the reader seek a cause. Again and again, the puzzle leads to the control of women's bodies by the law.

Lady Vane, the subject and supposed narrator of the "Memoirs," and Lady Altham, the mother of the Annesley claimant, were historical characters whose stories had engrossed public attention before Smollett included them in his novel. Apart from their sensational appeal, which we will consider in due time, the stories of these "real" women destroy any notion that female physicality always is, or always should be, compatible with the laws that regulate women. Moreover, the idea that these tales are instructive and contain object lessons, not only for the reader but for Peregrine himself, is supported by the way in which they are framed. Before Lady Vane narrates her story, she is established as a worthy, charitable individual who deserves and earns Peregrine's respect. The second story Peregrine hears in the humiliating confines of the debtors' prison. In discussing the epistemology and form of *Peregrine Pickle,* John M. Warner observes that the interpolated tales represent a "realism of assessment," which Smollett's attempt to achieve formal realism "vitiates."[18] The first part of this statement is un-

18. "The Interpolated Narratives in the Fiction of Fielding and Smollett: An Epistemological View," *Studies in the Novel* 5 (1973): 279.

questionably true. I would suggest, however, that what the interpolated tales represent and assess "realistically" is the vexed position of the female body under the law, and that they do it strongly enough to undermine any reassurances on this matter the novel elsewhere offers.

Two weeks before Smollett's novel appeared, the *Monthly* reviewed an anonymous pamphlet (now attributed to John Hill) entitled "The History of a Woman of Quality, or The Adventures of Lady Frail": "Whether these memoirs have any foundation in fact, we know not; nor who is the person designed to be understood under the name of Lady Frail. The public, ever ready enough to be caught by such baits, have, on this occasion, agreed to mention the name of a lady, who is creditably reported to have given real memoirs of herself, to the author of a famous novel, entitled, *The Adventures of Roderick Random* to be inserted and made public in a new work of his."[19] The lady whose name the public had "agreed to mention" was Lady Vane, born Frances Anne Hawes, and she excited interest through her notorious infidelities. Hill's titillating romp, ostensibly a "warning to the female sex," exploits, and comes fairly close to exhausting, the stereotype that "every woman is at heart a rake." His heroine is governed solely by an omnivorous sexual appetite, which she satisfies with anything that wears "the Habit of a man" (58). She is equally comfortable in her husband's brother's bed and cavorting in the heather with a "lusty highlander" she happens to meet while out for a stroll (38, 43). Hill both exploits female sexuality and denies the female person—in one of the scandal sheet's most telling passages, Lady Frail's husband (shortly to die from grief at her adultery) confronts, and instantly forms an attachment to, the "lusty highlander." As the two men converse (quickly forgetting Lady Frail, the only thing they have in common), we realize that even in eighteenth-century pornography the female body could not be certain of sustained attention. In contrast, the representation of Lady Vane's body in Smollett's "Memoirs of a Lady of Quality" makes her (as John Hill somewhat bemusedly remarked), "A Model for the rest of the Female World."[20]

19. *Monthly Review* 4 (1751): 307–8.
20. Kelly, *Tobias Smollett,* 73. The provenance of "Memoirs of a Lady of Quality" has occasioned much scholarly debate. H. S. Buck contends that Lady Vane wrote the memoirs herself and that Smollett merely inserted them in the

The first marriage of Frances Anne Hawes, to Lord William Hamilton, was a love match, and his death left her in a "stupification of sorrow" (448). After an interval, his widow "yielded to the importunity" (450) of her friends and married Lord Vane, the "very reverse" of her late husband (449). In the "Memoirs" Lady Vane's compliance in marrying a man she cannot love, not her subsequent affairs, occasions guilt. Felicity Nussbaum discusses the genre of the scandalous memoir as one in which the female speaker acknowledges and explains her crimes while trying to "escape the moral and social system which requires that very explanation."[21] The system against which Lady Vane justifies herself is that which makes a woman's body the property of her husband in matrimony, and the argument she uses against it is her own physical experience.

Lady Vane, speaking as one whose head may have "erred" but whose heart "hath always been uncorrupted" (433), seeks the approval of those who identify virtue with intense physical response to others. Smollett stages Lady Vane's narration by introducing her to the reader as a "charitable gentlewoman" (430), "breathing sentiment and beneficence, and softened into the most inchanting tenderness of weeping sympathy" (431). Lady Vane's "thousand acts of uncommon charity" (538), caused by the "deep impression" the "misery of [her] fellow-creatures" makes on her heart (537), demonstrate a virtue that flawlessly unites physical experience and moral response.

Each event in Lady Vane's life has a physical correlative. On

---

novel (*A Study in Smollett: Chiefly Peregrine Pickle* [1925; reprint, Mamaroneck, N.Y.: Appel, 1973], 47). Rufus Putney, on the other hand, argues that no contemporary thought Lady Vane capable of such an exercise and that "there is a considerable body of opinion . . . to support the view that Lady Vane furnished the materials which Smollett whipped into form" ("Smollett and Lady Vane's Memoirs," *Philological Quarterly* 25 [1946]: 126). Putney relies on mere sexism ("We are confronted in the 'Memoirs' with a masculine vocabulary and style" [122]), and his arguments from internal evidence are inconclusive (he isolates the rich vocabulary and heavy use of alliteration as "two mannerisms characteristic of Smollett" [126]), but the consonance between the themes of *Peregrine Pickle* and the memoirs suggests to me that Smollett had a significant role in shaping them for publication.

21. *The Autobiographical Subject: Gender and Ideology in Eighteenth-Century England* (Baltimore: Johns Hopkins University Press, 1989), 180.

first realizing she is loved, "my colour changed, my heart throbbed
with unusual violence" (435); when her lover falls ill, "grief and
anxiety became so conspicuous in my countenance . . . that every
body in the house perceived the situation of my thoughts" (455);
abandoned by a lover, she is "overwhelmed with . . . sorrow and
surprize," undergoing near fatal "violent agitation" (469–70); as
the victim of her husband's schemes she is "fretted and frighted
into sundry fits of illness" (491). Indeed, Lady Vane's narrative is
one in which strong passion often results in illness. Grief for her
stillborn first child precipitates a "dangerous fever" (446), and her
first husband's death plunges her into a "languishing distemper"
(448). The worry engendered by the "caprice and barbarity" of
Lord Vane causes an illness in which her life is "thought in danger"
(514). Lady Vane's body is one in which passion and expression are
thoroughly connected. Her story manifests the "sudden and remarkable effects of the passions" to an audience aware that "excess
of passion hath often proved fatal both to men and women."[22]
When she finishes her account, Peregrine is most amazed not at her
morals but at her survival of adventures "sufficient to destroy the
most hardy and robust constitution" (538).

Lady Vane's physical susceptibility makes her "uncorrupted
heart" legible and supports her contention that "the affections are
altogether involuntary" (473). Her sensations, whether they are
those of benevolence or love, can be neither avoided nor disguised.
Her "indiscretion" is a form of "candour" (432) that springs from
her sensibility. She commits her first infidelity because her heart
was "naturally adapted for the tender passions, and had been so fortunate, so cherished, in its first impressions, that it felt with joy the
same sensations revive, when influenced by the same engaging
qualifications" (457). Lady Vane is distinguished from her contemporaries not by her sexual transgressions, but by her "primitive
way of thinking" (456) in a society addicted to duplicity and disguise. Her sensibility not only justifies her sexual adventures; it also
satirizes a social world governed by "ceremonial visits, and empty
professions" (463). In Lady Vane's account of herself, virtue, sensibility, and sexuality are all united through their common origin in

22. Tobias Smollett, *Essay on the External Use of Water,* ed. Claude E. Jones
(Baltimore: Johns Hopkins University Press, 1935), 57.

the body, and they all partake of a primitive naturalism that ill accords with the corrupt society in which she moves.

Lady Vane's exemplary body is, however, a site of conflict because it is the property of her husband. In keeping with the association of charity and sexuality upon which the "Memoirs" insist, and in contrast to his charitable, passionate wife, Lord Vane is both devoid of "the impressions of humanity and benevolence," and, the narrative implies, sexually impotent. On his first visit to his future wife, Lord Vane makes a grotesque, unnatural appearance: "Whether it was with a view of screening himself from the cold, or of making a comfortable medium in case of being overturned, . . . I know not; but certain it is, the carriage was stuffed with hay, in such a manner, that when he arrived, the servants were at some pains in rummaging and removing it, before they could come at their master, or help him to alight" (449). From the first we see Lord Vane as a creature protected from the world of sensation, incapable of receiving impressions of any kind. Immune to physical urges, he spends his wedding night "moping in a corner, like a criminal on execution-day" and later forces his wife to endure his "shadowy, unsubstantial" (451) approaches. After this, the only desire he enunciates is that she "lie a whole hour every morning, with [her] neck uncovered, that by gazing he might quiet the perturbation of his spirits" (454). Lord Vane's physicality, on those rare occasions we are aware of it, is perverse and problematic. Incurably dependent, he supports and supplements his weak presence with a retinue of servants. We are told how he once interrupted a conversation with his wife and "called up three of his servants, whom he placed as centinels upon the stair" (496). After they separate, Lord Vane only appears to his wife with a "formidable band" (497), or "several domesticks armed" (514), or with "auxiliaries, reinforced with a constable" (520).

Throughout her narration, Lady Vane takes pains to erase what physical presence her husband does possess. We see a full-blooded and responsive wife tied to a mere cipher: a man who is defined solely by the powers the marriage contract confer on him, "a mere non entity" and "nominal husband" (456). Yet, finally, Lord Vane's powers as husband supply all his personal deficiencies. Lady Vane's narrative artfully points a paradox: the most "nominal" husband, the most pronounced "non entity," exerts legal power over

even the most superior wife. Two admissions underscore this paradox: Lady Vane is an instrument for the transmission of property
(had her affair produced a child, she would not have allowed it to
inherit "to the detriment of the right heir" [456]), and she is once
again living under her husband's roof (536). Lady Vane orchestrates her story so we become painfully aware of a clash between
the validity of female physical experience and oppression of matrimonial law. In the cult of sensibility the body generates meaning,
but in political terms that body has already been assigned a meaning as the foundation of property. Ideally, for the purposes of social
regulation, both meanings should be identical, but the "Memoirs,"
dividing Lady Vane's body into an object of property and a sensible, virtuous being, records an incongruity between her sensible
experience and legal definitions of her body. Speaking of the
importance, during this period, of "organic liaisons" to "political
rule," Terry Eagleton reminds us that "[t]o rely on sentiment as a
source of one's social cohesion is not as precarious a matter as it
looks. The bourgeois state, after all, still has its coercive instruments at the ready should this project falter; and what bonds could
in any case be stronger, more unimpeachable, than those of the
senses, of 'natural' compassion and instinctive allegiance?"[23] Eagleton's insight is pertinent here for a number of reasons. Lady
Vane establishes a sort of "social cohesion" through her natural
compassion. This social good cannot, however, be separated from
the very sexuality that estranges Lady Vane from her society and
subjects her to the "coercive instruments" of the law. In her case,
property and sensibility cannot be reconciled, and their conflict exposes the rhetoric by which writers on law, using the language of
sentiment, "naturalized property by associating it with the
body."[24]

    Throughout *Peregrine Pickle* female bodies suffer because of
their implication in property relations. That suffering becomes
most apparent in the most literal "organic liaison" of all: that between mother and child. As readers of *Peregrine Pickle* we monitor

    23. *Ideology of the Aesthetic*, 23–24.
    24. Judith Frank, "'A Man Who Laughs Is Never Dangerous': Character
and Class in Sterne's *A Sentimental Journey*," *English Literary History* 56
(1989): 103.

several pregnancies, each of which is a bizarre source of confusion and uncertainty.[25] The peculiarities of these pregnancies, which are rendered in both comic and tragic versions, are directly related to the fact that the expected child is also an heir. For example, Mrs. Trunnion, Peregrine's aunt, congratulates herself "on the symptoms of her own fertility" (47) and, having enjoyed her "sweet delusion" (50) for several months, discovers she has never been pregnant at all. Her intense desire to increase her own importance and gratify her husband with "an heir of his own begetting" (47) causes her to produce a phantom pregnancy.

Mrs. Pickle does gives birth to a healthy baby, but her relationship with Peregrine never approaches normality. First, she tortures him by washing him in freezing water, and, later in his young life, she inexplicably and brutally rejects him completely. The scenes in which Mrs. Pickle recoils from her own flesh parody those of sensible recognition celebrated elsewhere in the eighteenth-century novel: "no sooner was he presented to his mother than her countenance changed, she eyed him with tokens of affliction and surprise, and bursting into tears, exclaimed her child was dead, and this was no other than an impostor whom they had brought to defraud her sorrow" (64). Throughout the text Mrs. Pickle continues to entertain a "monstrous prejudice" against her son and will not offer him "the least mark of maternal regard" (108). At novel's end, Peregrine can take possession of his father's estate only by ousting his younger brother and various servants and confining his mother to her chamber. He learns that his mother sought to exclude him as heir (769) and hears her beg "pardon of God for having brought such a monster into the world" (768).

Why, when she looks at a man regarded by others as elegant, charming, and distinguished, does his mother see only a "monster"? The answer does not lie in Peregrine's physical constitution, but in his relationship to his father's estate. The household into which Peregrine is born values property over all else. His father, Gamaliel Pickle, is "little subject to refined sensations" (2) and sees

25. G. S. Rousseau notes that *Peregrine Pickle* is the first novel to "refer to heated controversies about the role of imagination in abnormal pregnancy" ("Pineapples, Pregnancy, and *Peregrine Pickle*," in *Tobias Smollett: Bicentennial Essays Presented to Lewis M. Knapp*, ed. P.-G. Boucé and G. S. Rousseau [New York: Oxford University Press, 1971], 82).

the human body as a form of property like any other. The "mercantile plainness" of Gamaliel's comic proposal to Sally Appleby, his future wife—"[u]nderstanding you have a parcel of heart, warranted sound, to be disposed of, shall be willing to treat for said commodity, on reasonable terms" (14)—reminds us that, if marriage is a contract like any other, then the heart is a "commodity" brought to market.

From several hints in the novel it seems clear that Peregrine's mother hates him because he is not her husband's son and represents her sin against property.[26] We are told that, when Gamaliel proposed, Sally's father "recommended the immediate execution of the project with . . . eagerness," suggesting a fear that his daughter's temperament might not keep "much longer cool" (13). We are further told that Mr. Pickle's celebration of his nuptials leaves him on his wedding night "deprived of all manner of sensation," a "misfortune" his new wife accepts "like a discreet woman, perfectly well acquainted with the nature of her own situation" (18). Mrs. Pickle successfully imposes her illegitimate son on her husband, but consciousness of her crime makes that son repellent to her.

Accounts of pregnancy in the eighteenth century, both popular and professional, devoted much attention to the effects of the mother's imagination and desires upon the fetus. A maternal longing for strawberries, for example, might mark the unborn child's body. In *Peregrine Pickle* Smollett exploits these theories for comic effect. Peregrine's aunt, anxious to protect her brother's heir, determines to watch over the pregnancy. To this end she equips herself with Culpepper's *Directory for Midwives* and, to prevent danger, endeavors to gratify her sister-in-law's every longing. Noting that *Peregrine Pickle* is the first English novel to refer to controversies surrounding pregnancy, G. S. Rousseau remarks that in many texts the mother's imagination or desire was seen as accounting for monstrous births, including those of "Hermaphrodites, Dwarfs or Gyants."[27] Providing a "socio-economic context" for writings on monstrous births, P.-G. Boucé concludes that "all the controversial eighteenth-century polemics about the force of pregnant women's imagination over the foetus may well be construed as a devious la-

---

26. R. G. Collins marshals the evidence for Peregrine's illegitimacy ("The Hidden Bastard: A Question of Illegitimacy in Smollett's *Peregrine Pickle*," *PMLA* 94 [1979]: 91–105).

27. "Pineapples, Pregnancy, and *Peregrine Pickle*," 82.

tent antifeminist discourse."[28] According to Mrs. Pickle—though
to no one else—she has given birth to a monster. In this case, however, female imagination acts as it does only because of Mrs.
Pickle's internalization of property relations. When she reviles Peregrine,
she does so in the voice of property, according to which he is, indeed, a monstrous imposter. Mrs. Pickle's implication in property
law prohibits a natural relationship to her son. If Peregrine's wife
harmonizes the natural and the legal selves, his mother's rejection
of her own flesh and blood intimates that the law is responsible for
the destruction of tender bonds.

　　While Smollett does not try to enlist the reader's compassion
for Mrs. Pickle's perversion of maternal feeling, her difficulty is
given added weight by the emphasis mother/child relationships are
given in the novel's second interpolated tale: the story of the
Annesley claimant. Even given that many eighteenth-century
novels prominently feature either illegitimate children or children
whose origins are shrouded in obscurity and mystery (one need
only think of *Moll Flanders, Tom Jones,* and *Evelina*), *Peregrine
Pickle* has a large population of actual, or imputed, illegitimate off-
spring. An illegitimate child is not recognized by the law. He or she
is "the son of nobody"; as Blackstone explains, "[T]he incapacity of
a bastard consists principally in this, that he cannot be heir to anyone" (1:416). The fate of a child who has no legal claim on its parents is considered by Lady Vane on the death of her "dear hapless
infant" who "had ingrossed a greater share of my tenderness than
perhaps I even should have paid to the offspring of a legitimate contract, because the circumstance of her birth would have been an
unsurmountable misfortune to her thro' the whole course of her
life, and rendered her absolutely dependent on my love and protection" (468). In all three sections of *Peregrine Pickle*—the story of
Peregrine himself, Lady Vane's "Memoirs," and the account of the
Annesley claimant, children embody the conflict of maternal "tenderness" and "legitimate contract." Not all virtuous feeling is rat-
ified by the law; we are forced to acknowledge a disparity between
society as "fellowship of feeling" and "political society."[29] Smollett
sustains his concern with illegitimacy, with individuals who can ex-

28. "Imagination, Pregnant Women, and Monsters, in Eighteenth-Century
England and France," in *Sexual Underworlds of the Enlightenment,* ed. G. S.
Rousseau and Roy Porter (Manchester: Manchester University Press, 1987), 99.
　29. Mullan, *Sentiment and Sociability,* 34.

ert only moral claims, throughout his career. His final novel, *The Expedition of Humphry Clinker,* is, despite its happy resolution, a particularly disturbing treatment of this problem, exploring on several levels the ways in which property determines and limits moral response.

In *Peregrine Pickle*'s second interpolated tale, the workings of property make bodies spectral and ghostly. James Annesley claimed to be the son of Lord Altham, who had died in poverty in Dublin in 1727. He further claimed that his uncle, Lord Anglesea, had, in order to gain control of lands entailed to Annesley, transported the boy as an indentured servant to America. In *Peregrine Pickle* Annesley's case is introduced as "a cause every way the most important that ever came under the discussion of the courts of law in these kingdoms." This sense of magnitude was expressed in the courtroom itself. Addressing the jury, the judge before whom the case was heard in November 1744 said that their verdict would "determine a question of as great consequence both as to property and title, as ever came before a *jury.*"[30] Having heard the story, Peregrine observes that "inhuman neglect" has deprived Annesley of "all the benefit of society; the sole end of which is, to protect the rights, redress the grievances, and promote the happiness of individuals" (732).

In their first attempt to discredit Annesley, Anglesea's lawyers claimed he was Altham's natural child, and strove to keep the distinctions between love and tenderness and legal rights clearly before the jury's mind: "no Family could be safe, if the Care of a natural Child should receive the Construction which the Plaintiff's Counsel contended for, and should such Circumstances of Kindness be worked by artful Men into Evidence, come ever to have Weight, there would be an End of all certainty in Successions of Estates, and a Door be opened to endless Perjury" (494). Kindness is not evidence. Lord Altham's care of his "natural" son does not make that child legitimate.

The second line of the defense was that Lady Altham had never had a child at all. We tend to think of pregnancy as an unmis-

---

30. "An Account of the Great Trial between James Annesley and Richard, Earl of Anglesey," *Gentleman's Magazine* 14 (1744): 541. Further references to this account will be given parenthetically in the text.

takable experience. Women soon know they are pregnant; their loved ones know a child is expected; the social world recognizes and remembers that a pregnancy is occurring or has occurred. Lady Vane shatters the commonsense notion that pregnancy, when it does occur, is eventually clearly visible, by telling us that within a week of giving birth to her lover's child she concealed her condition from her husband, "a man of no great penetration" (465). In Lady Altham's case a court of law is required to establish that she actually gave birth. Witness flatly contradicted witness. Those for the defendant swore that they had "never observ'd the Lady to be with Child" (318); that they "never heard of a publick christening of a Child of my Lady's" (320); and that they had "never heard my Lady say, she was with Child, but heard her wish it" (320). Those for the plaintiff claimed to have seen Lady Altham "big-bellied" and to have dressed her in that condition (27); that "there were three or four present, when Lady Altham was brought to Bed" (28); that "there was a Bonfire made and other Rejoicings" (27); that, when she parted from her husband, Lady Altham "begged very hard that she might have the Child, but my Lord took it out of the Chariot, and swore she should not" (28). Eventually, the case revolved not around what witnesses claimed, but who those witnesses were. One of the major arguments of the defense was that "not one Person of Rank had appeared to support the Reputation of the Cause" (492). Smollett numbers among Annesley's misfortunes the fact that "no gentleman of fashion lived in that parish" (*Pickle,* 712) at the time of his birth. Lady Vane's story opposes sensibility and property, whereas Emilia's story unites them. The second interpolated tale suggests that even conflict between these terms is extraordinary in a society where property ratifies not only the experience, but the very existence, of bodies.

At one point in her narration, Lady Vane speaks of how the circumstances of her illegitimate infant's birth "would have been an unsurmountable misfortune to her thro' the whole course of her life, and rendered her absolutely dependent on my love and protection." Peregrine is not technically illegitimate, and he is saved those kinds of misfortune by his mother's marriage to Gamaliel Pickle. He suffers, though, when his mother attempts to balance her sin against property by denying her son her love and protection. Given these circumstances, and the fact that the narrator finds Peregrine's own irregular attitudes to the human body "unaccountable," we might plausibly argue that the mystery of his birth is connected to his odd treatment of the human form. Forced to go through life without the "least mark of maternal regard," and castigated by his mother as an "impostor" and a "monster," Peregrine uses satire to demonstrate that the bodies of others are, like his own, not what they seem. There is, after all, a link between Peregrine's story and the stories of the novel's women. Ultimately, Peregrine's "ruling passion" leads us back to questions of the female body under the law.

Locke's *Essay concerning Human Understanding* erodes epistemological distinctions between human and monstrous forms; *Roderick Random* demonstrates that social distinctions make monsters of some men. In *Peregrine Pickle* these issues are given a domestic turn because it is within the sanctuary of the home, and not on the road or in the city, that Peregrine's body is most problematic. When Mrs. Pickle looks at Peregrine and begs "pardon of God for having brought such a monster into the world," she demonstrates that there is no area of life, and no aspect of female physicality, that the law does not reach and inform. Her inability to, in Hume's words, "give a loose to love and tenderness" and her desire to disown her own child are never explained to the reader. Yet her troubled maternity, accompanied as it is by that of Lady Vane and Lady Altham, provokes speculation. When we begin to think about the female figures of *Peregrine Pickle,* we see how they disturb and undermine any complacent celebration of female sensibility and physicality. Writing about the ideological contradictions of sensibility, John Mullan says that it cannot be simply interpreted as a "triumphant 'bourgeois' model of social being" because it involves a "sociability whose fate is isolation."[31] In *Peregrine Pickle* it is the law that isolates women and destroys tender bonds.

31. *Sentiment and Sociability,* 234–35.

CHAPTER FIVE

"THE RIGGERS OF AUTHORITY":
FATHOM AND *GREAVES*

Roderick Random and Peregrine Pickle are clearly physical entities moving through very specific social and political milieux. In his first two novels Smollett isolates and emphasizes sensation, its immediacy, authenticity, and possible pains, and he sharply defines the boundaries between sentient self and all that is not the self: other bodies, falling objects, penetrating sounds. Bodies subject to the laws of impact, collision, and explosion, Smollett's early figures are additionally, albeit more subtly, confined by the laws and institutions of their time and place. Relating their adventures, Smollett also delineates the ways and circumstances in which sensations acquire or are denied social and political significance. Bodies in the world are as vulnerable to interpretation as they are to blows and injury.

The novels of Smollett's midcareer offer two very different versions of the human body: the rogue Ferdinand, who seems almost ethereal, able to evade the constraints of physicality; and the gentleman Sir Launcelot, whose rhetoric is that of the English constitution but who travels eighteenth-century England in armor, participating in (though never suffering from) an economy of violence. If *Fathom* almost erases the body, *Greaves* returns us to a brutal physical world. What is going on in these peculiar novels? Both works function, I would argue, as a bridge to Smollett's final fictions: *The History and Adventures of an Atom* and *The Expedition of Humphry Clinker*. In different ways, both *Fathom* and *Greaves* test the limits of the physical. *Roderick Random* initiates the material body of the hero into society, and *Peregrine Pickle* is much concerned with pregnancy. In contrast, the works that follow are colored by the presence of death and the terrors it induces. Smollett's exploration of this terror leads, in the brilliant political satire of the *Atom*, to a depiction of a society controlled by the individual's fear of annihilation. By *Humphry Clinker,* death appears only to limit, but not to detract from, the comic potential of the body as sign.

At first, though, *The Adventures of Ferdinand Count Fathom* seems of a piece with Smollett's earlier works. Given Smollett's representation of characters as visible, tangible, physical beings, comprising surfaces and angles, it is not surprising that he chose, in *Fathom,* to explain fictional process through an analogy with painting and to promise, by implication, distinctly visible characters with definite physical dimensions.

> A Novel is a large diffused picture, comprehending the characters of life, disposed in different groupes, and exhibited in various attitudes, for the purposes of an uniform plan, and general occurrence, to which every individual figure is subservient. But this plan cannot be executed with propriety, probability or success, without a principal personage to attract the attention, unite the incidents, unwind the clue of the labyrinth, and at last close the scene by virtue of his own importance. (4)[1]

Our tendency to accept this analogy is encouraged by the ease with which we can apply it to Smollett's previous fiction. We recall the exuberance and audacity of his visual effects: Roderick tied to the deck of the *Thunder;* Strap falling down the ordinary stairs; Trunnion's odd ride to his wedding. We are aware of Smollett's characters first as bodies—each an expressive knit of fiber and physiog-

---

1. Jerry C. Beasley argues that while these comments have been "dismissed by critics as conventional and trite . . . they exactly describe the intentions with which their author approached each of his five novels." Smollett's imagination "apprehended experience directly in the scattered fragments by which it presented itself to his observing eye" ("Smollett's Art: The Novel as 'Picture,'" in *The First English Novelists: Essays in Understanding,* ed. J. M. Armistead [Knoxville: University of Tennessee Press, 1985], 143).

nomy. We expect Fathom to be as substantial, and as visible, as his successors. In fact, however, the dedication to *Fathom* poorly prepares us for the text itself because the large diffused pictures of *Fathom* present only a vague shadow where the body of the hero should be. Compared to Roderick, whose unfashionable carroty-red hair makes him a laughing stock in London, or to Peregrine, whose moral rehabilitation is expressed in physical symptoms, Ferdinand simply does not have a strong physical presence. Even taking the early references to Ferdinand's cowardice and his eventual punishment into account, he remains an oddly immaterial hero, who is, for the central sections of the novel, peculiarly nebulous and elusive, seemingly unconfined by his physicality. This non-representation of the body, anomalous in Smollett's work, is directly related to the novel's other singularities: the thoroughgoing villainy of the hero and the novel's explicit didacticism.

Smollett justifies his choice of villain as hero by claiming that those who "hesitate on the brink of iniquity, may be terrified from plunging into that irremeable gulph, by surveying the deplorable fate of FERDINAND Count FATHOM" (5). We are assured that Ferdinand's deceit, rapacity, treachery, and imposture will finally be punished, and that Ferdinand will serve as a "beacon for the benefit of the unexperienced and unwary" (5). Ferdinand's body is emblematic and exemplary and will become an iconic representation of vice justly punished. Indeed, the expectations aroused by the dedication are fulfilled towards the end of the novel when we discover the "wretched hero of these memoirs"

> stretched almost naked upon straw, insensible, convulsed, and seemingly in the grasp of death. He was wore to the bone either by famine or distemper; his face was overshadowed with hair and filth; his eyes were sunk, glazed and distorted; his nostrils dilated; his lips covered with a black slough, and his complexion faded into a pale clay-colour, tending to a yellow hue; in a word, the extremity of indigence, squalor and distress, could not be more feelingly represented. (347)

With its strong visualization of the subject, and careful attention to physical being, this scene accords perfectly with the dedication's definition of the novel form; we "survey" the deplorable fate of Ferdinand in distasteful detail. We also know, from the dedication, how we are supposed to respond. Smollett intends that, on seeing what happens to Ferdinand, we "may be terrified" from plunging into iniquity. Ferdinand's disgrace will serve as an "example of extensive use and influence" because it "leaves a deep impression of terror" upon the mind.

The nature and operation of terror is vital to Smollett's didacticism, and he takes pains to justify its use: "The impulses of fear which is the most violent and interesting of all the passions, remain longer than any other upon the memory; and for one that is allured to virtue, by the contemplation of that peace and happiness which it bestows, an hundred are deterred from the practice of vice, by that infamy and punishment to which it is liable, from the laws and regulations of mankind" (5).[2] Despite Smollett's hopes, noticeably unterrified readers have unanimously rejected the punishment of Ferdinand as merely formulaic and convenient. At the same time, many readers, including Hazlitt, have been impressed by Smollett's ability, elsewhere in the novel, to explore the passion of terror as it is experienced by Ferdinand's victims. In fact, *Fathom* vacillates between two very different understandings of terror, the kind of terror characters experience within the novel and the kind of terror the novel is supposed to generate in the reader. Each of these understandings generates a particular approach to fictional representation on Smollett's part, and his representation of Ferdinand's body and physicality therefore becomes a focus for our discussion of the tensions operative in the novel.

Fathom was a crucial novel for Smollett. *Peregrine Pickle* had not been particularly successful, although its themes and structures are very similar to those of *Roderick Random*. That Smollett, as he approached his third novel, was both particularly self-

2. As Thomas R. Preston usefully points out, this formula "totally inverts the sentimental exemplary formula" ("Disenchanting the Man of Feeling," in *Quick Springs of Sense: Studies in the Eighteenth Century,* ed. Larry S. Campion [Athens: University of Georgia Press, 1974], 227). While I agree with Damian Grant that Smollett's tone towards the reader at the beginning of the novel is both ironic and angry, the innovations of *Fathom* make me reluctant to dismiss Smollett's declaration as an "expedient" used "to give his novel an appearance of conformity to standards in which he himself did not believe" (*Tobias Smollett: A Study in Style* [Manchester: Manchester University Press, 1977], 26).

conscious about his fiction and anxious to assert authority as author is demonstrated by the fact that *Fathom* contains one of Smollett's few pieces of explicit critical theory—the definition of novel form at which we have already looked. Smollett's addresses to the reader also suggest authorial self-consciousness, and significantly, their major topic is the representation of human physicality. Right from the start, the human body is an explicit problem in this text. In a tone at times testy and defensive, Smollett quarrels with his reader, anxious both to justify the physicality of his earlier work and to expose readers who delight in the scatology and scurrility of Swift and Rabelais but who will, when faced with a "production of these days" unstamped with these names, "stop their noses with all the signs of loathing and abhorrence" (10). In the early pages of *Fathom,* Smollett alternatively rounds on and defers to such critics, assuring them that all distasteful physicality will be effaced from the production they are about to read. In this novel no umbrage will be given to the "gentle, delicate, sublime, critic" (9). The opening sections of *Fathom* leave us in no doubt that Smollett's grudging determination to submit to current literary taste will cause some deviation from his past literary practice, particularly from the low, coarse physicality with which his (failing) reputation is identified.

At first, however, that seems unlikely. Ferdinand, born to a camp follower five times married, a being without country or father, is more outrageously picaresque than any of his Smollettian predecessors, and his author's sarcastic promise that he will be "gradually sublimed" seems hardly credible. Nonetheless, while the first chapters of *Fathom* actually contain more "low" material than Smollett's earlier work (for example, the promiscuity of Ferdinand's mother, his birth in a wagon, and the sordid commercial transactions of camp life), Smollett keeps his distance from this material through use of a mock-heroic idiom. The sublimity of the mock-heroic also offers valuable opportunity for moral commentary, as had been apparent in Fielding's *Jonathan Wild,* a book whose style Smollett echoes here.[3] Smollett's treatment of Ferdi-

3. George M. Kahrl states that in *Fathom* Smollett indulges for the first time in a "conscious elaboration of his style, quite clearly after the example of Fielding" (*Tobias Smollett: Traveler-Novelist* [Chicago: University of Chicago Press, 1945], 53).

nand's mother, for example, demonstrates his ability to use incongruity between content and style for moral purposes. This woman, who makes her living by stripping the battle-dead, literally sees the human body as a form of refuse. In describing her death Smollett deliberately contains her reduction of human bodies to "splendid bundles," which she plunders, within a sublime narrative where her own body is identified with a mythic and transcendent figure. Already loaded with her spoils, Ferdinand's mother spots another bundle lying on the ground.

> This was no other than an unhappy officer of hussars; who, after having had the good fortune to take a Turkish standard, was desperately wounded in the thigh, and obliged to quit his horse; finding himself in such an helpless condition, he had wrapped his acquisition round his body, that whatever might happen, he and his glory should not be parted; and thus shrouded among the dying and the dead, he had observed the progress of our heroine, who stalked about the field, like another Atropos, finishing, wherever she came, the work of death: he did not at all doubt, that he himself would be visited in the course of her peregrinations, and therefore provided for her reception, with a pistol ready cock'd in his hand, while he lay perdue, beneath his covert, in all appearance bereft of life. He was not deceived in his prognostic; she no sooner eyed the golden crescent, than inflamed with curiosity or cupidity, she directed thitherward her steps, and discerning the carcase of a man, from which, she thought, there would be a necessity for disengaging it, she lifted up her weapon, in order to make sure of her purchase; and in the very instant of discharging her blow, receiv'd a brace of bullets in her brain. (19)

In this scene, Smollett controls his low material through a sublime idiom. The representation of Ferdinand's mother as Atropos assures the "delicate reader" that the narrator, at least, is not a low creature, even as it makes the death of Ferdinand's mother, from a "brace of bullets in her brain," more shockingly effective.

The same justification for low material can be offered for a scene later in the novel. Ferdinand, imprisoned for debt, discovers the king of Corsica, a fellow prisoner, playing at soldiers. Whereas Ferdinand's mother discards the body, taking only its trappings, the king takes pieces of refuse and invigorates them. Looking through a keyhole, Ferdinand sees "the sovereign and his minister sitting on opposite sides of a deal board table, covered with a large chart or map, upon which he saw a great number of muscle and oister-shells, ranged in a certain order, and at a little distance, several regular squares and columns made of cards cut in small pieces. The prince himself, whose eyes were reinforced by spectacles, surveyed this armament with great attention, while the general put the whole in action, and conducted their motions by beat of drum" (186–87). The incongruity between the sovereign and what he oversees, and that between Atropos and the work in which she delights, depends upon a visualization of the external world, and each incongruity, in turn, generates a moral response to the horrors of war and the perfidy of politicians. While these scenes use bullets and the shells of oysters and mussels, such "low" materials facilitate elevated reflections on the part of the reader.

Initially, we are encouraged to believe that Ferdinand's career will be an amplified version of his mother's, that he too will be connected with greatness so that the reader may realize his truly sordid nature. Smollett associates Ferdinand with the heroes of antiquity, saying that, like them, he might "have laid claim to divine extraction, without running the risque of being claimed by any earthly father" (8), and, of Ferdinand's birth in a wagon, his author says that deciding which country owned him would be as difficult as "ascertaining the so much contested birth-place of Homer" (9). Both Smollett and Fielding use the mock-heroic to show how easily their rogues, sons of ignorance and misrule, born to promiscuous, thieving mothers, can be deflated and mastered. The author's allegiance to the classical tradition separates him from the low physicality that the villain perforce experiences. In the early passages of *Fathom* Smollett transcends the physicality he describes, and propitiates his "sublime reader," by constant reference to the world outside the body: the world of myth and history. The cadences of the opening chapters are not maintained, however, and eventually fade altogether. Moreover, as the novel progresses, the sublimity offered by the mock-heroic is replaced by sublimity of a different order, which, unlike the mock-heroic, threatens the moral foundations of Smollett's enterprise.

This second understanding of sublimity is related to Ferdinand's ability to generate terror, and that ability, in turn, is related to his freedom from physical constraint. The most dramatic instance of this freedom, and one charged with symbolic significance, is the novel's famous Gothic interlude. Prior to this episode, Ferdinand is a fairly typical rogue, seducing chambermaids, cheating those who trust him, and betraying all and sundry. He also has a fairly ordinary physical definition: he is scared when he finds himself in the army, and so on. As the Gothic episode begins, Smollett emphasizes both Ferdinand's physical vulnerability and his cowardice: our hero is "by no means a man to set fear at defiance" (83). Making his way through a dark wood at night, Ferdinand experiences a threatening physical world much as had other Smollett characters before him. Rain leaves him "invaded to the skin" (84), and, after he takes off through the woods, the "succession of groves, and bogs, and thorns and brakes" causes his skin to suffer in "a grievous manner" (84). Ferdinand's physical discomfort and vulnerability is accompanied by mental suffering. He is "harrowed" by apprehension and fearful of robbers. Eventually, he arrives at an isolated cottage where he is given shelter by an old woman and concludes that, at last, his "person [is] quite secure" (84). His suspicions are aroused with the old woman locks him in, however, and discovering there is no bolt on his side of the door, Ferdinand "proposed to take an accurate survey of every object in the apartment, and in the course of his inquiry, had the mortification to find the dead body of a man, still warm, who had been lately stabbed, and concealed beneath several bundles of straw" (85). Smollett's prose momentarily switches the corpse, which is "still warm," and Ferdinand, who suffers "mortification." Ferdinand's fear is so extreme that it seems to extinguish life itself. The corpse in the isolated cottage is a graphic memento mori that impresses upon Ferdinand his basic nature and inevitable end: "Then his heart began to palpitate, his hair to bristle up, and his knees to totter; his thoughts teemed with presages of death and destruction; his conscience rose up in judgment against him, and he underwent a severe paroxysm of dismay and distraction. His spirits were agitated into a state of fermentation that produced a species of resolution a-kin to that which is inspired by brandy or other strong liquors, and by an impulse that seemed supernatural, he was immediately hurried into measures for his own preservation" (85). Here the terrified Ferdinand achieves the kind of moral realization Smollett claims for the emotion: "his thoughts teemed with presages of death and destruction; his conscience rose up in judgment against him." Briefly, Ferdinand reads the horrific scene as a dutiful and pious reader of emblems might—as, indeed, the reader of this novel is supposed to read Ferdinand's eventual fate. At this point, however, the narrative swerves away from morality and towards the uncanny. After his dismay and distraction, Ferdinand, under an impulse that "seems supernatural," begins to dismantle the moral tableau. He measures the full extent of his danger and manages to evade it. He undresses the corpse and, placing it in his own bed "in the attitude of a person who sleeps at his ease" (85), takes for himself "possession of the place from whence the body had been removed" (86). When the thieves arrive, they stab the corpse and retire, "with a design to return and rifle the deceased at their leisure" (86). The substitution works. Ferdinand lives by having the corpse "die" again in his stead.

This scene is a crux in the novel because it displaces one mode of representation with another. The discovery of the corpse and Ferdinand's reaction to it—both rendered in pictorial form and the latter charged with a moral perspective—accord with the precepts of the dedication. Ferdinand, however, by taking the position of the corpse, evades the "death and destruction" that the dedication seems to promise. Feigning death, Ferdinand renders death impotent. Death is the most definitive physical restriction, the body's final limitation. Ferdinand's triumph over death signals his incorporation into an economy that is not primarily visible or physical and is not, therefore, amenable to pictorial clarity.

Maximillian E. Novak, who reads this scene as consistent with the mock-heroic opening section of the novel, dismisses its Gothic aspects, arguing that "we never forget that Ferdinand is a rogue toward whose antics the reader feels a sense of superiority."[4] In fact, however, the confusion of bodies and corpses is a significant trope in the novel. Death is the most absolute of physical facts, and in the

4. "Gothic Fiction and the Grotesque," *Novel* 13 (1979–80): 58.

"picture of the novel" a corpse should be the most easily read element of all. Nonetheless, the distinction between the quick and the dead is a difficult one to make clearly in this text. Ferdinand's mother, driven by her desire for plunder, mistakes an officer of Hussars "shrouded among the dying and the dead" for a "carcase." In the climax of the novel, Renaldo—Ferdinand's virtuous counterpart—mistakes his vision of Monimia for a ghost. At the novel's turning point, Ferdinand manages to survive by having a dead man die again in his stead. Three confusions of this kind suggest that physicality is unusually problematic in this novel. In addition, a fictional pattern in which the very fact of life is difficult to ascertain does not bode well for the value of pictures and exhibitions.

It is clear that, after the initial chapters of the novel, Smollett, far from considering Ferdinand a simple puppet to be moved through his adventures in the cadences of mock sublimity, wishes instead to associate him with a more authentic form of the sublime. Various verbal parallels encourage us to associate Fathom with Milton's Satan, a literary figure who is, like Ferdinand himself, noticeably free from physical restraints. For example, Ferdinand looks upon England "as the land of promise, flowing with milk and honey, and abounding with subjects on which he knew his talents would be properly exercised" (77).[5] As the scene of Ferdinand's most distinctive exploits, England is represented as a kind of Eden. When he first views England's cliffs, Ferdinand's "heart throbbed with all the joy of a beloved son, who after a tedious and fatiguing voyage, reviews the chimneys of his father's house: he surveyed the neighbouring coast of England, with fond and longing eyes, like another Moses reconnoitring the land of Canaan from the top of mount Pisgah" (127). This recalls, very strongly, Satan's first view of earth in Book 3 of *Paradise Lost*. He looked at the world

5. Ferdinand's attitude towards his native land is similar to that expressed by Beelzebub towards Eden, at Satan's prompting, during the debate in hell: "There is a place / . . . another World, the happy seat / Of som new race called *Man*, about this time / To be created like to us . . . Thither let us bend all our thoughts, to learn / What creatures there inhabit, of what mould / Or substance, how endue'd, and what thir Power, / And where thir weakness, how attempted best, / By force or suttlety" (*Paradise Lost*, in *The Poetical Works of John Milton*, ed. Helen Darbishire [Oxford: Clarendon Press, 1952], 2.345–59).

> *As when a Scout*
> *Through dark and desart wayes with peril gone*
> *All night; at last by break of chearful dawne*
> *Obtains the brow of some high-climbing Hill,*
> *Which to his eye discovers unaware*
> *The goodly prospect of some forren land*
> *First-seen. (3.543–49)*

Smollett's use of typology elevates Ferdinand and places his adventures in the context of an archetypal battle between good and evil. This elevation markedly contrasts with the mock-heroic "sublimation" of the novel's opening. Moses reconnoiters the "land of Canaan" and regains for his people the Paradise that was originally lost by Satan's incursion. Ferdinand, poised to descend on England, is figured both as Moses and as Satan. Smollett's choice of iconography at once recalls both the loss and partial recuperation of Eden. Of course, Moses never sets foot in Canaan; both Satan the archetype and Ferdinand his emulator arrive in a Paradise that they subsequently despoil.

More significantly, both Satan and Ferdinand triumph because they isolate their victims from a clear perception of the external world and from the guidance of reason. Explaining Ferdinand's technique, Smollett remarks: "There is an affinity and short transition betwixt all the violent passions that agitate the human mind: they are all false perspectives, which though they magnify, yet perplex and render indistinct every object which they represent: and flattery is never so successfully administred, as to those who know they stand in need of friendship, assent and approbation" (141). The most violent passion is, as Smollett states in the dedication, terror, and its most powerful effect is that it renders "indistinct" every object in the external world. Like Satan, Ferdinand can manipulate the passions of his victims through his linguistic skill. Smollett might have appended to any one of Ferdinand's speeches the Miltonic comment "So spake the false dissembler unperceived" (3.681), while Milton's explanation of Satan's ability to hoodwink Uriel also applies to Fathom's relationship to Renaldo: "goodness thinks no ill / Where no ill seems" (3.688–89).[6]

6. Critical discussions of Smollett's Renaldo center on the adequacy of his judgment. Thomas R. Preston claims that *Fathom* is "an educational novel in

Throughout the novel we are aware of Ferdinand primarily as
a voice, a manipulator of language. The novel teems with references
to Ferdinand's articulate villainy, and Smollett's representation of
his powers further dissociates Ferdinand from the limitations and
constraints of physical experience. *Fathom* is the first Smollett
novel in which the relationships between characters, especially
those between Ferdinand and his victims, are not primarily visible
and physical. In the early novels, characters are endangered by
their material environment: by blows and bad food, by falls and
fights. These dangers may be severe, but at least one can see them
coming.

The vulnerability of Ferdinand's victims, among them
Celinda, Elinor, and Renaldo, was to be explained several years
later by Edmund Burke. Having announced that "[w]hatever is
fitted in any sort to excite the ideas of pain, and danger, that is to
say, whatever is in any sort terrible, or is conversant about terrible
objects, or operates in a manner analogous to terror, is a source of
the *sublime;* that is, it is productive of the strongest emotion which
the mind is capable of feeling."⁷ Burke goes on to elaborate on
the role of apprehension of sublime experiences. He argues that
"[w]hen we know the full extent of any danger, when we can accus-
tom our eyes to it, a great deal of the apprehension vanishes. Every
one will be sensible of this, who considers how greatly night adds to
our dread, in all cases of danger, and how much the notions of
ghosts and goblins, of which none can form clear ideas, affect
minds, which give credit to popular tales concerning such sorts of

which the virtuous man learns from the villain that the world is a place of fraud
and deceit calculated to destroy virtuous men. The novel's structure derives less
from the tradition of rogue biography than from the eighteenth-century tradition of the man of feeling" ("Disenchanting the Man of Feeling," 224). On the
other hand, Joel J. Thomas holds that, while *Fathom* "contains probably the
harshest satiric 'world' of all of Smollett's prose fiction, it most clearly manifests
his adherence to the ethics of feeling generally as well as the ethical principle of
sympathy propounded by Hume" ("Smollett and Ethical Sensibility: *Ferdinand
Count Fathom," Studies in Scottish Literature* 14 [1979]: 150). As we have
seen from the discussion of *Roderick Random,* Smollett's "adherence" to the
principle of sympathy was only partial.

7. *A Philosophical Enquiry into the Origin of Our Ideas of the Sublime and
Beautiful,* ed. James T. Boulton (Notre Dame, Ind.: University of Notre Dame
Press, 1968), 39.

beings" (58–59). Implicit in this passage is a distinction between the reassuring life of sensation and the body—what our eyes can see—and the dreadful nature of apprehension, when the subject is beset by dangers of which he or she can form no distinct idea. Dread and apprehension affect the human mind so strongly because they are intimately connected with the inevitability of our own dissolution. Ferdinand's ability to engender dread and terror in his victims is a consequence of his own invulnerability to these passions; in the novel's Gothic interlude he confronts, and emerges triumphant from a confrontation with, his own death.

Smollett's representation of Ferdinand keeps bodily definition in abeyance. This character's most pronounced traits, "insinuation" and "sagacity," suggest alike an ability to penetrate beneath the skin of his victims, somehow to destroy them from within. Johnson defines "to insinuate" as "to steal into imperceptibly; to be conveyed insensibly," and he offers as example Harvey's use of the word: "Pestilential miasms insinuate into the humoral and constituent parts of the body." One meaning of "insinuating" given in the OED is "penetrates by sinuous windings between the particles of a body." Ferdinand gains power over a succession of individuals in the novel because, like Harvey's "pestilential miasms," he can penetrate his victims "imperceptibly" and "insensibly."

Significantly, Ferdinand's most prominent intellectual trait is "sagacity," which is nothing other than the ability to penetrate the purposes of others: to participate in the drama beneath the skin. It is not insignificant that "sagacity," throughout the eighteenth century, still referred to an acute sense of smell and was associated with hounds in pursuit: "With might and main they chas'd the murd'rous fox / Nor wanted horns t'inspire sagacious hounds" (Dryden). Ferdinand has much of the bloodhound in him and can discover his prey from afar. Of course, "sagacity," as Douglas Lane Patey has pointed out, is also "the faculty of reading signs," and Ferdinand's wisdom is certainly derived from the skill with which he reads the body language of his victims.[8] After Ferdinand has perpetuated a juvenile deceit, Smollett asks: "If he exhibited such a proof of sagacity in the twelfth year of his age, what might not be expected from his finesse, in the maturity of his faculties and expe-

8. *Probability and Literary Form,* 182.

rience?" (25). As a youth, we are told, "He dived into the characters of mankind, with a penetration peculiar to himself" (30). Diving, insinuating, penetrating: Ferdinand's activities are a form of conquest in which the other is first entered and then completely subsumed. He expresses his lawlessness through a constant attempt to collapse the distance between self and other. He seeps into the consciousness of a victim and makes resistance unlikely or impossible. No barrier is proof against him as he works his way into the hidden, internal economies of those he chooses to despoil. In *Fathom* the edges that define individuals are softened, the boundary enforced by the skin relaxes, and the absolute privacy of characters is broached.

Smollett's representation of Ferdinand is of the utmost consequence for the moral scheme of the novel. Crucial episodes in the latter half of the novel—Ferdinand's seductions of Elinor and Celinda, and his betrayal of Renaldo, his former patron—only make didactic sense if the reader can see what Ferdinand's victims cannot; that is, that the "invasion" of sensory impressions can be controlled and withstood by applying the "consolations of philosophy." The moral the narrator intends us to draw from these battles is that, faced with Ferdinand's machinations, characters who are superstitious become almost permeable, whereas the reinforcements offered by philosophy and reason would have made them "impregnable." Ferdinand's treatment of Celinda and Elinor creates "impressions of terror" that thematize Smollett's stated intentions in the dedication.[9] Somehow, we as readers are supposed to distinguish the groundless terror these women experience from our own entirely rational terror at Ferdinand's punishment and his emaciated, wrecked body. One reason, among many, for our inability to make this distinction is Ferdinand's constitution. Smollett gives him powers of penetration and insinuation; he allows him to

9. John F. Sena sees a symmetry between Fathom's activities and those of his creator: "By permitting Fathom to give form and substance to the malevolent potential that resides in any artist, Smollett is able to rid himself of that potential before it becomes actualized in his art. Ultimately, self-portrait becomes self-catharsis" ("Fathoming Fathom: Smollett's Count as Malevolent Artist," *Forum for Modern Language Studies* 1 [January 1980]: 9). While Smollett does draw attention to Fathom as an artist, I don't see this as having the salutary effects that Sena notes.

permeate and overwhelm the minds of his victims. His ability to
steal into his victims imperceptibly, and insensibly take possession
of them, gives him affinities with the supernatural and the sublime.
As readers, we are unable to form a clear, distinct image of Ferdinand, and therefore we are all the more sympathetic to his victims'
terror.

Despite himself, Smollett does represent terror as a kind of
theft for which the subject cannot be held liable. He does represent
Celinda, and others, as victims. Fathom first attacks Celinda
through her love of music, soothing her sense of hearing "even to a
degree of ravishment" (157). Celinda can only explain Ferdinand's
effect on her by recourse to the supernatural, but the vocabulary of
sexual "ravishment" that Smollett uses here is similar to Burke's
language about a sublime aural experience.[10] In each instance the
subject is passive and completely possessed by the sensation of
sound. Celinda is also superstitious, and Ferdinand tells her "dismal stories of omens, portents, prophecies and apparitions" until
her mind is filled with "unceasing terrors": "Many sleepless nights
did [Celinda] pass amidst those horrors of fancy, starting at every
noise, and sweating with dreary apprehension, yet ashamed to own
her fears, or sollicit the comfort of a bed-fellow, lest she should in-
cur the ridicule and censure of her father's wife; and what rendered
this disposition the more irksome, was the solitary situation of her
chamber, that stood at the end of a long gallery scarce within hearing of any other inhabited part of the house" (158). Even though the
narrator clearly states that Celinda's horrors are those of "fancy,"
he goes on to give a detailed description of the very real physiological experience of fear. The girl is sleepless; she starts at every noise,
and sweats with "dreary apprehension." We are also drawn into
Celinda's isolation. She suspects that she is being ridiculous; she
can certainly imagine the "ridicule and censure" that a confession
of her fears would generate, yet she cannot alter her state of mind.
Ferdinand now orchestrates strange symphonies outside Celinda's

10. "[T]he ear-drum suffered a convulsion, and the whole body consented
with it. The tension of the part thus increasing at every blow, by the united
forces of the stroke itself, the expectation, and the surprise, it is worked up to
such a pitch as to be capable of the sublime" (*Origin of Our Ideas*, 140).
Smollett at one point describes Celinda's sensations as being "whetted to a most
painful keenness" (160).

door, and the girl is "overwhelmed with awful terror" (160). The narrator distances the reader from Celinda by intrusive remarks on her credulity and "superstition." At the same time, we are given a detailed account of her misapprehensions and the effect they have on her. The detail with which Smollett describes Celinda's fear validates it as a form of human experience worthy of scrutiny. Ferdinand gains access to Celinda's room on pretense of comforting her. She listens to him because he "diverts the gloomy ideas of her fear," and there is an "interesting transition" from the "most uneasy to the most agreeable sensation of human breast" (161). Smollett here emphasizes that passions, like ideas, are associated, and suggests that this movement between passions is a source of human vulnerability. As readers, we are all the more attentive to the "interesting transition" between extreme emotional states because it recapitulates Smollett's account, only twenty pages earlier, of Ferdinand's seduction of Elinor. Newly arrived in England, Ferdinand meets the young country girl on the London stagecoach and, by stealing her letters of introduction and her purse, places the girl in a state of panic. Disoriented with "false perspectives," Elinor is an easy victim.

In rehearsing these incidents of his plot, Smollett recognizes the subjectivity of moral experience. Speaking of the "gothic romance," J. M. S. Tompkins says, "[W]e never behold the naked form of terror, but always its image obscurely reflected in the victim's mind."[11] In *Fathom* we know that there is no "naked form of terror." Celinda is the victim of a trick, not of a supernatural agency, but the image "obscurely reflected in the victim's mind" is felt no less powerfully because it is an illusion. It is not surprising that Hazlitt, in commenting on this novel, singled out "the seduction in the west of England" for its "power of writing" and argued that it would be difficult to find, in any other author, "passages written with more force and mastery."[12] The story of Celinda is impressive because it completely involves us in the susceptibility of the character and forces us, however briefly, to inhabit her fears.

Smollett's moralizing on Celinda and Elinor fails to reassert

11. *The Popular Novel in England, 1770–1800* (1932; reprint, Lincoln: University of Nebraska Press, 1961), 253.
12. "On the English Novelists," 117.

the moral economy. The harsh fates that he inflicts on these women are, I think, an attempt to overcompensate for his sympathy with their positions. Smollett's narration allows the reader to enter so fully into their respective states of mind that condemnation becomes difficult. This being the case, only the most severe punishment can impress upon us the gravity of their fault. Smollett's desire to wash his hands completely of these two characters—who between them wreck the moral economy of his novel—is one of the most shocking elements of the work. Elinor is abandoned by Ferdinand and is conveyed to Bedlam, where we "leave her for the present, happily bereft of her reason" (146). Celinda, who has been introduced to alcohol by Ferdinand, "grew every day more and more sensual and degenerate, and contracted an intimacy with one of the footmen, who was kind enough to take her to wife, in hope of obtaining a good settlement from his master" (163). When he fails, the footman takes Celinda to London and abandons her to prostitution. Such punishments suggest that Elinor and Celinda are fundamentally "sensual and degenerate" characters bound to transgress sexually. But the author's effort at containment does not work. Instead of dismissing Celinda and Elinor as fallen women, the reader is still caught up in the circumstances of their fall. Celinda's seduction shares many of the characteristics of the Gothic tale, a genre that "reinforces a woman's sense of herself as an essentially sexual creature."[13] The eighteenth century, of course, was quite given to thinking (in a fairly negative way) of women as "essentially" sexual creatures. In its punishment of Celinda, *Fathom* seems to associate misapprehension with inveterate female rakishness. But, finally, the novel does not see the "false perspectives" from which Celinda and Elinor suffer as a peculiarly female problem.

In this novel, "false perspectives" are an inescapable element in male and female mental life. We see this most clearly in Renaldo's transformation of Monimia, his virtuous, beautiful beloved, into an object of horror. Renaldo, beset by financial difficulties and powerless to claim his patrimony in Hungary, is overcome by despair: "He began to be seized with horror at the sight of poor Monimia, whom

13. Cynthia Griffin Wolff, "The Radcliffean Gothic Model: A Form for Feminine Sexuality," in *The Female Gothic,* ed. Juliann E. Fleenor (Montreal and London: Eden Press, 1983), 209.

he therefore shunned as much as the circumstances of their correspondence would allow; and every evening he went forth alone to
some solitary place, where he could unperceived give a loose to the
transports of his sorrow, and in silence meditate some means to
lighten the burden of his woe" (208). The situation finally reaches
the point where Renaldo, coming upon his lover by accident, starts
back with horror, "like a traveller who chances to tread upon a
snake" (216). Renaldo personifies virtue; no character is closer to
the "consolations of philosophy," yet this does not preserve him
from distorted perceptions of others, or from yielding to terror.[14]
This psychological susceptibility, although it has been given little
critical notice, is much more interesting than Renaldo's brush with
the "explained supernatural" at the novel's end. It exemplifies a variety of male vulnerability that had not previously been the subject
of fiction. As Margaret Anne Doody observes: "[M]en could not be
fully present in the novel until they could be shown as self-divided,
wary, torn by their own unconscious and divided motives, even
weak, erring and guilty—and shown thus without being exhibited
as villains or failures."[15] Like the Gothic novels of which Doody
speaks, *Fathom* gives its characters "the freedom to have—and to
live in—nightmares." Because Renaldo's experience has so much
in common with that of Ferdinand's female victims, the novel
breaks down, rather than reinforcing, gender boundaries.

Smollett does attempt to contain the experiences of terror he
relates. His intrusive commentary distinguishes vice and virtue; it
provides clarity and then apportions blame. But it does not answer
our questions. We are told Celinda should have avoided "particular
correspondence with perfidious man" (162), but we want to know
why the narrator validates her isolation and vulnerability. We are

14. In pointing out that there are more disturbing phenomena in *Fathom*
than the attitude of its most obviously moral character to corpses, I am reminded of Terry Castle's argument about *The Mysteries of Udolpho*. Although
the novel uses the "explained supernatural," Castle points out that, if we read all
of *Udolpho*, the "supposedly ordinary parts . . . may begin to look increasingly
peculiar." She calls this phenomenon the "supernaturalization of everyday life"
("The Spectralization of the Other in *The Mysteries of Udolpho*," in *The New
Eighteenth Century*, ed. Felicity Nussbaum and Laura Brown [London and New
York: Methuen, 1987], 233, 234).

15. "Deserts, Ruins, and Troubled Waters: Female Dreams in Fiction and the
Development of the Gothic Novel," *Genre* 10 (1977): 572.

told that Renaldo was duped by the "artful serpent Fathom," but his transformation of Monimia into an object of horror is not explained. The text of *Fathom,* then, betrays an ambivalent attitude towards the "false perspectives" of its characters. The narrator wants to rationalize the emotions of fear and terror by associating them with internal weakness. There are aspects of the narrative, however, that reveal Smollett's uneasiness with this arrangement. Chief among them is his representation of Ferdinand. Despite all the care Smollett takes of the reader, this is an instance where he forces us to participate in the "false perspectives" of the novel's characters. Indeed, it is through his representation of Ferdinand that Smollett acknowledges the limitations of clarity and rationality. It is not only Celinda's superstition that makes Ferdinand into "something supernatural." His incorporeality, his lack of substance, his powers of insinuation and penetration not only give him a tremendous advantage in his nefarious plotting; they also deny the reader the visual clarities on which the novel's moral scheme relies. In the dedication we are promised a picturelike novel in which the clearly visible hero will further the author's "uniform plan." But the plan of this novel goes awry. Ferdinand's constitution establishes a logic whereby false perspectives seem inevitable and in which the mind cannot protect itself from terror.

The psychology of terror that Smollett discovers in *Fathom* is inimical to his moral project. The tension between what Smollett initially takes terror to be, and the varieties of terror he discovers in the novel itself, is latent in the dedication. In this passage Smollett emphasizes terror as one of the novelist's tools, but the terror that he has in mind is that produced by "the disgrace and discomfiture of vice" (5). Smollett's eagerness to justify his choice of villain as hero, and his insistence that this representation will disgust the reader, implicitly defines *Fathom* by Johnsonian prescripts. In "Rambler 4" Johnson argues: "In narratives where historical veracity has no place, I cannot discover why there should not be exhibited the most perfect idea of virtue; of virtue not angelical, nor above probability, for what we cannot credit we shall never imitate, but the highest and purest that humanity can reach . . . Vice, for vice is necessary to be shewn, should always disgust."[16] Smollett's

---

16. *The Rambler,* ed. W. J. Bate and Albrecht B. Strauss, Yale Edition of the Works of Samuel Johnson (New Haven: Yale University Press, 1969), 3:24.

use of the familiar literary vocabulary of example and verisimilitude in his dedication minimizes the actual experimental nature of
Fathom, because ultimately the reader the novel constructs is at
odds with that projected in *The Rambler.* Johnson bases his remarks about the representation of vice and virtue on the understanding that reading is a form of judgment that allows the individual reader to regulate his conduct. Johnson's putative reader
responds intellectually to the "perfect idea of virtue," which he first
"credits" and then "imitates." Such a concept of fictional exem-
plarity requires a continuity between the text and the world in
which it is read. Only examples grounded in a world recognized by
the reader can be imitated. This whole cycle of imitation, in which
verisimilitude plays a crucial role, is based on cognitive, rational
acts. Johnson's prescriptions for didactic fiction require a clarity of
perspective on two levels: the reader should be able to identify the
patterns of the fiction in the pattern of his own experience, and vice
and virtue should be clearly divided.

In the dedication to *Fathom* Smollett suggests that terror is
amenable to such clarity; he discusses it as a passion different in
strength, but not in kind, from other passions: the impulses of terror are among "the most violent and interesting of all the passions"
and its effects "remain longer than any other on the memory." In a
further step to normalize terror and present it in a context of rational, daily life, Smollett draws attention to his dependence upon the
power of secular law to resolve his plot. The only punitive machinery at his command is the "infamy and punishment" to which vice
is liable "from the laws and regulations of mankind" (5). In this passage Smollett both creates and elides a difference between what he
is doing and what literary history sees as the conventional didactic
practice of the period. He emphasizes the uses of fear, but then he
presents the impressions of terror and the operation of the law as
being two versions of the same thing: they share a regulative social
role. David Punter, in a brief discussion of *Fathom,* has argued that

> [t]he Gothic quality of *Fathom* rests on a number of
> points: the attempt to embody a theory of the social
> purposes of terror; the portrayal of the misery of separa-
> tion from civilized norms, and the inadequacy of most
> of the characters to deal with extreme situations; the
> interest in the perverse tendencies of sensibility; the in-

sistence on the power of guilt; the realistic treatment of
loathing and disgust. And it is interesting that these are
features which could be grafted on to a literary form
which was largely realist in form and socially critical in
intention.[17]

It is the nature of this "grafting" and the effects it has on a "largely
realist" literary form that presently concern us. In the course of
Fathom, Smollett's conception of terror deepens and becomes
more complex; it gains an importance apart from its assigned narrative function, and finally overwhelms the novel's didactic objec-
tives. Critics have argued that, whereas eighteenth-century poets
used terror to "prepare the mind for whatever moralizing the poet
might choose," prose writers soon lost this moralistic purpose, and
the "emotion comes to be the important factor, to be enjoyed in and
for itself."[18] This is only a partial truth; in *Fathom,* at least, the de-
ployment of terror causes the prose writer to recognize its incom-
patibility with moral purposes. The experience of terror, Smollett
argues, will restrain the reader from vice; he then begins to represent scenes of terror within the narrative itself—only to find that
they do not accord with his narrative theory. The dedication of
Fathom would have us define terror as a particularly strong form of
cognitive activity, the effects of which would remain a long time in
the memory. The text of the novel, however, eventually leads us towards an idea of terror similar to that offered by Edmund Burke:
"No passion so effectually robs the mind of all its powers of acting
and reasoning as fear. For fear being an apprehension of pain or
death, it operates in a manner that resembles actual pain" (57). For
Burke, fear and terror cause the suspension of the intellect and
make cognition impossible. If terror is, as Burke suggests, a form of
robbery, then it must be an undesirable instrument of social regulation. Burke is important to us here because he emphasizes, as
Smollett as yet cannot, the political abuses of terror. In defining the
sublime, Burke says that "whatever . . . operates in a manner analogous to terror, is a source of the sublime; that is, it is productive of
the strongest emotion which the mind is capable of feeling" (39).

17. *The Literature of Terror: A History of Gothic Fictions from 1765 to the
Present Day* (London and New York: Longman, 1980), 49.
18. S. H. Monk, *The Sublime: A Study of Critical Theories in Eighteenth-
Century England* (New York: Modern Language Association, 1935), 90.

But no sooner has he defined this emotion, than he points to the possibility of its political abuse: "I am in great doubt, whether any man could be found who would earn a life of the most perfect satisfaction, at the price of ending it in the torments, which justice inflicted in a few hours on the late unfortunate regicide in France" (39). The spectacular execution of "the late unfortunate regicide" creates an atmosphere of fear and apprehension that facilitates social regulation. Burke reminds us, when speaking of obscurity, that "[t]hose despotic governments founded on the passions of men, and principally upon the passion of fear, keep their chief as much as may be from the public eye" (59). In *Fathom* Smollett keeps his chief, Ferdinand the hero, from the public eye. But *Fathom*, unlike *Roderick Random*, is not concerned with the nature of political narrative and political power. For the moment, Smollett avoids the political implications of his fictional experiment. In *Greaves*, where he suggests that England itself is, in some measure, a "despotic government founded on the passions of men," he begins to confront them.

Seven years separate *Fathom* (1753) and *The Life and Adventures of Sir Launcelot Greaves*, but despite this interval, and the obvious contrast between Ferdinand, the deservedly punished rogue, and Launcelot, the justly rewarded gentleman, the two books are intimately connected. At first, however, *Greaves* seems a deliberate attempt to deny the vision and technique of the earlier novel. Whereas the most typical scenes in *Fathom* involve private, often isolated individuals engaged in moral interpretation, the equivalent scenes in *Greaves* are insistently public and communal. In keeping with this emphasis, Smollett avoids the subjectivity of Gothic innovation, and returns in *Greaves* to quixotic and romantic motifs. Most obviously, *Greaves* reinstates a physical economy of sensation. In contrast to the elusive Fathom, Greaves is physically conspicuous, a character who is anachronistically prepared to participate in a social economy of violence and physical damage. He makes his first appearance "cased in armour, such as hath been for above a whole century disused in this and every other country in Europe" (12). Nonetheless, *Greaves* continues the explorations of the earlier novel. The novel's very title points both to the greaves of armor that protect the hero and to his internal wound, the griev-

ing for lost love that initiates his chivalric quest. The novel begins
in the cheerful companionship of the Black Lion, but it continues in
the isolation of Bernard Shackle's private madhouse, including
scenes in which, as Allan Ingram says, "language itself is interro-
gated."[19] Despite all its affirmations of community, of warmth, and
of physicality, *Greaves* finally develops the discoveries of *Fathom*,
and, being Smollett's most public novel, it becomes a meditation on
the institutional and public uses of terror, apprehension, and mental infirmity.

The opening of *Greaves* exchanges the shadows and obscu-
rities of *Fathom* for the brightly lit kitchen of the Black Lion, "remarkably clean, furnished with three or four Windsor chairs,
adorned with shining plates of pewter and copper sauce-pans
nicely scoured, that even dazzled the eyes of the beholder; while a
chearful fire of sea-coal blazed in the chimney" (1). In keeping with
this pleasant domestic scene, Smollett addresses the reader several
times in terms of affable equality, cultivating the reader's "co-
operation and collaboration."[20] The general assertion of community in *Greaves*, of which Smollett's attitude to the reader forms a
part, represents his desire to counter the uncomfortable conception of the individual that emerges in *Fathom*.

Consonant with this understanding of the novel as a collaborative and not a private form, *Greaves* is dominated by the discourse in which social relationships are most explicitly and
confidently recorded and promulgated: the law. The novel may begin with a comic parody of legalese, but as it advances, the law becomes not only a mechanism by which elements of the plot are
resolved but also a matter for serious debate. Of the group seated in
the Black Lion, one traveler, Tom Clarke, is an attorney, though he
never owns himself as such "without blushing"; his uncle, Samuel
Crowe, the seafarer of this novel, is embroiled in a dispute over an
inheritance, while a third member of the group, Ferret, is a hack
writer who has felt the "rod of power" and is now trying to evade a

19. *The Madhouse of Language: Writing and Reading Madness in the Eighteenth Century* (London: Routledge, 1991), 101.

20. J. V. Price, "Smollett and the Reader in *Launcelot Greaves*," in *Smollett:
Author of the First Distinction*, ed. Alan Bold (Totowa, N.J.: Barnes and Noble,
1982), 205.

warrant for his arrest. These characters, whose discussion of the
legalities of inheritance is interrupted by Launcelot's abrupt appearance, are self-conscious citizens who define themselves in relationship to the law and its powers over them, and it is with the
legal implications of the hero's actions that they become immediately concerned. Launcelot explains to the company that he is an
aspiring knight-errant, determined "to honour and assert the efforts of virtue; to combat vice in all her forms, redress injuries,
chastise oppression, protect the helpless and forlorn, relieve the indigent, exert [his] best endeavours in the cause of innocence and
beauty, and dedicate [his] talents, such as they are, to the service of
[his] country" (12). He intends, that is, to serve the law by remedy-
ing evils "which the law cannot reach" (14). As Launcelot's explanation unfolds, it becomes clear that his peculiar appearance is
connected to his class politics. As a "gentleman" Launcelot is allowed by law to wear armor in his own defense, and as his quixotic
vocation may make him the victim of "attempts of treachery,"
"combat against odds," and assaults by a "multitude of plebeians,"
he has chosen to protect himself with "the armour of [his] fore-
fathers" (14). Launcelot's armor symbolizes his belief that social
order puts the law, and its gentlemanly "coadjutors," in opposition
to plebeian multitudes. In the course of the novel, he will both cast
off his armor and change his understanding of how the law works.

Ferret, performing a useful metacritical role for Smollett, issues the first challenge to Launcelot's scheme when he denounces
the plan of the "modern Don Quixote" as being both "stale and extravagant" (12). More importantly, Ferret makes the case that there
is no area beyond the "reach of the law," and that Launcelot might
easily find himself overcome by some "determined constable, who
will seize your worship as a vagrant, according to the statute" (13).
In Ferret's view of the world, quixotes and constables compete
against each other. As one who has suffered for his outspoken political opinions, Ferret believes that all activities—even the whimsical
one of wandering around in ancient armor—fall under the control
of the law. In the heated debate that ensues, Greaves has to prove
that his quixotic conduct will not expose him to charges such as
vagrancy, disturbing the peace, and riding in disguise. This detailed
legal discussion focuses a major theme of the novel. The law, as
Ferret sees it, is comprehensive and exerts an impressive, even

oppressive, amount of control over citizens; yet, according to Launcelot, the law does not have sufficient reach, and many evils go undetected and unpunished. Ferret understands the law as an instrument of terror; Launcelot insists on its public utility. In their debate Launcelot wins the day, but the novel never entirely relinquishes Ferret's perspective on the law, and Launcelot will later accept some of Ferret's contentions.

The debate between Ferret and Launcelot is also important because it establishes the limits of Launcelot's chivalric infatuation. Despite his appearance, Launcelot's rhetoric is that of citizenship, not chivalry. His social code is clearly that of an eighteenth-century English gentleman who believes that the law provides adequate safeguards and protection for those who live under it. His peculiar costuming is designed to gain an audience for constitutional truths. Launcelot distinguishes himself from Don Quixote, to whom he alludes while insisting on his own mental health.[21] Nor is Greaves attached to the chivalric code per se. Certainly, when issued a challenge in orthodox chivalric manner by his rival for the hand of Aurelia, Launcelot "began to reflect, not without mortification, that he was treated as a lunatic by some person who wanted to amuse himself with the infirmities of his fellow creatures" (148–49). Greaves's model of chivalry does not violate the "suggestion[s] of reason." When he follows Aurelia to London, he abruptly abandons his quixotic behavior and leaves his armor in the care of an innkeeper. Towards the end of the novel, incarcerated in a private madhouse, Greaves "heartily repented of his knight-errantry, as a frolic which might have very serious consequences" (186). Once Smollett has established Greaves's quixoticism, he only mentions knight-errantry and chivalry in order to modify and qualify his hero's attachment to its laws and forms. The irony is that Greaves, who is both sane and passionate and cleaves to the reason of the law, discovers through his own imprisonment and incarceration

---

21. "I am neither an affected imitator of Don Quixote, nor, as I trust in heaven, visited by that spirit of lunacy so admirably displayed in the fictitious character exhibited by the inimitable Cervantes. I have not yet encountered a windmill for a giant; nor mistaken this public house for a magnificent castle . . . I see and distinguish objects as they are discerned and described by other men. I reason without prejudice, can endure contradiction, and, as the company perceives, even bear impertinent censure without passion or resentment" (13).

that the law he so much admires is prepared to prey on infirmity, apprehension, and madness.

Launcelot's allegiance to English law is clearly seen when he participates in a county election. The ignorance of the Tory candidate and the mercenary attitude of the Whig cause Greaves to address his fellow citizens and remind them of their constitutional rights and obligations: "You, the freemen of England, are the basis of that excellent constitution, which hath long flourished the object of envy and admiration. To you belongs the inestimable privilege of choosing a delegate properly qualified to represent you in the high court of parliament. This is your birth-right, inherited from your ancestors, obtained by their courage, and sealed with their blood" (75–76).[22] Shortly after this impassioned speech, Greaves's abstract admiration for the law is put to practical application. Falsely imprisoned by the officers of Justice Gobble, Launcelot uses his legal knowledge to demand his rights: "I now demand to see the information in consequence of which I was detained in prison, the copy of the warrant of commitment or detainer, and the face of the person by whom I was accused. I insist upon a compliance with these demands, as the privileges of a British subject; and if it is refused, I shall seek redress before a higher tribunal" (94). Launcelot's knowledge does not, however, sway the judge—whose stupidity and ignorance are invincible—and his release is secured by other means. The jail is not, however, the most severe test of the constitution. That role is reserved for the private madhouse in which Launcelot later finds himself incarcerated: "How little reason (said he to himself) have we to boast of the blessings enjoyed by the British subject, if he holds them on such a precarious tenure: if a man of rank and property may be thus kidnapped even in the midst of the capital; if he may be seized by ruffians, insulted, robbed, and con-

22. Greaves goes on to list the qualifications necessary for a member of Parliament, who "ought not only to be endued with the most inflexible integrity, but should likewise possess a fund of knowledge that may enable him to act as a part of the legislature. He must be well acquainted with the history, the constitution, and the laws of his country . . ." (76). An acute awareness of the law is also a requirement for the role of knight-errant, as Launcelot explains to the aspirant, Crowe: "A knight-errant ought to understand the sciences, to be master of ethics or morality, to be well versed in theology, a compleat casuist, and minutely acquainted with the laws of his country" (61–62).

veyed to such a prison as this, from which there seems to be no possibility of escape" (190). Once in the madhouse Launcelot realizes that the armor worn to defend his body may be used to prove his mental infirmity. He further realizes that under such a pretext "the most innocent person upon earth is liable to be immured for life" (190).

The value of citizenship is asserted just as Launcelot doubts it. At the very moment of his disillusioned reverie, Clarke and Crowe have gained knowledge of his whereabouts and have, upon application to a judge, gained a warrant to search the establishment. The details of Launcelot's release are given by Smollett with some care; moreover, they are recapitulated a few pages later when Launcelot restores his Aurelia—whom he has heard singing in the asylum—to freedom: "There was no room for hesitation or choice; he attended [Aurelia's kinswoman] immediately to the judge, who upon proper application issued another search-warrant for Aurelia Darnel. The constable and his posse were again retained; and Sir Launcelot Greaves once more crossed the threshold of Mr. Bernard Shackle" (196). The events of *Greaves*, at least in part, and the fact that various resolutions in the novel are facilitated by legal action, validate its hero's rhetoric and his faith in the law. Aurelia, who has been abused and wrongfully imprisoned by her uncle, has "immediate recourse" to "eminent lawyers" so that she can choose a new guardian for the remaining months of her minority (201). While her uncle's death renders this unnecessary, the reader has been reminded of the protection the law affords. Even the secondary characters benefit from a legal resolution: Crowe gains his inheritance after all.[23]

Smollett's validation of Launcelot's constitutional enthusiasm is only partial, however, and is balanced by satiric portraits of legal officials at work. Justice Gobble, the novel's most notorious character in this respect, responds to Launcelot's citation of his rights as audacious behavior for which he might well be trounced. Launcelot is saved only by his social standing, as Mrs. Gobble comically elucidates.

---

23. It turns out that the aunt who docked the entail on Crowe's property was not entitled to do so, as she had undergone a secret marriage and was therefore a "couvert femme" at the time she took the action.

Thank God, we have been used to deal with gentlefolks,
and many's the good pound we have lost by them; but
what of that? Sure we know how to behave to our bet-
ters. Mr. Gobble, thanks be to God, can defy the whole
world to prove that he ever said an uncivil word, or did a
rude thing to a gentleman, knowing him to be a person
of fortune. Indeed, as to your poor gentry and riff-raff,
your tag, rag, and bobtail, or such vulgar scoundrelly
people, he has always behaved like a magistrate, and
treated them with the rigger of authority. (96)

In exposing the selective, and self-interested, "rigger of authority,"
Smollett forces his reader to consider that not even the most admi-
rable constitution can transcend its daily interpretations. To this
point, we can compare *Greaves* to a novel like Fielding's *Amelia*
and argue that, while both novels satirize legal abuses and the corruption of legal institutions, they nonetheless share a faith in legal
process and, as their respective plots evidence, hold that eventually
the law of the land is sufficient to protect the innocent and punish
the guilty. Smollett and Fielding are reformers who use the medium
of the novel to educate readers about details of the law and to suggest necessary corrections of the system. But *Greaves,* despite its
golden conclusion, is a much darker novel than *Amelia.*

Launcelot's own relationship to the law is troubling. In the
scene above, Launcelot self-righteously translates Mrs. Gobble's
words into the confession that her husband has "tyrannized over
the poor, and connived at the vices of the rich" (96). What Launcelot cannot admit here, or at any other point in the novel, is the
derivation of his own power from exactly the same kind of social
discrimination that the Gobbles (who are ignorant upstarts) inex-
pertly apply. Launcelot's behavior and beliefs demonstrate the
limits of constitutional rhetoric as fundamentally, if more obliquely,
as the Gobbles'. Even as he addresses those he meets as "fellow citizens" and celebrates the laws and customs that unite Englishmen,
Launcelot remains conscious of the social differences that separate
them. Launcelot's ability to fulfill the law, to serve as "coadjutor,"
is, paradoxically, related to his own impunity. Clarke, when he
recounts the "golden age" Greaves has brought about on his estate, relates that "his generosity seemed to overleap the bounds of
discretion; and even in some cases might be thought tending to a

breach of the king's peace" (40). As a "general redresser of grievances," Launcelot's method was to take "the law in his own hands":
"If a woman complained to him of being ill treated by her husband,
he first inquired into the foundation of the complaint; and if he
found it just, catechised the defendant. If this warning had no effect, and the man proceeded to fresh acts of violence; then this
judge took the execution of the law in his own hands, and horse-
whipped the party. Thus he involved himself in several law-suits,
that drained him of pretty large sums of money" (40). Launcelot
can institute direct and equivalent punishment—horsewhipping
for wife beating—because he can afford to pay large amounts of
money in damages. More importantly, the very offense he punishes,
wife beating, reveals the class-based nature of the law itself. Blackstone records that by the "old law" a man "might give his wife mod-
erate correction": "But, with us, in the politer reign of Charles the
second, this power of correction began to be doubted: and a wife
may now have security of the peace against her husband; or, in return, a husband against his wife. Yet, the lower rank of people, who
were always fond of the old common law, still claim and exert their
antient privilege: and the courts of law will still permit a husband to
restrain a wife of her liberty, in case of any gross misbehaviour"
(1:433). In Blackstone's passage we get the feeling that obeying or
not obeying the law (itself the product of more or less polite reigns)
is a matter of personal taste and station in society. Those "fond" of a
particular illegality can continue to perform it. But, even though
Launcelot takes a progressive view of the wife-beating issue, no real
progress is made, as violence against the wife is answered by violence against the husband.

Launcelot's use of violent punishment far exceeds his legal
right to correct, with moderation, his servants. His first action after
he is dubbed a knight is to give Crabshaw a "thwack with his launce
across the shoulders" (44), and he follows this up with a horsewhipping. In Crabshaw's words, Launcelot has "a mortal good hand at
giving a flap with a fox's tail" (63). When Crabshaw crosses the
hounds at a hunt, Greaves, "instead of assisting the disastrous
squire, exhorted his adversaries to punish him severely for his insolence" (47). Other lower-class characters who fail to recognize social distinctions are denounced as insolent and are immediately
and brutally punished. When Launcelot is jeered by a soldier, he
announces that he would "chastise the fellow on the spot for his in-

solence, were it not out of the respect I bear to his majesty's service." After further abuse, Greaves orders Crabshaw to "beat in that scoundrel's drum-head" (48). The incident ends when the parties involved appear before the local justice of the peace. But, even though the soldiers have a case against Launcelot and Crabshaw, who are the aggressors in the fray, they choose not to pursue it.

> They were not, however, so fond of the law as the justice seemed to be. Their sentiments had taken a turn in favour of Sir Launcelot, during the course of his examination, by which it appeared that he was really a gentleman of fashion and fortune; and they resolved to compromise the affair without the intervention of his worship. Accordingly, the serjeant repaired to the constable's house, where the knight was lodged; and humbled himself before his honour, protesting with many oaths, that if he had known his quality he would have beaten the drummer's brains about his ears, for presuming to give his honour or his horse the least disturbance; thof the fellow, he believed, was sufficiently punished in being a cripple for life. Sir Launcelot admitted of his apologies; and taking compassion on the fellow who had suffered so severely for his folly, resolved to provide for his maintenance. (49–50)[24]

In this instance, the mere fact that Greaves is a gentleman of "fashion and fortune" justifies his act of aggression. Those he has injured "humble" themselves before him rather than take advantage of the law. The sergeant's speech, which urges that a lifelong disability is a fair punishment for lower-class rudeness, would not be out of place in *Candide.* But, given the rest of the novel, it is difficult to argue

24. This is the most brutal punishment of insolence in the novel, but there are further incidents. At a wayside inn two officers demand the supper that is being prepared for Launcelot's party. Crabshaw remonstrates with them and gets a bloody nose. Launcelot's response is that he has been saved the trouble of punishing Crabshaw's "insolence and rusticity" himself (108). It is only when the officers treat the other residents with "insolence and contempt" (109) that Greaves intervenes. Even then he is prepared to forgive them because they are "probably of good families." However, when the "officers" admit they are disguised apprentices, Tom Clarke and Crabshaw attack them and punish them for their "presumption." Essentially, the apprentices are punished not for their boorish behavior but for their low social status.

with any degree of assurance that Smollett is being completely satiric. Although Launcelot distances himself from the sergeant's brutality by "taking compassion on the fellow who had suffered so severely for his folly," the sergeant's attitude to the drummer is only a more extreme version of Launcelot's attitude to Crabshaw.

It would be a mistake, however, to isolate the violence of the upper class in a novel whose every turn depends on physical force and bodily damage. The plot progresses by way of brawls, affrays, and assaults. All participate. Moreover, they participate without authorial comment or remark. In this novel there are two modes of social regulation: the law and violence. While the function and operation of the first is the subject of self-conscious debate, no rationale or justification of the second is ever offered. Occasionally, Launcelot opposes legal recourse and violent action and argues that the existence of the one obviates the other.[25] In so doing, he accepts the Lockean premise that civil societies exist to provide impartial justice in place of personal vengeance. Such an opposition only makes us realize (as Launcelot does not) that, despite all the discussion of the law in the novel, there is constant violence, most of which cannot be justified by reference to "natural right" or personal vengeance. In *Roderick Random* and *Peregrine Pickle* Smollett uses the body and its experience of the world to investigate and comment on social and political conditions. Both novels have their share of violence, but in neither is violence so general, so repetitious, so severe, and so weakly motivated as it is in *Greaves*. In the society of this novel, spasms of violence are endemic, yet it is precisely this violence that elaborate legal codes are supposed to replace.

The world of *Greaves* is characterized by imperfect human institutions, constant brutality, and the dim promise of "Eternal Justice." The configuration of these terms suggests a novel like *Guzmán de Alfarache*. Unlike Launcelot, who is on a mission, Guzmán sees his whole life as a punishment for his restlessness: "being as it were in Paradise, I would goe abroad into the world; and like my first fore-fathers, could not see when I was well."[26] But what the

25. For example, in his speech before Gobble, where Launcelot speaks of arming himself with the "right of nature" to "exterminate such villains" (98).

26. Mateo Alemán, *Guzmán de Alfarache,* trans. James Mabbe (London, 1623), 61.

two texts have in common is the ability to entertain seeming contradictions silently. In *Greaves* the contradiction is between law
and violence; in *Guzmán* it is between spirituality and violence.
Guzmán's experiences give him both a form of spiritual knowledge
and an intense desire for very physical revenge on those who have
injured him. He uses the words of Paul's letter to the Ephesians to
describe the effects of adversity: "I plainly began to perceive, how
Adversitie makes men wise: in that very instant, me thought, I discovered a new light; which as in a cleare Glasse, did represent unto
mee things past, things present, and things to come" (104). But
Guzmán's religious observances and rhetoric do not prevent him
from having the most graphic dreams of revenge. Within pages he is
describing his resolve to be revenged on a woman who has mistre-
ated him, and he sees himself "treading on the very necke of her,
and setting my foot on her old withered windpipe, throwing her first
to the ground, as thou woudst a Dish-clout" (105). The ability of the
hero to entertain both religious aspirations and violent impulses,
without any sense of contradiction or hypocrisy, is a complex one.
In the society of Alemán's novel a character must be either the per-
petrator or the victim of violence; there is simply no perspective
from which violence can be judged and assessed. Furthermore, the
religious background of the novel is dominated by the vengeful God
of the Old Testament and imbued with an early modern Catholic
understanding of the insignificance of the flesh and physical pain.
Guzmán brings both of these elements together when he speaks in
the cadences of Ecclesiastes: "Mans life is a warre fare upon earth,
there is no certainty therein; no settled assurance, no estate that is
permanent; no pleasure that is perfect; no content that is true; but
all is counterfeit and vaine" (57). *Guzmán* makes the reader un-
comfortably conscious of what "warre fare upon earth" means. The
law in this novel is completely arbitrary, hypocritical, and corrupt.
This being the case, characters can either satisfy themselves with
personal vengeance or solace themselves with the possibility of a
more permanent estate where the dictates of justice obtain.

  Smollett had explicitly spoken of *Guzmán* as a possible model
for his own work in chapter 1 of Fathom. It makes sense that,
having "sublimed" Ferdinand out of the low physicality of the picaresque with disturbing results, Smollett would return to that novel's
point of origin and see what reassurance the blunt, material world

would offer. *Greaves,* though far removed from the world and events of *Guzmán,* is infused with its spirit and juggles the same notions of secular law, spiritual justice, and incredible violence. Launcelot, it is true, entertains a reverence for the law that is related specifically to English society, and events in the novel go some way towards justifying his faith. But a more fundamental reality of the novel is violence. Neither constitutional rhetoric nor Christian belief provides an efficient social language.

The brutality of *Greaves* indicates that Smollett, in many ways a gentleman of the Enlightenment, shared with the author of *Guzmán* a deep suspicion of human institutions and progress. But, although the most obvious similarity between *Guzmán* and *Greaves* is their violence, there is a more profound connection. Each novel has a vision of the terrors of religion. Alemán's visions of eternal damnation are not unexpected, but Smollett is a resolutely secular writer, who generally uses religious references for the purposes of comic exaggeration.[27] We know little, apart from his distaste for bigotry, about his own religious beliefs. Yet in *Greaves* only the gloomy idea of final judgment gives any hope. Launcelot, wrongfully imprisoned himself, asks his fellow inmates for an account of the magistrate.

> This request was no sooner signified than a crew of naked wretches crowded around him, and, like a congregation of rooks, opened their throats all at once, in accusation of justice Gobble. The knight was moved at this scene, which he could not help comparing, in his own mind, to what would appear upon a much more awful occasion, when the cries of the widow and the orphan, the injured and oppressed, would be uttered at the tribunal of an unerring Judge against the villainous and insolent authors of their calamity. (86)

Launcelot is moved at the scene, but his invocation of religious terror is private. Reading this passage, we see the pathetic spectacle— the "naked wretches" and the vulnerability of their birdlike naked throats. But the vindication of these creatures occurs only in Launcelot's private vision of "a much more awful occasion."

27. I say this even with the Christian primitivism of the character Humphry Clinker in mind.

Alone among major eighteenth-century writers, Smollett avoids overt religious references. Why does this one occur here? The answer, I think, has to do with the political implications of the relationship of mind and body. Smollett tried to answer the troubled subjectivity of *Fathom* by a return to the external world, but although *Greaves* opens in a cheery domestic light, it closes with the darkness of the mind. In *Greaves*, unlike *Fathom*, the frailty of the human mind is a matter of public concern. Even in the madhouse, Launcelot tries to distinguish between the operations of the state and the illegality of his imprisonment, but his very effort to tell them apart only proves how close they are. When first kidnapped, Launcelot believes he is "apprehended on suspicion of treasonable practices, by a warrant from the secretary of state" (185). He consoles himself with the notion that he is entitled to the privilege of habeas corpus, "as the act including that inestimable jewel, was happily not suspended at this time" (185). After an interval has passed, the madhouse and the instruments of despotic government move closer together in Launcelot's mind: "People may inveigh against the Bastile in France, and the Inquisition in Portugal; but I would ask if either of these be in reality so dangerous or dreadful as a private mad-house in England" (190).[28] Launcelot may "demand the protection of the legislature" (193), but he knows the legislature will not protect him should corrupt physicians (such as the one now in attendance) claim he is mad. In addition, and even more disturbing, the government itself treats those suspected of treason as madmen. "False perspectives" are not just a matter of private horror. The fragility of the human mind can be used as an instrument of public terror. The lessons of *Greaves* are made explicit in later fiction. In Wollstonecraft's *Maria, or The Wrongs of Woman* the heroine, incarcerated in a private madhouse, considers her imprisonment merely as a literalization of female oppression under the law. The law sometimes salves its citizens with reasonable intervention, but it can also manipulate private terror. Confronted with the terrifying spectacle of the law, the citizen can summon up images of a "far more awful" solemnity, but it is only in the privacy of the mind that the citizen can oppose legal with grander terrors.

28. Comparison of Launcelot's sober reflections here with Peregrine's boredom when imprisoned in the Bastille reveals Smollett's growing awareness of the sinister operations of state power.

Fathom and *Greaves* result from Smollett's concern with the nature and efficacy of social order. His intention in *Fathom* was to manipulate the passion of terror in the interests of morality. Instead, he himself was ensnared by the intricate workings of a passion not amenable to rational explanation and graphic display. Smollett sought to balance the understanding of the passions he achieved in *Fathom* by striving in *Greaves* for external, public perspective. The hope in the latter novel is that the rational system of the law, allied with the warmth of human community, can save the subject from dread and apprehension. In his strivings Smollett did not, however, deny his own better knowledge. The curiously nonphysical Fathom and the armor-encased Greaves seem to be polar opposites, but through them Smollett explores two versions of the same terror. In the *Atom* Smollett gives that terror a contemporary cast. One of the most scathing satires in English, this late work represents politics and state power as the ability not only to damage bodies but to force them to inhabit images of their own vulnerability.

CHAPTER SIX

THE POLITICS OF MATTER:
THE HISTORY AND ADVENTURES
OF AN ATOM

To render his punishment more public and conspicuous, he was removed to Paris there to undergo a repetition of all his former tortures, with such additional circumstances as the most fertile and cruel dispositions could devise for encreasing his misery and torment. Being conducted to the concergerie, an iron bed, which likewise served for a chair, was prepared for him, and to this he was fastened with chains. The torture again was applied, and a physician ordered to attend, to see what degree of pain he could support. Nothing, however, material was extorted; for what he one moment confessed, he recanted the next. It is not within our province, and we consider it a felicity, to relate all the circumstances of this cruel and tragical event. Sufficient it is, that, after suffering the most exquisite tortures that human nature could invent, or man support, his judges thought proper to terminate his misery by a death shocking to imagination, and shameful to humanity.

Smollett, A Continuation of the Complete History of England

The death that Tobias Smollett goes on to describe is indeed "shocking to imagination." Most horrific of all is the knowledge that, during the application of red-hot pincers, boiling oil, and melted lead and the protracted attempt at dismemberment, Robert Damiens, attempter of the life of Louis XV, "preserved his senses." It is difficult to read Smollett's account of Damiens's death, and almost impossible to quote from it at length. Elaine Scarry has written that our sense of the incommensurability of pain makes us reluctant to discuss torture, and means that "the very moral intuitions that might act on behalf of the claims of sentience remain almost as interior and inarticulate as sentience itself."[1] Any moral intuitions we may have about the execution of Damiens are, in an important sense, redundant. Smollett, however, described Damiens's ordeal within a couple of years of its occurrence and at a time when exacerbated forms of capital punishment were under discussion in England. Each detail in Smollett's description of Damiens's death contributes to the condemnation of extreme state power and furthers the account's political purpose.

Smollett's condemnation of what is done to Damiens is strengthened by his understanding of its logic. When he says that Damiens was removed to Paris to "render his punishment more public and conspicuous," he prefigures the analysis of Michel Foucault, whose account of Damiens's execution in the opening pages of *Discipline and Punish* has made the event part of contemporary literary theory. Describing the "juridico-political function" of public execution, Foucault argues that it brings into play

> as its extreme point, the dissymmetry between the subject who has dared to violate the law and the allpowerful sovereign who displays his strength . . . the punishment is carried out in such a way as to give a spectacle not of measure, but of imbalance and excess; in this liturgy of punishment, there must be an emphatic affirmation of power and of its intrinsic superiority. And this superiority is not simply that of right, but that of the physical strength of the sovereign beating down upon the body of his adversary and mastering it.[2]

Smollett also understands that the spectacle of such executions depends on a "dissymmetry" between the subject who has violated the law and the "all-powerful sovereign," and he elucidates this dissymmetry for the reader. He ends his account by saying the regicide was of disturbed mind, and that the detestation "justly due to the enormity of his crime ought now to have been absorbed in the consideration of his misfortune, the greatest that can befall human nature." Smollett's comment that the procedure against Damiens and

1. *The Body in Pain,* 60.
2. *Discipline and Punish,* trans. Alan Sheridan (New York: Vintage Books, 1979), 48–49.

his family ended "in a manner not favourable to the avowed clemency of Louis, or the acknowledged humanity of the French nation" puts one in mind of the time he boarded a prison galley berthed at Nice and said that the "miserable wretches" in chains were "a sight which a British subject, sensible of the blessing he enjoys, cannot behold without horror and compassion" (*Travels*, 128). But the extremity of foreign penal systems provided only relative comfort.

The "emphatic affirmation of power" that the spectacle of public punishment allowed was, at this time, receiving renewed attention in England. J. M. Beattie has delineated the ways in which punishment by public exposure, in the pillory or by whipping, was central to a penal system in which neither magistrates nor judges "seem to have thought of incarceration as a useful punishment."[3] The increase in violent crime at midcentury created a desire to make the spectacle of punishment more terrifying and so frighten the populace into abiding by the law.[4] In the middle years of the century, when Damiens was executed in Paris, the English authorities were "adding aggravating circumstances" to execution, which heightened its "disgrace and terror": "These turned out to be further attacks on the convict's body . . . by denying to the convict the comfort of a decent and Christian burial and denying to his family and friends the possibility of the customary forms of bereavement. These resulted from decisions to mutilate the convict's body after death by ordering it to be either hanged in chains or dissected by surgeons."[5]

That Smollett knew the centrality of spectacular punishment to domestic order can be judged from *The Present State of All Nations* (1768–69), his socioeconomic compendium. Smollett begins his account of England: "The English constitution is a limited monarchy" (2:161). In thirteen pages he describes the functions of the

3. *Crime and the Courts in England, 1660–1800* (Oxford: Clarendon Press, 1986), 460. A concise list of the entire range of eighteenth-century punishments is given in Chamber's *Cyclopedia* (London, 1728): "Among us the principal *Civil Punishments* are Imprisonment, the Stocks, Pillory, Burning in the Hand, Whipping, Cuching-stool, Hanging, Beheading, Quartering, Burning, Transportation, etc. see Fine, Pillory, Cuching Stool, Gallows, Gibbet, Etc."

4. See, for example, Henry Fielding, *Enquiry into the Causes of the Late Increase of Robbers* (London, 1751).

5. Beattie, *Crime and the Courts in England*, 526–27.

king, the House of Commons, the House of Lords, the constitution (both major strengths and defects), the judges, various courts, and sheriffs. At the end of this rapid enumeration of the offices of power, he devotes three pages to a detailed account of the "punishments inflicted on civil criminals in England." His distaste for "aggravating circumstances of execution" is clear: "In atrocious cases of murder and robbery, the criminal's body is, after execution, hung in chains upon a gibbet, by the road side, where it continues to rot, to the great annoyance of travellers, and the prejudice of those who possess houses and lands in the neighbourhood" (2:176).

Various scholars have demonstrated how Smollett drew on his nonfiction works from the 1750s and 1760s in writing his least-known and most problematic work: *The History and Adventures of an Atom* (1769).[6] Those same nonfiction works—among them *The Complete History of England* and *The Present State*—also suggest another dimension to Smollett's satirical allegory of English political life: a concern with the material effects of power. In the *Atom* Smollett's insistence on bodily experience allows him to expose the workings of what Althusser would call the repressive state apparatus: the power of the state to coerce its members and inflict pain upon their bodies.[7] Repression has, however, a secondary ideological component to which bodies moving in time and space are subject. Throughout the *Atom* Smollett teases out the relationships between the individual, who is made of matter and generates abstractions, and the material institution of the state, which resides on an abstract foundation. His satire recognizes, and negotiates between, two distinct sources of power: the power of the political system to maintain itself by translating its laws and regulations into the physical experience of malefactors, and the power of the individual to upset abstract political justifications, by upsetting the interpretation of physical reality from which such justifications are derived.

The *Atom* is Smollett's most obscure work—in every sense. Only recently made accessible by Robert Adams Day's scholarly

6. See especially Martz, *Later Career of Tobias Smollett,* 90–103, and Robert Adams Day's editorial apparatus to the University of Georgia edition.

7. Louis Althusser, "Ideology and Ideological State Apparatuses," in *Lenin and Philosophy,* trans. Ben Brewster (New York: Monthly Review Press, 1971), 127–86.

edition, the *Atom* was previously a work that, as Day observes in his introduction, "[o]nly a handful of living persons" (xxv) had read through. In explanation, it must be admitted that the *Atom* is not the most immediately attractive of texts. Some readers will be repelled by its scatology;[8] more will find the work's sequence of events impenetrable. A detailed account of English politics from 1754 to 1768 (including the years of the Seven Years' War), told as though it were a history of Japan beginning in "the year of the period Foggien one hundred and fifty four" (27), makes considerable demands on a modern reader. Moreover, the narrator is the eponymous atom, and its reflections on its own epistemological status may seem, at first, somewhat abstract. Ultimately, however, the *Atom* rewards its reader: scatological, topical, full of learned wit, this story is also a testament to the reality of political power and its concrete effects upon the body.

　　To begin its narrative, the atom assembles its cast, and gives a brief explanation of each character. Among the chief actors are

8. The graphic details of physical dysfunction and perversion with which Smollett infuses his satire have so distressed critics that they have strenuously attempted to deny that Smollett wrote the work at all. In 1950 Francesco Cordasco published a letter in which Smollett speaks of the "anxiety and apprehension" that his supposed authorship of the piece has caused and insists that he will take measures to protect his name: "[W]ere I in England it should be meet to lash the pestilence which has shrouded my name. With the fond anticipation that Misery stalk your presence, and W[ilkes] drown in Stygian bile . . . With Refusal and Anger, Ts Smollett" (*The Letters of Tobias George Smollett* [Madrid: Avelino Ortega, 1950], 35). The letter was a forgery. Other critics have contented themselves with saying that the work is "unnecessarily disgusting" and that it merely evinces Smollett's "ample pornographic abilities" (Arnold Whitridge, *Tobias Smollett* [New York: Arnold Whitridge, 1925], 97, 117). Lewis Knapp is reluctant to attribute the work to Smollett: "The *Atom* does contain in its method and material much that is Smollettian . . . Yet it should be remembered that we lack the external evidence necessary to prove conclusively that he wrote it" (*Tobias Smollett: Doctor of Men and Manners* [Princeton: Princeton University Press, 1949], 283). James R. Forster marshals the "presumptive evidence" for Smollett's authorship ("Smollett and the *Atom*," PMLA 68 [1953]: 1032–46). The evidence for Smollett's authorship that Robert Adams Day provides justifies his assertion that, "while we still lack an affidavit of authorship in Smollett's hand, nothing further remains to be desired to corroborate the attribution of the *Atom* to him" (liii). Particularly convincing is Adams Day's dry observation (supported by the textual notes) that "[i]f Smollett did not write the *Atom*, its author was a person unknown who devoted himself to plagiarizing the works of Smollett with unexampled pertinacity and thoroughness" (lvi).

Thomas Pelham-Holles, the duke of Newcastle (Fika-kaka), who was first lord of the treasury for much of the war; William, duke of Cumberland, third son of George II, and military commander at Culloden (Fatzman); and Philip Yorke, earl of Hardwicke, the lord high steward at trials of the rebel lords and primarily responsible for repressive legislation after the Forty-five (Sti-phi-rum-poo).

Having characterized its major actors, the atom proceeds to "a plain narration of historical incidents" (27). This account begins with French (Chinese) encroachments on English (Japanese) lands in America (Fatsissio). It continues with a description of the fall of Minorca to the French in 1756, Admiral Byng's (Bihn-goh's) failure to engage the French fleet in battle, and his subsequent execution (1757) (32–36). At this point, William Pitt, first earl of Chatham (Taycho), enters the narrative, and we reach the heart of the satire. Pitt had initially gained his public following for his determined opposition to the subsidies England paid to its German allies; the atom introduces him as one distinguished by "fluency of abuse" who did not hesitate to throw out "personal sarcasms against the Dairo [George II] himself": "He inveighed against his partial attachment to the land of Yesso [Hanover], which he had more than once manifested to the detriment of Japan: he inflamed the national prejudice against foreigners; and as he professed an inviolable zeal for the commons of Japan, he became the first demagogue of the empire. The truth is, he generally happened to be on the right side" (37). Pitt did not, however, remain on the right side. The most dynamic episode the atom relates is Pitt's betrayal of his original political principles in favor of Hanoverian policy and the pursuit of the German war. Taycho's manipulation of the mob (Blatant Beast), his reconciliation with George II, and his management of the campaign in Fatsissio are described by the atom with salacious relish. The atom's account is designed to convince the reader of political views Smollett himself held strongly: Pitt has persuaded the people to "beggar themselves" pursuing a Continental war "all for the sake of Yesso" (78), when it is in the American war that the interests of England are "chiefly concerned" (101). After the confirmation of the Peace of Paris (119), Smollett's narrative becomes less detailed, though the atom does give some attention to the fall of Lord Bute (Yak-strot), the unpopular Scottish advisor of George III (Gio-Gio), and to increasing unrest in the American colonies.

The predictable response to the rotund and bulging world of

such a work is to flatten it into a series of correspondences between
fictional characters and their real-life counterparts. Read in this
way, the satire can best be discussed in terms of justice and accu-
racy. Is Smollett fair in his portrayal of Newcastle, a man who, despite his intellectual failings, did serve the public for almost half a
century without making any personal gain? Why does he give us
such a negative picture of Pitt (to whom, after all, he had dedicated
his enormously successful *Complete History of England* only a decade before)?[9] Exclusive focus on the parallels between Smollett's
"Japan" and England during the Seven Years' War blinds us to the
complexity of the satire's drama. In the *Atom* Smollett defines the
political individual through the body—its needs, its weaknesses,
the reality of its discomforts, and the oddities of its power. In telling
the history of England as a sequence of physical, corporeal events,
Smollett acknowledges the body's vulnerability as an object of
repression, but he also uses the body as a powerful ideological
weapon. In the *Atom* Smollett is governed entirely by "the desire to
destroy through words and by the satirist's savage delight in his own
powers."[10] Savage and destructive the satiric transformations of
the *Atom* certainly are, but they spring from Smollett's anger at the
political abuse of the body.[11]

The enabling fiction of the *Atom* is that matter can speak and
make its perspective heard. The *Atom* begins when an atom—lodged
in the body of Nathaniel Peacock, impoverished haberdasher—
becomes articulate, confronting the body of which it is part with
the intricacies of its own physical makeup ("What thou hearest is
within thee—is part of thyself" [5]). The atom resides in a particularly crucial, yet obscure, part of Nathaniel's anatomy: his pineal
gland. Descartes had chosen this small gland in the brain as the
place in which the soul, "united to all the portions of the body con-
jointly," exercises its function "more particularly than in other

9. Lewis Knapp usefully summarizes Smollett's references to Pitt in
"Smollett and the Elder Pitt," *Modern Language Notes* 59 (April 1944): 250–57.
10. Adams Day, introduction to the *Atom*, xxv.
11. The satire of the *Atom* is not, of course, entirely disinterested. For example, the satire of Bute's "liberality in patronizing genius and the arts" (102) is
obviously driven by Smollett's sense that his polemical attempts on Bute's behalf, especially in his management of the *Briton,* have not been sufficiently acknowledged and that his merit has been overlooked.

parts."[12] Within Nathaniel's body the atom's task is that of integration; it negotiates between matter and spirit and unites mind and body into one distinct identity. Within the structure of the satire as a whole, the atom is similarly concerned with transactions between matter and the consciousness of matter, but its fictional function is a reversal of its corporeal role. The text of the *Atom* opens with a moment of division when the tiny particle in Nathaniel's head asserts its "actual, independent existence," and thrusts itself forward as an object of consciousness. The atom explains to Nathaniel that, although they are endowed with reason, atoms can communicate only "once in a thousand years, and then only, when we fill a certain place in the pineal gland of a human creature" (6). According to Descartes, an atom so placed enjoys a privileged perspective on the connection of body and soul. When Nathaniel's atom seizes its millennial chance to converse, it disrupts the hitherto silent unity of the haberdasher's corporeal and spiritual principles. The shrill sound of the atom in Nathaniel's garret signals an opposition of matter and consciousness. Both through what it does, and more subtly through what it is, the atom forces Nathaniel, and by extension the reader, to mind his matters, to become more fully conscious of our own materiality.

In giving priority to matter, the narrative reverses traditional categories in which mind and spirit are accorded greater value. The story we are about to hear has, then, a different orientation from those with which we are familiar, and this difference is further emphasized by other atomic attributes. Eighteenth-century science regarded the atom as the smallest possible modification of matter and understood that its minuteness placed it beyond human visualization. All objects, animate and inanimate, were composed of atoms, but any one atom was, literally, too insignificant to be considered. The atom's "small voice," silent for so long, will therefore make comprehensible and significant a vital story that has, for var-

12. *Philosophical Works of Descartes,* 1:345. Descartes explains the functioning of the gland by saying that it exists "so suspended between the cavities which contain the spirits that it can be moved by them in as many different ways as there are sensible diversities in the object, but that it may also be moved in diverse ways by the soul, whose nature is such that it receives in itself as many diverse impressions, that is to say, that it possesses as many diverse perceptions as there are diverse movements in this gland" (1:347).

ious reasons, been elusive. The particle has asserted itself because it requires an amanuensis. Nathaniel is the obvious choice, and the story he writes at the atom's command is the major portion of the *Atom.*

The atom's own nature allows it to gloat over its freedom from the material effects of government and thereby makes the tale of political vulnerability it unfolds even more striking. As one of those "constituent particles of matter, which can neither be annihilated, divided, nor impaired" (5–6), the atom is immune to physical punishment, and throughout its narration it goads and taunts Nathaniel by contrasting their constitutions.

> Nathaniel, You have heard of the transmigration of souls, a doctrine avowed by one Pythagoras, a philosopher of Crotona. This doctrine, though discarded and reprobated by christians, is nevertheless sound, and orthodox, I affirm on the integrity of an atom. Further I shall not explain myself on this subject, though I might with safety set the convocation and the whole hierarchy at defiance, knowing, as I do, that it is not in their power to make me bate one particle of what I advance: or, if they should endeavour to reach me through your organs, and even condemn you to the stake at Smithfield, verily, I say unto thee, I should be a gainer by the next remove. I should shift my quarters from a very cold and empty tenement, which I now occupy in the brain of a poor haberdasher, to the nervous plexus situated at the mouth of the stomach of a fat alderman fed with venison and turtle. (10)

The string of puns with which the atom expresses itself emphasizes its own imperishable, inviolate qualities. It affirms what it says on the "integrity of an atom," and it will never "bate one particle" of what it advances. The atom cannot be hanged, drawn, and quartered for attacking the state; it cannot be burned at Smithfield for unorthodox views. Its physical definition gives it a privileged relationship to the political system. Digressive and opinionated, the atom taunts Nathaniel with its peculiar physical superiority. By definition the atom is indivisible and irreducible; in contrast, Nathaniel, as instances of his life history alluded to by the atom show, is physically weak and vulnerable. The atom's definitions and recollections provide a commentary on the political events it narrates. Smollett's division of his satire into the political arena of "Japan" and the garret room of Nathaniel Peacock emphasizes the fear of punishment common to both narratives.

The atom's account of England during the Seven Years' War is haunted by events that occurred more than a decade earlier. Smollett's attention to the repression of the Forty-five in the *Atom* shows that he understood it, in Foucault's words, as "an emphatic affirmation of power" in which the physical strength of the sovereign beat down on the bodies of his adversaries. At the time of the rebellion, Smollett transmuted his anger and pain into "The Tears of Scotland," a poem that mourned, not those fallen in battle, but "the naked and forlorn" forced to live under Cumberland's brutal repression.

> *Yet, when the rage of battle ceas'd*
> *The victor's soul was not appeas'd;*
> *The naked and forlorn must feel*
> *Devouring flames, and murd'ring steel.*[13]

When friends advised Smollett that the verses were a little too warm and high in tone, he immediately added a concluding verse.

> *Whilst the warm blood bedews my veins,*
> *And unimpair'd remembrance reigns;*
> *Resentment of my country's fate,*
> *Within my filial breast shall beat;*
> *And, spite of her insulting foe,*
> *My sympathizing verse shall flow,*
> *"Mourn, hapless Caledonia, mourn*
> *Thy banish'd peace, thy laurels torn."*

Two decades later, Smollett's resentment at his country's fate was still strong enough to cause him to include the rebellion in the *Atom*. Introducing the chief politicians of the midfifties, the atom carefully includes their involvement in the aftermath of the rebellion. Hardwicke is remarkable for the cruelty of his counsels and "the

13. *Poems, Plays, and "The Briton,"* ed. Byron Gassman (Athens: University of Georgia Press, 1993), 26.

rancorous pleasure he seemed to feel in pronouncing sentence of death" (20).

> Sti-phi-rum-poo [Hardwicke], and other judges in the South, were condemning such of their parents and husbands as survived the sword, to crucifixion, cauldrons of boiling oil, or exenteration; and the people were indulging their appetites by feasting upon the viscera thus extracted. The liver of a Ximian [Scotsman] was in such request at this period, that if the market had been properly managed and supplied, this delicacy would have sold for two Obans a pound, or about four pounds sterling . . . This new branch of traffick would have produced about three hundred and sixty thousand pounds annually: for the rebellion might easily have been fomented from year to year; and consequently it would have yielded a considerable addition to the emperor's revenue, by a proper taxation. (24)

The prolonged savagery of this passage is clearly inspired by the punishment for high treason. Blackstone describes the final stages of that sentence thus: "3. That his [the offender's] entrails be taken out, and burned, while he is yet alive. 4. That his head be cut off. 5. That his body be divided into four parts. 6. That his head and quarters be at the king's disposal" (4:92). The logic of Smollett's account is that if the state is going to play the butcher it should do so thoroughly, and that eating a man's entrails is no less obscene, and a good deal more profitable, than burning them before his face. The arbitrariness and unjustifiable excess of the death sentences imposed after the rebellion horrified neutral and sympathetic observers. In *The Present State* Smollett refers to the executions after the rebellion while making a case against the punishment for treason: "This punishment, which is a disgrace to humanity, was executed literally, with every circumstance of barbarity, upon the convicted rebels in 1746" (2:175). The excessive nature of the capital punishment for treason is captured in the variety of deaths Smollett imagines for his Ximian rebels. His historical references to the rebellion stress the anachronistic, as well as the barbaric, nature of the punishment. Moreover, as historians of crime and punishment in eighteenth-century England attest, the spectacle of execution could not always be controlled by the authorities. At times it elicited a public response very different from that intended. Describing the execution of Dr. Cameron, a Jacobite rebel who had escaped at the time of the rebellion but was captured on his return to England, Smollett remarks: "[T]he populace, though not very subject to tender emotions, were moved to compassion, and even to tears, by his behaviour at the place of execution; and many sincere well-wishers to the present establishment thought that the sacrifice of this victim, at such a juncture, could not redound either to its honour or security" (*Continuation,* 1:73). The excesses of the death penalty, as a ritualistic readjustment of the body politic, cannot be justified. The Jacobite rebellion focuses and clarifies Smollett's condemnation of the entire system of capital punishment.

The vindictiveness of the administration did not cease with its treatment of the leaders of the rebellion. After the Forty-five, leading politicians seriously suggested that Scotland be blockaded and the innocent forced to starve with the guilty. Smollett's image of trading in human flesh realizes and makes tangible a prevailing attitude.[14] Yet, even if such treatment of Scotland had never been suggested, we can still see the reasoning behind Smollett's passionate imagery. The literary source for Smollett's postrebellion representation is, of course, Swift's *Modest Proposal* (1729). The extremity of both satires is justified by a situation in which society, a supposedly protective institution, becomes simply a more organized form of destruction than can be had in the state of nature. Smollett imposes on his Ximians the sentence imposed on English traitors, the only difference being that the "Japanese" emperor makes some use of the bodies at his disposal.

In *The Complete History of England* Smollett ends his account of the rebellion by saying how, after Culloden, Cumberland "detached several parties to ravage the country": "Those ministers of vengeance were so alert in the execution of their office, that in a few days there was neither house, cottage, man nor beast, to be seen in the compass of fifty miles; all was ruin, silence and desolation. The humane reader cannot reflect upon such a scene without

14. Bruce Lenman, *The Jacobite Risings in Britain, 1689–1746* (London: Methuen, 1984), 262.

grief and horror; what then must have been the sensation of the fugitive prince, when he beheld those spectacles of woe, the dismal fruit of his ambition" (4:674). Smollett is careful here to distance himself from the Jacobite cause: Charles Stuart, surveying the dismal fruit of his ambition, recalls Milton's Satan, confronting the results of his rebellion as he views his fallen comrades on the burning lake. As a historian, Smollett's tone is elevated and poetic: "all was ruin, silence and desolation"; and he explicitly appeals to a "humane reader" who will respond with horror to the scenes he describes. In the *Atom* the same events are rendered in visceral, graphic terms calculated to rouse the reader's revulsion. The satire is savage because Smollett wants us to be revolted by the collision of material man and material state.

In the extended preliminary section of the *Atom,* the characterization of major actors (11–27), the rebellion serves as a definitive political moment. Once the atom begins its "plain narration of historical incidents," a further example of the state's power over the bodies of its citizens immediately occurs. The example is the fate of Admiral Byng. Byng had been sent to the Mediterranean to protect English interests on the isle of Minorca. The island subsequently fell to the French, and the ships commanded by Byng failed to engage in sea battle. A public outcry ensued. Byng's trial unleashed one of the most virulent pamphlet wars England had yet seen.[15] If Byng's judgment only was at fault, then the Newcastle administration should accept responsibility for appointing him in the first place. If cowardice was at the bottom of the naval failure, then the law held that Byng should die. The court-martial that tried Byng found that he had not done his utmost to relieve St. Philip's Castle on Minorca, and that he had not done all he could to take enemy ships, but, as they thought neither cowardice nor disaffection responsible for these failures, they recommended clemency. Both king and Parliament ignored the recommendation, and Byng was executed in 1757. The extent of Byng's responsibility for naval failure is not an issue with which the atom is concerned. In the *Atom* Byng becomes a sacrificial victim, whose body the administration

15. The detailed cases made for and against Byng by his contemporaries are accessible in R. D. Spector's *English Literary Periodicals* (The Hague: Mouton, 1966), 16–34.

uses to deflect public anger and indignation. Smollett, through the atom, claims that Byng was turned into "[a] sop, [a] barrel, [a] scapegoat," and describes the end of the drama thus:

> Agents were employed through the whole metropolis to vilify his character, and accuse him of cowardice and treachery. Authors were enlisted to defame him in public writings; and mobs hired to hang and burn him in effigie. By these means the revenge of the people was artfully transferred, and their attention effectually diverted from the ministry, which was the first object of their indignation. At length, matters being duly prepared for the exhibition of such an extraordinary spectacle, Bihn-goh underwent a public trial, was unanimously found guilty, and unanimously declared innocent; by the same mouths condemned to death and recommended to mercy: but mercy was incompatible with the designs of the ad—n. The unfortunate Bihn-goh was crucified for cowardice, and bore his fate with the most heroic courage. His behaviour at his death was so inconsistent with the crime for which he was doomed to die, that the emissaries of the Cuboy [prime minister] were fain to propagate a report, that Bihn-goh had bribed a person to represent him at his execution, and be crucified in his stead. (36)

In this passage Smollett exposes the administration's transformation of Byng's living body into a sop thrown to the mob. According to the atom, the spectacle of public punishment, far from being used for the public good, is being cynically manipulated to save the administration. Byng's bravery, however, discredits the charges against him. His ability to maintain his spiritual integrity even as his physical integrity is violated frustrates the intentions of the administration. In the atom's satiric account Byng's courage forces the administration to argue that the executed man was not Byng but a bribed substitute. The stupidity of the libel is itself a significant comic stroke, for it implies that the administration has no sense of the absolute nature of death, and no understanding of the gravity of its own measures. If the power of death can be equaled by the power of a bribe, then the spectacle of public punishment is just that: a spectacle without any absolute consequences. The libel is also a perfect inversion of the bed trick of comedy in which it is the fact of consummation and not the experience of consummation that is of significance. The public execution is carried out and the desire of the administration is consummated in deed, but Byng's behavior draws attention away from the spectacle and towards an interpretation of his own character. He plays the role assigned, but not in the manner the administration requires. His acceptance of his fate is a paradoxical form of resistance to the transformation the administration wishes to effect upon his body, and through his body upon his reputation.

Admiral Byng and the Scottish rebels are extreme examples of how the body suffered within the eighteenth-century political system, but Smollett also uses physicality to expose more mundane workings of government. In a passage that strongly recalls *A Tale of a Tub*, Smollett insists that Pitt's war oratory is no replacement for solid fare.

> He composed a mess that should fill their bellies, and, at the same time, protract the intoxication of their brains, which it was so much his interest to maintain.—He put them upon a diet of yeast; where this did not agree with the stomach, he employed his emissaries to blow up the patients *à posteriori,* as the dog was blown up by the madman of Seville, recorded by Cervantes. The individuals thus inflated were seen swaggering about the streets, smooth and round, and sleek and jolly, with leering eyes and florid complexion . . . He declared as if by revelation, that the more debt the public owed, the richer it became; that food was not necessary to the support of life; nor an intercourse of the sexes required for the propagation of the species. (60–61)

The successes of the war were a heady mixture for the English populace, but they absorbed the national wealth. Moreover, according to the atom, huge territorial accessions left England "in danger of being ruined by her conquests" (117). In the *Atom* Smollett uses the severe grain shortage of 1766 to suggest that the war has given only empty satisfactions and denied the people their material necessities.

The effects of the yeast potions which [Legion] had
drank so liberally from the hands of Taycho, now wore
off. The fumes dispersed; the illusion vanished; the flat-
ulent tumor of its belly disappeared with innumerable
explosions, leaving a hideous lankness and such a ca-
nine appetite as all the eatables of Japan could not satisfy. After having devoured the whole harvest, it
yawned for more, and grew quite outrageous in its hunger, threatening to feed on human flesh, if not plen-
tifully supplied with other viands. (129)

Smollett's satire draws attention to the vulnerability of the human
frame, and the effects of government policy on material bodies.

Matter, as represented by the atom, is also the starting point
for an exposure of that system's ideology. Invisible and indivisible,
the atom is a material being beyond the reach of the political system. In contrast, Nathaniel is a ridiculous caricature of hidebound
man, whose every attempt to get beyond his own material being (including his most ambitious effort, a projected rendezvous with the
devil in Norway) is a comic failure. Yet those passages in which the
atom satirizes Nathaniel for his inability to escape his corporeal
limitations also make us aware that the imagination can, in some
instances, free the body. Particularly significant is Nathaniel's
comic failure to join the Rosicrucians: "I remember your poring
over the treatise *De volucri arborea,* until you had well-nigh lost
your wits; and your intention to enrol yourself in the Rosicrusian
society, until your intrigue with the tripe-woman in Thieving-lane
destroyed your pretensions to chastity" (64). Nathaniel is undone
by entanglements of the flesh. The uneasy sensation of lust destroys his philosophic and metaphysical ambitions, and, even more
galling, he must sit and hear a tiny, invisible atom, which itself possesses hardly any physical characteristics, narrate his limitations.
The Rosicrucian Brotherhood—the only evidence of which is a
body of texts published in the early seventeenth-century—was as
ethereal a human body as can be imagined. Known as the Invisible
Brotherhood because its members were impossible to identify, the
writings associated with the order were an amalgamation of scientific, mystical, and cabbalistic thought. Even the idea of the order
engendered notions of a renovated political state based on a revised

spiritual and intellectual understanding of man.[16] Pathetic as it is, Nathaniel's interest in the Rosicrucians marks a longing to understand differently his own place in the world. Locked inescapably within his own skin, and within a political system that uses his limitations to control him, Nathaniel still clings to the possibility of freedom. Oddly enough, this is precisely what the atom offers him, for along with the atom's mocking commentary goes a reconceptualization of the material world.

Throughout the 1750s and 1760s inanimate or eccentric narrators—like the atom—were a popular fictional device. Apart from their novelty value, they also allowed an author to estrange the reader from familiar understandings of how the world worked and to reconstruct the social world according to different principles. In 1760 Charles Johnstone's *Chrysal, or The Adventures of a Guinea* had been narrated by the spirit of gold. The novel's readers were taken from South America to almost every court in Europe, and the guinea's particular vantage point allowed Johnstone to demonstrate all the evils he attributed to a monetary economy: the corruption of logic, the overturning of hierarchy, and the complete rejection of natural order. *Chrysal* was an enormous popular success, and in 1765 the guinea's itinerary was expanded in response to public demand. In a matter of years, corkscrews, pincushions, and shoes had all appeared to human scribes and divested themselves of their insights and wisdom. The proven acceptability of nonhuman narrators probably encouraged Smollett in creating an atomic narrator at the decade's end, but corkscrews and pincushions, no matter how adroitly used, do not in themselves pose a social threat. The atom, however, did.

The atom subverted eighteenth-century ideology through its association with atheism and the importance it assigned to chance. Dryden, for example, often uses images of "jarring atoms" and "atoms casually together hurl'd" as antithetical to order in general and artistic order in particular.[17] Furthermore, the difficulty of

16. Frances A. Yates, in her fascinating and intensely readable account of this matter, traces "a chain of tradition leading from the Rosicrucian movement to the antecedents of the Royal Society" (*The Rosicrucian Enlightenment* [1972; reprint, New York and London: ARK Paperbacks, 1986], 183).

17. "A Song for St. Cecilia's Day"; "To My Honored Friend Sir Robert Howard."

imagining the atom in the first place exposed the analogical process whereby human physical experience is used to support the social order. Resemblances between the ancient materialist doctrines of Epicurus and Lucretius and the mechanist philosophies of Descartes and Gassendi made the writings of the ancient atomists particularly important in the seventeenth century. Pierre Gassendi, the contemporary of Descartes, took as his philosophical task the renovation of Epicurean doctrine. He believed with Epicurus that the world was made up of matter, void, and movement, but he added to this explanation of matter Christian beliefs in a nonmaterial soul and a prime mover. In *Syntagma* (1658) Gassendi asserted:

> It may also be supposed that the individual atoms received from God as he created them their corpulence, or dimensions, however small, and their shapes in ineffable variety, and likewise they received the capacity requisite to moving, to imparting motion to others, to rolling about, and consequently the capacity to disentangle themselves, to free themselves, to leap away, to knock against other atoms, to turn them away, to move away from them, and similarly the capacity to take hold of each other, to attach themselves to each other, to join together, to bind each other fast, and the like, all this to the degree that he foresaw would be necessary for every purpose and effect that he destined them for.[18]

While atomism became rapidly acceptable in England, a process aided by such reformers as Walter Charleton who followed Gassendi in combining atomic natural history and Christian theology, the troubling aspects of the philosophy remained obdurate.[19] The

18. *Selected Works of Pierre Gassendi,* trans. and ed. Craig Bush (New York and London: Johnson Reprint, 1972), 400.

19. For a concise history of atomist thought in England see R. H. Kargon, *Atomism in England from Harriot to Newton* (Oxford: Clarendon Press, 1966). C. T. Harrison notes that "[b]oth the device of offering systems which opposed those of the materialists and the device of directly attacking materialistic tenets were conscientiously employed during the latter half of the seventeenth century. The attacks were especially thorough; there is no prominent section of ancient atomistic philosophy which was not systematically examined and refuted" ("The Ancient Atomists and English Literature of the Seventeenth Century," *Harvard Studies in Classical Philology* 45 [1934]: 26).

connection between atomism and atheism still lingered. The eerie
spaciousness of Lucretius's *De rerum natura* (first translated into
English in 1656) continued to haunt and disturb readers convinced
that the implications of atomic physics were inimical to a well-run
society. Richard Blackmore, in the preface to his own counter-
Epicurean philosophical poem *Creation,* says of Lucretius: "The
Harmony of Numbers engages many to read and retain what they
would neglect if written in Prose; and I persuade myself the *Epicurean* Philosophy had not liv'd so long, nor been so much esteem'd, had it not been kept alive and propagated by the famous
Poem of *Lucretius.* "[20] In his preface Blackmore elucidates the social effects of atomism, and states as his unabashed agenda the interpretation of the natural world in accordance with social
cohesion. Blackmore's poem is a good example of how inextricably
observation of physical data and the maintenance of social structure were intertwined in the eighteenth century.

> If any Man should declare he believes in a Deity, but af-
> firms that this Deity is of human Shape, and not Eter-
> nal; that he derives his Being from the fortuitous
> Concourse and Complication of Atoms; or though he al-
> low's him to be Eternal, should maintain, that he show'd
> no Wisdom, Design or Prudence in the Formation, and
> no care or Providence in the Government of the World
> . . . Such a Person is indeed, and in Effect, as much an
> Atheist as the former [i.e., one who denies God out-
> right]. For tho' he owns the Appellation, yet his De-
> scription is destructive of the Idea of God. (ix–x)

Blackmore further argues that atheists, having no faith in divine
law, can set no store on the Oath of Allegiance. It therefore follows
that "an Atheist must be the worst of Subjects . . . his Principles
subvert the Thrones of Princes and undermine the Foundations of
Government." The argument is straightforward and straightfor-
wardly expressed: those who derive their being from "the fortuitous
Concourse and Complication of Atoms" cannot play the role they
should in society. Blackmore's actual refutation of atomism is to in-
quire rhetorically if the manifest wonders of the created world,

20. *Creation: A Philosophical Poem in Seven Books* (London, 1712), xxxiii.

which he delineates with skillful detail, can be the result of chance alone.

> *Could Atomes, which with undirected flight*
> *Roam'd thro' the Void, and range'd the Realmes of Night,*
> *Of Reason destitute, without Intent,*
> *Depriv'd of Choice and mindless of Event,*
> *In Order March, and to their Posts advance,*
> *Led by no Guide, but undesigning Chance.*

Blackmore's attempt to make the world cozier is understandable, especially when one reads Lucretius's "propagation" of the Epicurean philosophy and experiences the chilly awe induced by his vision of pristine nature.

> *Again, Natures eternal Laws provide,*
> *That the vast All should be immensely wide,*
> *Boundless, and infinite, because they place*
> *Body as bound to Void, to Body Space*
> *By mutual bonding making both* immense
>
> . . . .
>
> *For sure* unthinking seeds *did ne'er dispose*
> *Themselves by counsel, nor their order chose,*
> *Nor any compacts make how each should move,*
> *But from Eternal thro the Vacuum strove,*
> *Variously mov'd and turn'd; untill at last*
> *Most sorts of* Motion *and of* Union *past,*
> *By chance to that convenient Order hurl'd*
> *Which frames the Beings that compose the World.*[21]

It is an odd sensation to read these lines and then to realize that the anticlimactic "convenient order" that ends the passage is the frame of our world. The resolution of the world is a poor recompense for the entrancements of the chaos we almost glimpse.

Our involvement with the atom does not stop there. For, as yet, we have formed no mental image of our narrator. No one in eighteenth-century England had ever seen an atom; it could only be approached indirectly, gingerly, through the claims that ancient philosophy and seventeenth-century science made on its behalf.

21. Lucretius, *De rerum natura*, trans. Thomas Creech (Oxford, 1682), 31.

According to the ancient atomists, atoms in and of themselves possessed only shape and mass, but in conjunction with one another,
through local motion, made up the entirety of visible objects. Epicurus states: "We must suppose that the atoms possess none of the
qualities of visible things except shape, mass, and size, and whatever is a necessary concomitant of shape. For every quality changes;
but the atoms do not change in any way."[22] Both the teachings
of Epicurus and the mechanical philosophies of Descartes and
Gassendi strip visible reality of quality after quality until they arrive at the simple, necessary form of matter. This is clearly the
method of Descartes: "the nature of matter, or of body in its universal aspect, does not consist in its being hard, or heavy, or coloured,
or one that affects our sense in some other way, but solely in the
fact that it is a substance extended in length, breadth and depth"
(1:255–56). At the core of Smollett's narration is an entity that no
one had ever seen. Its very existence and properties had to be taken
on trust from those inventive and assertive enough to declare its
nature. The atom is that without which nothing can exist; but our
apprehension of the atom exists only as abstraction that cannot
be proved. The eighteenth-century reader who accepts that he is
made of atoms is forced by Smollett's satire to acknowledge that
this most fundamental particle of his body is beyond his grasp, and
this realization is crucial to the satire's overall effect. For, just as we
are confronted with the undeniable reality of the pain experienced
by the human body, so also are we confronted by the way in which
our knowledge of the body is controlled by others. Our understanding of matter differs from our experience of it. Through its choice of
narrator, Smollett's satire elicits our recognition, not simply of the
state's material power over the body, but also of that power's more
abstract ramifications.

The mental distance between the undirected, endless universe of Lucretius and the bureaucratic, compact, modern state
is almost untraversable. Yet the system of metaphor chosen by
Smollett for his satire and represented by its narrator causes us to
bring the two together. This satire insists, without any of the ame-

22. Epicurus, *Letters, Principal Doctrine, and Vatican Sayings*, trans.
Russell M. Geer (Indianapolis and New York: Bobbs-Merrill, 1964), 18. Further
references are to this edition and are given parenthetically in the text.

liorative atomism provided by Gassendi and Walter Charleton, that politics—like nature itself—is matter in motion. As the atoms of Lucretius created the visible world through haphazard, ceaseless motion, the politicians of the *Atom* create history through physical contact. But whereas the motion of Lucretius and Gassendi is exultant and exuberant, the motions in Smollett's satire have some of the unpleasant nuances provided by the most notorious English atomist of all, Thomas Hobbes: "All which qualities called *Sensible,* are in the object that causeth them, but so many several motions of the matter, by which it presseth our organs diversely. Neither in us that are pressed, are they any thing else, but divers motions; (for motion, produceth nothing but motion)."[23] Reading Lucretius and Gassendi, we experience an almost unbridled liberty and excitement; in Hobbes and Smollett the experience is one of oppression. The world of atoms is no longer located outside us; it "presseth our organs diversely." The model of movement is still that provided by Lucretius, but the spectacle is now shrunk and tawdry.

Telling the story of contemporary English politics, Smollett's *Atom* uses the body to represent social and political chaos. The atom assumes that in each politician and public figure physical makeup and behavior are intimately connected, and to fulfill its satiric task it endows each of its victims with a unique physiology. Like the atom itself, Newcastle (Fika-kaka) has few inherent qualities. As the atom lacks color, gravity, and texture, so Newcastle is also defined by a series of negatives, and, as atoms achieve further characteristics through movement, so Newcastle only acquires positive qualities by his incessant fidgeting: "He had no understanding, no oeconomy, no courage, no industry, no steadiness, no discernment, no vigour, no retention. He was reputed generous and good-humoured; but was really profuse, chicken-hearted, negligent, fickle, blundering, weak, and leaky. All these qualifications were agitated by an eagerness, haste, and impatience, that compleated the most ludicrous composition, which human nature ever produced" (12). Lucretius argued that space must alternate with void; otherwise, motion would be impossible. The notion that matter and void border on each other in mutual definition provided Smollett with further details of Newcastle's constitution: "All this

23. *The Leviathan,* ed. Michael Oakeshott (Oxford: Blackwell, 1946), 7.

bustle and trepidation proceeded from a hollowness in the brain,
forming a kind of eddy, in which his animal spirits were hurried
about in a perpetual swirl. Had it not been for this *Lusus Naturae,*
the circulation would not have been sufficient for the purposes of
animal life" (12). It is the void that permits movement and thereby
allows matter to achieve further definition. Smollett adopts this
scene of elemental chaos and confines it within Newcastle's skull.
Only his empty-headedness makes his life possible.[24] Confronted
with a system that subjects the human body to ideological transformations and literal punishment, the revenge of the satirist is to
disembody, through a nonhuman system of metaphor, all the participants in the body politic.

In the *Atom* the model of simple chaos, before the evolution of
complex life-forms, situates the intentionless, unceasing movement of ruled and ruler alike. Like Newcastle, the citizens of England are satirized as Lucretian atoms, "harried and set in motion
with blows throughout the universe from infinity": "[They] are
such inconsistent, capricious animals, that one would imagine they
were created for the purpose of ridicule . . . They seem to have no
fixed principle of action, no certain plan of conduct, no effectual
rudder to steer them through the voyage of life; but to be hurried
down the rapid tide of each revolving whim, or driven, the sport of
every gust of passion that happens to blow" (8). The political world
of the *Atom* is literally mindless. Purely physical events determine
the choice of leaders, the establishment of policy, and the conduct
of war. For example, George II's choice of Newcastle as chief advisor
is depicted as an entirely mechanical event over which neither of
the parties had any control: "They were like twin particles of matter, which having been divorced from one another by a most violent
shock, had floated many thousand years in the ocean of the universe, till at length meeting by accident, and approaching within

24. Smollett was not the first to use this metaphysical tradition for satiric
purposes. Rochester's poem "On Nothing" also finds chaos a natural resource
for the satirist: "But Nothing, why does Something still permit / That sacred
monarchs should in council sit / With persons highly thought at best for nothing
fit, / While weighty Something modestly abstains / From princes' coffers, and
from statesmen's brains, / And Nothing there like stately Nothing reigns?" (*The
Complete Poems of John Wilmot, Earl of Rochester,* ed. David M. Vieth [New
Haven: Yale University Press, 1968], 119).

the spheres of each other's attraction, they rush together with an eager embrace, and continue united ever after" (13). The satire here does not point to some moral failure on the part of Newcastle and George II. There are no accusations of corruption or duplicity. Such personal qualities are simply not at issue. Smollett's vocabulary is that of the physical world, not that of moral responsibility. In this fantastic satire, politicians are atoms, and events unfold according to Blackmore's vision of the impossible. History is made as individuals "to their Posts advance, / Led by no Guide, but undesigning Chance." The random association of atoms, and the haphazard way they approach the "spheres of each other's influence," is offered as the most accurate representation of political reality. The consistent description of political events as the result of accident and physical attraction is, of course, paralleled by the historical account that provides the chronology of the atom's tale. Smollett takes the interpretation of the physical universe favored by atheists and others who put themselves outside the pale of the society, and makes this metaphysical threat the basis of his satiric reality. The contrast between the fantastic, mechanical caricatures of political leaders and the actual, historical events that these leaders directed gives a nightmarish edge to the *Atom*.

Smollett's atom argues against definition and demarcation: the very qualities that make social order possible. In introducing itself to Nathaniel, the atom states that there is a remarkable sameness beneath all the apparent variety in the world: "Of the same shape, substance, and quality, are the component particles, that harden in rock, and flow in water; that blacken in the negro, and brighten in the diamond; that exhale from a rose, and steam from a dunghill" (6). The atom casually mixes the animate and the inanimate and refuses to make any real distinctions between roses, dunghills, and human beings. Motion and action alone distinguish one entity from another. This incessant motion is a property of both matter and spirit. The atom's account of its own "vicissitudes" involves a journey through a grain of rice, a Dutch mariner, an English supercargo, a duck, Ephraim Peacock (father of the auditor), and finally Nathaniel Peacock himself. From the atomic perspective all distinctions are transitory, and in the helter-skelter pace of Smollett's prose they become almost momentary. The version of physical reality we get from the atom is one of continuous and profound change. The transformations and movement that are characteristic of the atom's narrative are both physical and metaphysical; they occur in any time scale one chooses to adopt. There is no end to this process. Nature is forever recycling itself, and as men and beasts exchange their animate matter, the chain of being begins to seem like an escalator, traveling at incredible speed, in which the steps are always changing places. It is not only on earth that matter constantly takes new forms. In the heavens the process continues. For, according to the atom, "metempsychosis, or transmigration of souls, is the method which nature and fate constantly pursue, in animating the creatures produced on the face of the earth." Nathaniel Peacock as Nathaniel Peacock is only a brief stage in the entire procedure: "For example, my good friend Nathaniel Peacock, your own soul has within these hundred years threaded a goat, a spider, and a bishop; and its next stage will be the carcase of a brewer's horse" (11). If a goat, a spider, and a bishop have shared the same soul, then any discussion of their physical differences, discussion that would lead to establishing some order among them, seems to be ill-placed.

Simple atomism did not completely obliterate the body politic. Even Hobbes, the archatomist, had defused the implications of his atomic theory, and artfully constructed a cohesive society. Smollett does not, however, accept the Hobbesian transformation of physical reality into the state. The creation of that "Artificial Man," as Part 2 of *The Leviathan* tells us, involves a deadening of activity, a reduction of variety, a cessation of motion.

> The only way to erect such a common power, as may be able to defend them from the invasion of Foreigners, and the injuries of one another . . . is, to confer all their power and strength upon one Man, or upon one Assembly of men, that may reduce all their wills, by plurality of voices, unto one Will: which is as much as to say, to appoint one Man, or Assembly of men, to beare their Person; and every one to own, and acknowledge himself to be Author of whatsoever he that so beareth their Person, shall Act, or Cause to be Acted, in those things which concern the Common Peace and Safety; and therein to submit their Wills, every one to his Will, and their judgements, to his Judgement. This is more

than Consent, or Concord; it is a real Unity of them all,
in one and the same Person, made by Covenant of every
man with every man . . . This done, the Multitude so
united in one Person, is called A Common-Wealth, in
latin *Civitas.* This is the Generation of that great Leviathan, or rather (to speak more reverently) of that *Mortal God,* to which we owe under the *Immortal God,* our
peace and defence. For by this Authority, given him by
every particular man in the Common-Wealth, he hath
the use of so much Power and Strength conferred on
him, that by terror thereof, he is inabled to form the
wills of them all, to Peace at home, and mutual aid
against their enemies. (111–12)

The formation of the state requires the relinquishment of personal
movement and volition. In the commonwealth an individual is literally carried by the figure appointed to "beare their Person." The
state is not merely an agreement, or a contract; it is a real physical
union, "a real Unity of them all, in one and the same Person." This
new physical entity, the Leviathan, is acknowledged by Hobbes to
be a creation of art, based upon an imitation of man, and it requires
a certain interpretation of man's material reality to work. The fiction that sustains the Leviathan is that men will cease to agitate on
their own behalf, and that there can be physical unity between
them. As man can be seen as a fortuitous collection of atoms, so the
Leviathan can be seen as a functional, physically combined collection of men.

In contrast, Smollett's semblance of the body politic is a rest-
less, uncomfortable being. In the *Atom* there is no cessation of motion, no moment of rest in which the affairs of state can be given
coherence. We have already seen Smollett describe political figures
as if they were atoms without sense of direction or any sense of control. The transition of atoms from one human being to another is a
parody of Hobbes's ideas of the "real unity" that exists between
men in the commonwealth. The *Atom* gives moments of connection, of encounter between individuals, extraordinary prominence.
Each instance of physical contact is exaggerated and described at
length. One can suggest a number of reasons for this. Given that
characters in the satire have been denied much identity, it makes
sense that the only time they have a profound sense of themselves

is when they rub surfaces with another human being. The second
reason is that such moments make it impossible to take the idea of a
body politic seriously. There is, all these ticklish, itchy, odd encounters tell us, no one body, merely a collection of distinct particles whose blind encounters and mutual agitation suggest the
impossibility of any "real unity." In the short "Advertisement" from
the "publisher" of the *Atom,* which precedes the satire proper, the
publisher expresses fear that his text, if misunderstood as a satiric
account of living politicians (which of course it is), will have unpleasant consequences: "In these ticklish times, it may be necessary to give such an account of the following sheets, as will exempt
me from the plague of prosecution" (3). The satire's very first ad-
jective presents political relationships in physical terms: the body
politic is "ticklish," and if irritated may release a "plague" of prosecution upon the publisher's head. The body politic is, the publisher suggests, unfixed and unstable and therefore vulnerable, but
it is also capable of spasmodic and violent reaction to those who
attack it.

   Nonetheless, while he denies satiric intent, the publisher in-
structs his reader in the methods of satire. The ludic note tells us
how to relate the narrative to the culture that produced it: "As to
the MS, before I would treat for it, I read it over attentively, and
found it contained divers curious particulars of a foreign history,
without any allusion to, or resemblance with, the transactions of
these times. I likewise turned over to Kempfer and the Universal
History, and found in their several accounts of Japan, many of the
names and much of the matter specified in the following sheets"
(3).[25] Insistence that the narrative, without any allusion to "transactions of these times," deals with a foreign land reminds the reader
of eighteenth-century travel accounts that were imagined and published precisely because of their relevance to domestic issues—the
most famous of such accounts being the "Travels into several Re-
mote Nations of the World" of Lemuel Gulliver. When political circumstances at home are "ticklish," as they were when the *Atom*
was published, the satirist protects himself by writing about "re-

---

25. A full discussion of the parallels between Smollett's *Atom,* Kaempfer's
History of Japan (1727–28), and the *Universal History* (1759–65) is available
in Martz, *Later Career of Tobias Smollett,* 90–103.

mote nations." The advantage thus gained is noted sardonically by Swift, quoted under "ticklish" in Johnson's *Dictionary.*

> *How shall our author hope a gentle fate,*
> *Who dares most impudently not translate;*
> *It had been civil in these* ticklish *times*
> *To fetch his fools and knaves from foreign climes.*

The foreign climes to which fearful authors resort are perfect sites for satiric impudence. In distant regions of the globe, authors shrink, expand, and transform the human body and thereby revise the relationship between physical reality and political organization. Swift shrinks man in *Gulliver's Travels* and in so doing challenges all the social meanings that have accumulated around his stature. The reconstituted satiric victim exposes his society's politics.

Various forms of the word "ticklish" appear constantly in the *Atom.* Ticklishness is an unreliable phenomenon: it can be pleasant at one moment and painful at the next. In the world of the *Atom* pleasure and pain, rather than external and functional characteristics, orient man in his society. Johnson defines "ticklish" as "sensible to titillation, easily tickled," and supplies as example a quotation from Bacon: "The palm of the hand, though it hath as thin a skin as the other parts, Yet it is not *ticklish,* because it is accustomed to being touched." Only parts of the body unaccustomed to being touched are ticklish. A ticklish nature, like a sexual nature, is not always apparent in a public, formal body; a ticklish nature, unlike a sexual nature, is something most adults vehemently deny. Our ticklishness is a significant, if overlooked, part of our humanity. Victims of tickling know they have a mind/body problem. Tickling causes convulsions, starts, grimaces, and peculiar movements. It militates against dignity and reminds us that complete self-control is impossible. A recurrent motif in eighteenth-century literature, especially satire, the connotations of "titillation" are varied and intense. Usually it suggests sexual indulgence, and the satiric object's absorption in gratification at all costs. Ticklishness is important to the satirist because it does not reinforce social organization, and supports an anarchic interpretation of human physicality.

Among the most graphic, and pornographic, of Smollett's pre-

sentations in the *Atom* is that of Fika-kaka (Newcastle), whose de-
votion to the "gratification of his master's prejudices and rapacity"
(14–15) involves the presentation of his posteriors to his master
"to be kicked as regularly as the day revolved." One day, the pleasure this gave Fika-kaka resulted in "a kind of tension or stiffness,
which began to grow troublesome just as he reached his own pal-
ace, where the Bonzas were assembled to offer up their diurnal
incense" (17).[26]

> At sight of a grizzled beard belonging to one of those
> venerable doctors, he was struck with the idea of a pow-
> erful assuager; and taking him into his cabinet, pro-
> posed that he should make oral application to the part
> affected . . . such a delectable titillation ensued, that
> Fika-kaka was quite in raptures . . . The transports thus
> produced seemed to disarrange his whole nervous sys-
> tem, and produce an odd kind of revolution in his fancy;
> for tho' he was naturally grave, and indeed over-
> whelmed with constitutional hebetude, he became, in
> consequence of this periodical tickling, the most giddy,
> pert buffoon in nature. All was grinning, giggling, laugh-
> ing, and prating, except when his fears intervened; then
> he started and stared, and cursed and prayed by turns.
> (17)

Confronted by this detailed account of "delectable titillation" and
"periodical tickling," the reader will understand why the *Atom* has
occasioned critical embarrassment and aversion, but such passages are, as we have seen, an integrated part of the satire's system
of imagery. Moreover, the ability to give offense is at the heart
of satiric efficiency. To justify the offensive nature of his satire,
Smollett has the "publisher" of the *Atom* invoke the very highest
authorities: "Finally, that I might run no risque of misconstruction,
I had recourse to an eminent chamber-council of my acquaintance,
who diligently perused the whole, and declared it was no more

---

26. Smollett is satirizing Newcastle's close relationship to, and cultivation
of, the ecclesiastical powers of the Church of England.

actionable than the Vision of Ezekiel, or the Lamentations of Jeremiah the prophet" (3). The Old Testament books provide a paradigm for the *Atom* and are present in the publisher's "Advertisement" as a cryptic justification of Smollett's satiric practice. Ezekiel and Jeremiah interpret the physical transformations their people have undergone; they explain ailments, aberrations, and the suffering of the entire natural world as outward signs of transgression. The people have not abided by the laws given to them by God, and they are now blasted and deformed; they have relinquished the law of God, and the strength of their bodies has been taken from them: "Jerusalem hath grievously sinned; therefore she is removed: all that honoured her despise her, because they have seen her nakedness: yea, she sigheth, and turneth backward. Her filthiness is in her skirts; she remembereth not her last end; therefore she came down wonderfully: she had no comforter" (Lam. 1:8–9). In the Lamentations of Jeremiah the lot of Zion is one of complete, physical devastation. The purpose of the prophetic books is to connect the advent of physical ills to the social role that God's people have neglected.

The prophet explains physical transformation as literal punishment brought about by the hand of God. These Old Testament books are concerned with physical signs; their God-given task is to interpret these signs, to make sense of this awful physical transformation and thereby bring God's people back to God. The eighteenth-century satirist is also concerned with physical signs. The surfaces he describes, the warped physicality he details, are the same as those found in the Old Testament books. Of course, the important distinction is that the physical marks and signs that make up the satirist's account are indications not of God's purpose but of the satirist's own intentions. The satirist plays both God and prophet. The prophet is impelled, against his own self-interest, to share with his people his God-given understanding of their affliction. The satirist also claims to be inspired with God-given clear-sightedness; of course, what he sees is a fantastic world of his own devising. Both the satirist and the prophet bring bad news. The "Advertisement" to the *Atom*, appearing to propitiate the authorities and to preempt any charges that may be made against those involved in the production of the work, defines the political position of the publisher as one of vulnerability, but it also firmly asserts the moral authority of the satirist.[27]

In his *Second Treatise of Civil Government* John Locke describes how, in the state of nature, the power every man has to punish the transgressions of others is "irregular and uncertain." It is for this reason that individuals are willing to give up their "single power of punishing" and enter into society. Locke defines political power as the power to punish, and raises the danger that the machinery of government may be used against the very individuals it is supposed to protect: "*Political power* then I take to be a *right* of making Laws with Penalties of Death and, consequently, all less penalties for the Regulating and Preserving of Property, and of employing the force of the Community on the Execution of such Laws, and in the defence of the commonwealth from foreign injury, and all this only for the publick good" (265). In the tale the atom tells to Nathaniel, the government is seen to pervert every task allotted to it by Locke: it exploits instead of protecting its citizens, it engages the country in foreign injury, and it does all this not for the public good but in order to perpetuate itself. In these circumstances the satirist is one who refuses the social pact, unravels the mechanisms of power, and reasserts, in a savage and fantastic way, his "single power of punishing."

The *Atom* never denies the reality of political power, and it leaves the reader with graphic images of bodies damaged and destroyed by the government's power to punish, but Smollett's satire works its own effective transformations of the body. In and of itself, the atom represents a subversive understanding of matter, and it is, throughout its narration, more than willing to explain the political

---

27. Traditionally, the power of the satirist was described as the ability to wreck vengeance on his satiric victims. In *The Power of Satire* (Princeton: Princeton University Press, 1960) Robert C. Elliott recounts the story of Archilochus, the first known satirist, who composed verses against his bride-to-be and her father when they decided against the marriage. Supposedly, both of Archilochus's satiric victims hanged themselves. Smollett's recurrent absorption with revenge, and the deep influence exerted upon him by Alexander Pope, who envisioned the satirist as an Archilochus figure, suggests that a sense of modern satiric impotence may be one of the implicit tensions in the *Atom*.

implications of its form to the unhappy Nathaniel Peacock. The atom knows that government is not only a question of gallows and gibbets, but also of how individuals think about their own corporeal frames: what gives the atom such self-delight is that it is free from the first and offers a significant challenge to the second.

CHAPTER SEVEN

"THE FROLICK MAY GO ROUND": BODIES AS SIGNS IN *HUMPHRY CLINKER*

"As pure sentience the body cannot signify."[1] Roland Barthes is completely unambiguous: bodies in and of themselves are insignificant. Pure sentience has no meaning. Much of Smollett's fiction is about how sentience acquires meaning, how feeling becomes significance, questions that are particularly prominent in his first and last novels. The plot and narrative structure of *Roderick Random* emphasize disjunctions between material forms and linguistic signs. Descartes saw the use of signs, both natural and linguistic, as the "true difference between man and beast," yet despite Roderick's attention to his body as a set of signs, and his ability to render those signs in language, his body only slowly becomes a form that his society consents to read as human. The form of Smollett's last novel, an epistolary work written by five different hands, offers multiple articulations of body as sign. At one extreme is the eponymous hero, Humphry, whose body—like Roderick's— is submitted to interpretative gazes he can do little to direct or alter. Humphry does not even appear until the novel is well advanced, and, alone among the novel's major characters, he writes no letters. His body is always read for us by others. By naming the novel for Humphry, Smollett ensures some critical attention for

---

1. Roland Barthes, *The Fashion System,* trans. Matthew Ward and Richard Howard (London: Cape, 1985), 258.

taciturn sentience, but the center of the novel is occupied by a character who enjoys a radically different relationship to language.

Matthew Bramble self-consciously attempts to control his body's translation into linguistic and social sense; he has, more-over, the cultural authority, social standing, and leisure to be suc-cessful. So satisfying is Bramble's reading of his body that it has won general endorsement from Smollett's critics, despite the fact— noted but not usually accorded central importance—that it de-pends upon, and defines itself against, negative versions of female physicality. Bramble's letters provide a revealing study of how cer-tain versions of physicality acquire authority, in this case from the discourse of eighteenth-century medicine and also from the struc-tures of the novel itself. Authoritative though it may be, Bramble's interpretation is not proof, finally, against slippage and contesta-tion. Bramble's body can never be just as he means. That the dis-course of sensibility through which Bramble represents himself is inherently contradictory, dividing his narration against itself, causes some problems. The more general difficulty, however, is that no attempt to render the body in language, as a system of signs, can ever be completely stable or perfectly achieved.

The most dramatic split in Bramble's narrative occurs to-wards the end of the novel, when he suddenly appears under a new name. In fiction, as in life, names fix ever-changing physical forms, permitting recognition and continuity. In *Roderick Random* a ca-sual "are you asleep, Rory" from Captain Bowling initiates a reu-nion between father and son: "Before I had time to reply, Don Rodriguez, with an uncommon eagerness of voice and look, pro-nounced, 'Pray, captain, what is the young gentleman's name?'— 'His name (said my uncle) is Roderick Random.'—'Gracious Powers!' (cried the stranger, starting up)—'And his mother's'—'His mother (answered the captain, amazed) was called Charlotte Bowling.'—'O bounteous heaven! (exclaimed Don Rodriguez, springing across the table, and clasping me in his arms) my son! my son! have I found thee again?'" (413). And so, Roderick is claimed by his father and becomes an object of paternal care. Towards the end of *Humphry Clinker* we witness a similar scene, but one where the child must claim the father, forcing him to acknowledge both a different name and his implication in an entirely new scheme of meaning. "'Matthew Loyd of Glamorgan!—O Providence!—

Matthew Loyd of Glamorgan!' . . . 'Your worship must forgive me—
Matthew Loyd of Glamorgan!—O Lord, Sir!—I can't contain
myself!—I shall lose my senses.'" Humphry Clinker irrupts because he recognizes the name of his father. That Matthew Bramble
and Matthew Loyd signify one and the same body forces narration
of a past that has been covered over and obscured. "'I took my
mother's name, which was Loyd, as heir to her lands in Glamorgan-
shire; but, when I came of age, I sold that property, in order to clear
my paternal estate, and resumed my real name; so that I am now
Matthew Bramble'" (318). Bramble's actions are innocent enough,
but they have unfortunate consequences. Resuming his "real
name," he not only gives up his maternal inheritance but also
makes it impossible for the mother of his child to trace him. Clear-
ing his paternal estate requires that he give up his mother's land,
and causes him to evade his responsibilities to Dorothy Twyford,
"barkeeper at the Angel at Chippenham." The previously unspoken
transactions in Bramble's past—economic and sexual—radically
alter his narrative. Bramble represents this eventuality as a moral
failure. Confronted with Humphry Clinker, his offspring, he exclaims: "You see, gentlemen, how the sins of my youth rise up in
judgement against me" (318). What is at stake here, however, is
not so much a simple sin of the flesh, but an admission that the
flesh cannot be contained in any one narrative. Whereas Matthew
Bramble seeks to control the significance of his own corporeality,
Matthew Loyd, unknowing father of an adult son, can have no such
illusions. Under the sign of Matthew Loyd, Bramble acknowledges
the contribution women have made to his "paternal estate," and
begins to interpret himself differently.

Roland Barthes, when he asserts that the body as "pure sentience" cannot signify, goes on to suggest that "clothing guarantees
the passage from sentience to meaning." Bramble's representation
of self is hedged around with all sorts of guarantees—his gentlemanly style accessorized with various forms of cultural authority—
but it finally cannot be secured. As *Humphry Clinker* is a comedy, Bramble's realization of imperfect mastery is the cause for
embarrassed celebration: his discovery of the "free play of the sig-
nifier" is analogous to his discovery of his son. The comedy of the
novel is, however, muted and subdued, shadowed by death. If the
novel turns on the unexpected fecundity of the sign, it also inti-

mates that "[m]ortality may be that against which all discourse defines itself, as protest or as attempted recovery."[2]

The Expedition of Humphry Clinker is Smollett's last, best work, his "one indisputably canonical novel."[3] Critics like its fusion of historical matter and novelistic invention, and its sophisticated development of epistolary technique. The novel is constructed around a number of quests—for health, love, and order—and the chief quester is Matthew Bramble, a Welsh squire afflicted with ill health and the demands of his extended family: his wards, Jery and Lydia Melford; his sister Tabitha and her maid, Win Jenkins. The letters written by the five members of the Bramble entourage as they tour through England and Scotland amend, correct, and modify each other, and these partial and subjective accounts generate a greater whole.[4] The extent to which the novel honors multiple viewpoints, however, has been exaggerated. *Humphry Clinker* highlights not only differences between male and female expression but the superiority of the former.[5] Matthew Bramble and his

2. Brooks, *Body Work*, 7.
3. Robert Mayer, "History, *Humphry Clinker*, and the Novel," *Eighteenth-Century Fiction* 4 (1992): 240.
4. Smollett's mastery of epistolary devices is given vigorous and comprehensive treatment by P.-G. Boucé (*Novels of Tobias Smollett*, 191–99). J. V. Price (*The Expedition of Humphry Clinker*) and Eric Rothstein (*Systems of Order and Inquiry in Later Eighteenth-Century Fiction* [Berkeley and London: University of California Press, 1975], 109–53) provide incisive commentary on the form of the novel. Wolfgang Iser lucidly describes the generic composition of the text and discusses how the form of *Humphry Clinker* affects its reception: "For the reader, the succession of letters brings about a telescoping of situations in which—paradoxically enough—the characters reveal themselves and their surroundings through the very fact that they see everything from their own limited point of view. Consequently, the task of coordination is handed over to the reader, for he alone has all the information at his disposal. The one-sidedness of these viewpoints gives a sharp outline to the world that is described, whereas their blending results in its modification" (*The Implied Reader* [Baltimore and London: Johns Hopkins University Press, 1974], 75).
5. Superficially, the structure of the novel suggests that *Humphry Clinker* is a fit candidate for Bakhtinian analysis, but as soon as such an examination gets under way, we realize that the novel only superficially meets the requirements of heteroglossia. For Bakhtin the "decisive and distinctive importance of the novel as genre" is that "the human being in the novel is first, foremost and always a speaking being" ("Discourse in the Novel," in *The Dialogic Imagination*, ed. Michael Holquist, trans. Michael Holquist and Caryl Emerson [Austin: Uni-

nephew, Jery, "write" the bulk of the novel, while the three women are afforded scant space.[6] The novel implicitly justifies this disparity by representing the women as feeble correspondents: Win Jenkins and Tabitha are almost illiterate, their mastery of linguistic signs haphazard at best, and Lydia's prose style, especially at the beginning, is entirely conventional. One of the major functions of *Humphry Clinker* is to render an account of England and Scotland at the close of the 1760s. Matthew Bramble, middle-aged, in pain, full of lament and complaint about the state of England, and Jery, a vigorous rake determined to be amused and distracted, complement each other in the performance of this task. The female voices in the novel do not seriously contest the expression of male perspectives. The reader is led, by the limited amount and nature of female expression in the novel, to accept the combined viewpoint of Matthew and Jery as the work's central perspective.[7]

---

versity of Texas Press, 1983], 332). But the presence of speech difference is only the first step in Bakhtin's narrative theory. Crucial to his definition of the speaking person is the idea of contest. In Bakhtin's view the "speaking human being" is a synecdochal expression of a political entity: "An independent, responsible and active discourse is *the* fundamental indication of an ethical, legal and political human being" (349–50). When the reader recognizes the multiplicity of human voices in a novel, she simultaneously appreciates political and ethical difference; the novel, denying "the absolutism of a single and unitary language," thereby achieves its generic function (366). The logic of Bakhtin's argument requires that the social languages expressed in any novel are all "equally capable of being 'languages of truth,'" and that they are all "equally relative, reified and limited" (367). The simple indication of linguistic difference does not in itself establish heteroglossia, or a verbal contest, in the novel. Each of the social languages must also have a unique claim on certain social, political, legal truths. Through the admission of the these various truths, the decentering of the "ideological world" is attained.

6. Between them, Bramble and Jery write 83% of the novel (Price, *Expedition of Humphry Clinker,* 9).

7. "[W]ith contemporary reviewers of the novel I have argued that the acceptable views expressed in the novel radiate from Bramble" (John Sekora, *Luxury: The Concept in Western Thought* [Baltimore: Johns Hopkins University Press, 1977], 240). Eric Rothstein modifies this view and argues that "[t]he five letter writers . . . form a kind of circle of shared characteristics, moving from Jery to Bramble to Tabby to Win and Liddy, and thence to Jery again; or, alternatively, the other way around. The relation between Jery and Bramble is the most important of these because the two men are the rhetors of the novel" (*Systems of Order,* 120). Rothstein defines rhetor as "source of a tone and formal patterns" (138).

As *Humphry Clinker* begins with scenes of illness, disorder, and upset and moves gradually towards health, regulation, and calm, criticism has concentrated on what P.-G. Boucé calls its "therapeutic function."[8] The body most urgently demanding a cure is that of the hypochondriacal Matthew Bramble.[9] Bramble's complaint that he is constipated and "equally distressed in mind and body" opens the novel (5). Jery's first letter reveals that his uncle is "tortured with gout," which has "soured his temper" (8). Soon after, however, Jery recognizes the "natural excess of mental sensibility" (17) that afflicts his uncle, and thereafter he gives a fuller account of his uncle's susceptibility: "He is as tender as a man without a skin; who cannot bear the slightest touch without flinching. What tickles another would give him torment; and yet he has what we may call lucid intervals, when he is remarkably facetious— Indeed, I never knew a hypochondriac so apt to be infected with good-humour" (49). Just before his departure from London, in which Bramble has suffered both the false arrest of his manservant and his sister's attempt to decoy her niece's suitor, he diagnoses his own condition: "I find my spirits and my health affect each other reciprocally—that is to say, every thing that discomposes my mind produces a correspondent disorder in my body; and my bodily complaints are remarkably mitigated by those considerations that dissipate the clouds of mental chagrin" (154). From this point on, Bramble's health steadily improves. In Edinburgh he begins "to feel the good effects of exercise" and enjoys a "constant tide of spirits, equally distant from inanition and excess" (219). By novel's end,

8. *Novels of Tobias Smollett*, 209. William A. West argues that Bramble's return to health supplies the "central development of the novel" ("Matt Bramble's Journey to Health," *Texas Studies in Literature and Language* 11 [1969]: 1197). B. L. Reid characterizes the novel as "Smollett's Healing Journey" in which "the action moves from negative to positive, from passive to active: sickness to health, constipation to purgation, irritability to sensitivity, anonymity to identity, distance to intimacy, doubt to trust, celibacy to marriage, ignorance to knowledge" (*Virginia Quarterly Review* 41 [1965]: 550).

9. "From Classical times to the turn of the eighteenth century, 'hypochondria' was primarily defined as a somatic abdominal disorder accompanied by a mystifying multiplicity of symptoms migrating around the body. Increasingly, however, these secondary symptoms moved stage-center; emphasis switched to the non-specific pains, and their relations to the ever-fecund imagination" (Roy Porter and Dorothy Porter, *In Sickness and in Health: The British Experience, 1650–1850* [London: Fourth Estate, 1988], 203).

Bramble is "disposed to bid defiance to gout and rheumatism" and begins to think he "put [him]self on the superannuated list too soon" (339). Bramble's ill health, then, is not a purely physical phenomenon; it is intimately connected to what "discomposes his mind" and is therefore connected to his apprehensions of disorder.

From the start Bramble presents himself not only as a patient, a suffering body, but as one able to identify and interpret his own physical symptoms. The very opening words of the novel abruptly dispute the judgment of his correspondent, Dr. Lewis ("Doctor, The pills are good for nothing").[10] Bramble's body, like his property, is something he himself will control: "I think, every man of tolerable parts ought, at my time of day, to be both physician and lawyer, as far as his own constitution and property are concerned" (23). Having studied his case with "the most painful attention," Bramble does not accept that there are any "mysteries in physick" (23). He not only knows what his body feels and undergoes, but can translate those feelings into social and symbolic meanings. Bramble consistently identifies his bodily malaise with social ills. Attacks of gout, abdominal disorder, swellings, and discomfort are responses, Bramble says, to the moral and social disorder of Bath, "the very center of racket and dissipation" (34), and London, a "center of infection" (118) and a "great reservoir of folly, knavery, and sophistication" (107).

Eighteenth-century medical texts support Bramble's claims to authority because they construct hypochondria and gout as marks of moral and social standing and its sufferers as able commentators on social affairs. Sydenham, writing in the late seventeenth century, describes hypochondriacs as "persons of prudent judgement, persons who in the profundity of their meditations and the wisdom of their speech, far surpass those whose minds have never been excited by such stimuli."[11] Bernard Mandeville, several

---

10. While there are exceptions, Bramble tends to address Lewis as "Doctor" when he is being disputatious or magisterial, as "Dear Lewis" when the mood is neutral, and as "Dear Dick" when the letter is particularly expansive or affectionate.

11. "Epistolary Dissertation to Dr. Cole," in *The Works of Thomas Sydenham, M.D.* (London: Sydenham Society, 1850), 2:89. Further references are to this edition and are given parenthetically in the text.

decades later, reiterates the connection between intense susceptibility and moral sense.

> Hypochondriacal People are generally Men of Sense,
> that's very true: Not that the Spleen is the cause of Both,
> or either indeed; but because Men of Sense, especially
> those of Learning, are guilty of Errors that, unless they
> are of a very happy constitution, will infallibly bring the
> Disease upon them, for all Men that continually fatigue
> their Heads with Intense Thought and Study, whilst
> they neglect to give the rest of their Bodies the Exercise
> they require, go the ready way to get it, as by undenia-
> ble Arguments I shall demonstrate hereafter: So that
> soft-headed People are no otherwise exempt from this
> Disease, than Eunuchs are from Claps, by being inca-
> pable of Performing what may occasion it.[12]

George Cheyne, whose *English Malady* (1733) provided the most
influential version of hypochondria, concurs with Mandeville: "For
I seldom ever observ'd a heavy, dull, earthy, clod-pated Clown,
much troubled with nervous Disorders."[13] He also notes that hypochondriasis particularly afflicted "People of condition." Both Mandeville and Cheyne introduce their case studies with encomia on
their patients, who are all persons of fine character and discernment. The prevalence of hypochondria among "those of the live-
liest and quickest Parts . . . whose Genius is most keen and
penetrating," suggests the moral authority of its sufferers (*English
Malady*, 262). Bramble's illness supports the contention that he is
the novel's "moral guide," flawed but nonetheless "acute and reliable."[14]

Under Bramble's guidance the reader begins to identify illness with women, particularly with Bramble's traveling companions. In fact, in his first letter he complains that a "ridiculous
incident that happened yesterday to my niece Liddy, has disor-

12. *A Treatise of the Hypochondriack and Hysterical Passions* (London,
1711), 95. Further references are to this edition and are given parenthetically in
the text.
13. *The English Malady* (London, 1733), 262. Further references are to this
edition and are given parenthetically in the text.
14. Sekora, *Luxury*, 242.

dered me in such a manner, that I expect to be laid up with another
fit of the gout" (5). Having reached London, Bramble reports that
"the complaints in my stomach and bowels are returned" and rhetorically asks, "What the devil had I to do, to come a plague hunting
with a leash of females in my train?" (141). As both of these incidents involve the matrimonial plans of Bramble's womenfolk, he
sets up a correspondence whereby the "cure" of Matthew Bramble
requires the containment of female sexuality.

Bramble's interpretation is corroborated, albeit unwittingly,
by his female companions. At the age of forty-five, Tabitha has left
no stone unturned to "avoid the reproachful epithet of old maid"
(60), but she seems condemned to name forever what she is increasingly unlikely to experience. Tabitha's sexual obsession be-
gets a linguistic corruption whereby she subconsciously insinuates
the female body, most particularly her own neglected body, into
places where it will attract attention. Her complaint to Dr. Lewis
about a lambskin that she regards as her property but that has been
given to a servant—"Give me leaf to tell you, methinks you mought
employ your talons better, than to encourage servants to pillage
their masters—I find by Gwyllim, that Villiams has got my skin; for
which he is an impotent rascal" (78)—effectively, if unconsciously,
protests the undesirability of Tabitha's own skin, the neglect or ridicule that her body routinely encounters, and her inability to dispose of herself on the marriage market. The impression created by
the letters of Tabitha, and those of her servant Win, is of the "raging
force of female sexuality," a source of energy that no form of sanctioned expression could contain.[15]

That management of the female person is crucial for male
health is further underlined by the development of Lydia Melford.
In contrast to both Tabitha and Win, Lydia gains insight and inde-
pendence as the summer progresses. Her approach to the type of
discourse that her brother and uncle have commanded from the
start is, however, indicated by misogynistic reflection on the desperate and intense matrimonial campaign of her aunt.

15. The phrase is that of Patricia Meyer Spacks, who continues: "Not all
male poets, playwrights, and novelists supported Pope's dictum that every
woman is a rake, but many hinted their belief in—or their hope or fear of—its
truth" ("Ev'ry Woman Is at Heart a Rake," *Eighteenth-Century Studies* 8
[1974]: 27).

My dear Willis, I am truly ashamed of my own sex—We
complain of advantages which the men take of our
youth, inexperience, sensibility, and all that; but I have
seen enough to believe, that our sex in general make it
their business to ensnare the other; and for this purpose, employ arts which are by no means to be justified
—In point of constancy, they certainly have nothing to
reproach the male part of the creation—My poor aunt,
without any regard to her years and imperfections, has
gone to market with her charms in every place where
she thought she had the least chance to dispose of her
person, which, however, hangs still heavy on her hands.
(259)

Lydia can be accommodated within the patriarchal economy because, although her unhappiness makes her ill and can therefore be
read by her companions, she will never articulate her own desires.
Even writing to her female confidant, she insists there is nothing to
be said: "You know my heart, and will excuse its weakness." Re-
united with her love, Lydia blushes, trembles, and states what is
only too obvious: "I really know not what I say—but I beg you will
think I have said what's agreeable" (330). Lydia properly represses
what Tabitha improperly betrays. Women, enthralled by their materiality and sexuality, are unable to enter fully the signifying order.
Like Lydia, they can either mimic the male voice, signifying their
own desire only by absence ("you know my heart," "I know not
what I say") or—like Tabitha and Win—they can become living
marks of disorder, whose sexuality interrupts and distorts linguistic
acts.[16] That Bramble's own health depends upon the containment
of his women folk is economically suggested when he explains his
decision to leave Bath sooner than expected. Tabitha has begun a
"flirting correspondence" with an impoverished Irishman, and
Lydia has "attracted the notice of some coxcombs." In a telling pun,
Bramble concludes: "You perceive what an agreeable task it must

16. W. A. Boggs provides detailed examination of Win's orthography in a series of articles, the last of which is "Dialectal Ingenuity in *Humphry Clinker*,"
Papers on Language and Literature 1 (1965): 327–37. Arthur Sherbo disputes
this ingenuity in "Win Jenkins' Language," *Papers on Language and Literature*
5 (1969): 199–204.

be, to a man of my kidney, to have the cure of such souls as these"
(48).

For Bramble, women in general signify the dangers of luxury
and corruption. Critics have, of course, noticed that "the influence
of women . . . recurs as a constant misogynous theme in Matthew
Bramble's letters," but the instrumental nature of that misogyny
has not been accorded sufficient attention.[17] As John Sekora demonstrates, Bramble's views on women and luxury derive authority
from a long-established literary mode: "the attack upon luxury had
for centuries depended upon an easy recognition of a series of contrasts elaborated into a typology: masculine-feminine, old-young,
country philosopher–city sharper, and so on."[18] Finding Bath in-
undated by an "irresistible torrent of folly and extravagance," Bramble complains of the "wives and daughters of low tradesmen" who
feed on those of fortune like "shovel-nosed sharks" (37). Attending
a ball, Bramble—bored and seeking to escape a "tiresome repetition of the same languid, frivolous scene"—makes his way to the
door, "when an end being put to the minuets, the benches were removed to make way for the country-dances; and the multitude ris-
ing at once, the whole atmosphere was put in commotion. Then, all
of a sudden, came rushing upon me an Egyptian gale, so impregnated with pestilential vapours, that my nerves were overpowered,
and I dropt senseless upon the floor" (65). The physician Bramble
consults explains that his swooning "was entirely occasioned by an
accidental impression of fetid effluvia upon nerves of uncommon
sensibility." Yet Bramble's disdain for the proceedings and his description of the "Egyptian gale," which overcame him, combine in
representing his faintness as a moral reaction to degenerate, tedious entertainment. Of course, as Bramble only attended the ball
at the instigation of Tabitha, both he and Jery hold her indirectly
responsible.

In the structure of the novel, other incidents, domestic and
foreign, endorse Bramble's identification of women with luxury. As
James Carson points out, even Lismahago's exotic, brutal narrative
of his capture by the Miami and marriage to Squinkinacoosta works
to this effect. Lismahago's response to Tabitha's inquiries as to his

17. Boucé, *Novels of Tobias Smollett,* 209.
18. *Luxury,* 249.

bride's wedding dress is that the Miami are "too virtuous and sensible to encourage the introduction of any fashion which might help to render them corrupt and effeminate" (194–95), but the information that Squinkinacoosta wore "the fresh scalp of a Mohawk warrior" around her neck implies that female fashion is everywhere the death of men.[19] The parallel between various forms of female violence is extended by Lismahago's gift to Tabitha of a purse that his wife had used "as a shot-pouch in her hunting expeditions" (197). Closer to home, the Brambles hear George Dennison reflect that in times of luxury and dissipation, "the pride, envy, and ambition of . . . wives and daughters" are the rocks upon which "all the small estates in the country are wrecked" (327). The end of the novel also includes a case history that justifies Dennison's opinion. Bramble visits his old friend Baynard, only to find him "meagre, yellow and dejected" and the once fruitful garden without the least "vestige . . . of trees, walls, or hedges" (286). Baynard's ill health and the ruin of his estate have been effected by his wife, whose modish improvements and taste for extravagant life have devastated both the land and its owner.[20]

Later in the novel Smollett takes desperate measures on Baynard's behalf: shortly after Bramble's visit, Mrs. Baynard catches a "pleuritic fever" and expires, an event at which Matthew Bramble is "exceedingly pleased" (341). The technical merit of Mrs. Baynard's character has been fully appreciated by John Sekora: "Placed unexpectedly at the close of the book, she can be

19. "Commodification and the Figure of the Castrato in Smollett's *Humphry Clinker,*" *Eighteenth Century: Theory and Interpretation* 33 (1992): 38. Carson states that in *Humphry Clinker* woman "seeks to become not only a consumer, but to make men the objects of exchange. But Smollett cannot imagine a man as a commodity, so emasculation must precede commodification" (35).

20. Smollett's extraordinary portrait of this extravagant, stupid, and completely unfeeling woman (291–93) has caused at least one of his critics some embarrassment. P.-G. Boucé disarmingly remarks: "It would be wrong to suspect Smollett of a shameless misogyny. Even if the case of Mrs. Baynard is farfetched, he takes care to observe that two other women in the neighborhood are driving their husbands to ruin by rivalling each other in idiotic ostentation" (*Novels of Tobias Smollett,* 213). While Boucé is to be applauded for suggesting that this aspect of the novel is misogynistic, I don't think Smollett's ability to make misogyny look reasonable, as well as farfetched, exonerates him from the charge.

vapid in and of herself yet potent enough to evoke memories and
resonances from everywhere in England. Her parts are entirely
negative, yet she becomes greater than the sum of those parts . . .
The fact that Mrs. Baynard does draw together so many strands of
the novel gives us a further instance of Smollett's achievement"
(264–65). Mrs. Baynard is vapid "in and of herself"; her function is
to draw together "many strands of the novel," which she does best
by expiring of a pleuritic fever. Sekora's words underline the extent
to which the formal success of *Humphry Clinker* depends upon the
containment of women. The female threat can be neutralized in
two ways: sex and death. Normally, sex is enough, but if it proves
insufficient, death will be necessary. In the structure of *Humphry
Clinker* the death of Mrs. Baynard is as important as the three marriages with which the novel ends.

The association of women with disorder and ill health is,
moreover, silently argued by their almost total exclusion from the
Scottish expedition. The description of Scotland is the literal and
symbolic heart of *Humphry Clinker,* for which Smollett prepares
the reader with some care. As the travelers approach the border, he
integrates detailed discussions of Scottish ways and culture into
the novel, and even creates a new character, Lismahago, a Scots officer on half-pay, to introduce the Bramble entourage to new views
on Scottish matters.[21] Through Bramble and Jery Melford, who are
agreeably surprised at the Scotland they discover, Smollett attempts to educate the English reading public away from anti-Scots
feeling. In his letters each man addresses specific prejudices and
records his surprise at their ill-grounded nature. For the entire duration of the Scottish interlude Jery and Bramble present their
womenfolk to us. We are given brief reports on Tabitha's "progress

21. Louis Martz has cogently argued that a deliberate contrast between
Scotland and England was "an essential inspiration" for *Humphry Clinker.*
Martz suggests that Smollett desired to placate those of his countrymen offended by the portrayal of Scotland in *The Present State,* and that he wished to
dilute anti-Scots feeling made even more intense by the Bute ministry (*Later
Career of Tobias Smollett,* 124–31). In a lively and informative article, Eric
Rothstein details the forms English prejudice against Scotland took and describes how Smollett uses the structure of *Humphry Clinker* to deflect such
prejudice ("Scotophilia and *Humphry Clinker:* The Politics of Beggary, Bugs,
and Buttocks," *University of Toronto Quarterly* 52 [1982]: 63–78).

in husband-hunting" (202) and are told that the "neglect of the male sex" in Edinburgh left her "malcontent and peevish" (225). Although Jery tells us that her failure to entrap a man has made her "the less manageable" (236), we gather that her recalcitrance has not seriously interfered with the success of the trip. Both Bramble and Jery make occasional references to Lydia's health and express concern about her, but it is not until the September letter that we get her version of her upset at the Edinburgh ball—an event that Jery had already described one month and many pages earlier. The almost exclusively male commentary we are given on things Scottish suggests that the order, harmony, and health that the place symbolically represents are incompatible with female nature and concerns. In fact, for a time the group splits up.

In the absence of the women, Bramble experiences the Highlands and gives way, for the only time in the novel, to an expression of awe and wonder: "This country is amazingly wild, especially towards the mountains, which are heaped upon the backs of one another, making a most stupendous appearance of savage nature, with hardly any signs of cultivation, or even of population. All is sublimity, silence, and solitude" (252). The appearance of the sublime coincides with the disappearance of women. Of course, as Edmund Burke's *Philosophical Enquiry into the Origin of Our Ideas of the Sublime and Beautiful* reminds us, sublimity *is* male, a modification of power that speaks of the authority of the father and is opposed to the weak delicacy of female beauty: "There is a wide difference between admiration and love. The sublime, which is the cause of the former, always dwells on great objects, and terrible; the latter on small ones, and pleasing; we submit to what we admire, but we love what submits to us" (113). Men may submit to the sublime, but they partake in its power: "The authority of a father, so useful to our well-being, and so justly venerable upon all accounts, hinders us from having that entire love for him that we have for our mothers" (111). Bramble's experience of the sublime further endorses his authority and marks his separation from women.

Controlling his body's passage from sentience into meaning, Bramble elaborates an account of his illness that holds women in some measure responsible, and in which his symptoms become a response to "the dissipation, follies and general moral corruption of society."[22] His account derives considerable authority from the discourses of eighteenth-century medicine, which represented hypochondriacs as persons of sound judgment and good sense, and from events within the novel itself—where women are seen as disorderly creatures who ruin estates and endanger health. Despite all this, Bramble cannot completely secure his wished-for interpretation. Notwithstanding his considerable cultural authority and adroit management, the signs are not entirely under his control.

Historians of medicine say that the advent of the hypochondriac as a cultural type marks an important moment: "It signals a stage in medicine itself, with lay desires generating a medical consumerism integral to the wider development of market society."[23] In fact, Smollett, in the *Critical Review,* tends to speak of medical consumerism as Bramble does of luxury in general. *Medical Observations and Enquiries, by a Society of Physicians in London* causes Smollett to bemoan the "inundation of medical books, by which the public has been lately overwhelmed," while Francis Home's *Medical Facts and Experiments* is bad-temperedly noticed in terms of "*holiday* writers, and such as read for amusement."[24] Medical texts were a part of eighteenth-century leisure just as Ranelagh was, and Bramble is as thorough a consumer as his niece, Lydia, or his sister, Tabitha. Whereas Lydia's subjectivity is formed by pulp fiction—according to her uncle she "has got a languishing eye, and reads romances" (12)—Bramble studiously turns his mind to "all that has been written on the Hot Wells" (23). As one of the laity, determined not to relinquish control of his body to a professional, Bramble seizes upon the opportunities for enlightenment presented by his culture. His discourse is to some extent generated by the very social circumstances that he most vehemently denounces. He uses his illness to castigate social developments, but as his consumption of medical texts is itself a luxurious process, his criticism only further develops the society he despises. Nor is this Bramble's only implication in the processes of luxury. Bramble is not only a consumer in his own right, but he is generous to his wom-

22. John F. Sena, "Smollett's Matthew Bramble and the Tradition of the Physician-Satirist," *Papers on Language and Literature* 11 (1975): 387.

23. Porter and Porter, *In Sickness and in Health,* 209.

24. *Critical Review* 4 (1757): 45; *Critical Review* 7 (1759): 529.

enfolk. In one of the best-judged jokes in the novel Smollett has Bramble lament the "flood of luxury and extravagance" (57) at Bath. The next letter, from Lydia, tells us "my uncle, who has made me a present of a very fine set of garnets, talks of treating us with a jaunt to London" (58). The joke is repeated when the group reach London. No sooner has Bramble described this "grand source of luxury and corruption" (87) than Lydia charmingly tells us that Bramble ("good-natured and generous, even beyond my wish") has made her a present of "a suit of clothes, with trimmings and laces, which cost more money than I shall mention" (94). Bramble's generosity exceeds Lydia's desires, and she is embarrassed by the amount of money he has spent. Certainly, in her new clothes and jewelry Lydia functions as a sign of luxury, but in this case luxury is driven by male generosity. To revise Mandeville, and the discourse of luxury itself, private virtues can have public benefits.

Bramble is implicated in luxury in ways that undermine his social analysis.[25] Not only that, but the medical discourse that he luxuriously deploys takes him even closer to the objects he castigates. John Mullan has written that, during the eighteenth century, hypochondria and acute sensibility always carried conflicting meanings: "by the middle of the century, a distinct ambivalence has become crucial; sensibility can produce either collapse or integrity, disorder or articulacy."[26] The ambiguities of hypochondria are such that Bramble's privileged affliction can either support or subvert his interpretative authority. The same medical texts that construct the hypochondriac as a man of sense and genius also describe the capacity of the disease to deceive and mislead its interpreters. Sydenham describes its symptoms as a "farrago of disorderly and irregular phenomena" (90) and was the first writer to explain why this was the case: "Few of the maladies of miserable mortality are not imitated by it. Whatever part of the body it attacks, it will create the proper symptom of that part. Hence, without skill and sagacity the physician will be deceived; so as to refer the symptoms to some essential disease of the part in question"

25. For another approach to Bramble's implication in luxurious processes, see Edward L. Schwarzschild, "'I Will Take the Whole upon My Own Shoulders': Collections and Corporeality in *Humphry Clinker*," *Criticism* 36 (Fall 1994): 541–68.

26. *Sentiment and Sociability*, 236.

(85). Almost a century later Robert Whytt praised his "sagacious" predecessor not only for the justness of his observation, but for the elegance of its expression: "the shapes of *Proteus,* or the colours of the *chamaeleon,* are not more numerous and inconstant, than the variations of the hypochondriac and hysteric disease."[27] While accounts of hypochondriasis tend to flatter the victim, they also suggest that the disease resulted from a life of extremes.[28] Bernard Mandeville's *Treatise* offers the case study of one Misomedon, who admitted to a "very irregular" youth. Similarly, George Cheyne, presenting his own tussle with the disease, attributes its onset to intense study in youth, followed by much dissipation on his arrival in London. Cheyne also tells us that the "Vulgar and Unlearned" do not understand this disease and take it for "a lower Degree of Lunacy, and the first Step towards a distemper'd Brain" (260).

Other understandings of hypochondria bear directly on gender ambiguities within the novel. For instance, a fundamental symptom of hypochondriasis is a lack of balance and perspective. This condition was sympathetically described by Sydenham in the mid–seventeenth century: "The patients believe that they have to suffer all the evils that can befall humanity, all the troubles that the world can supply. They have melancholy forebodings. They brood over trifles, cherishing them in their anxious and unquiet bosoms . . . there is no moderation. All is caprice" (89). An excessive concern with trifles and capricious behavior are, of course, the stuff of satire against women. Such a connection between Bramble and the weak women he castigates forces consideration of an important as-

27. *Observations of the Nature, Causes, and Cure of those Disorders which have been commonly called Nervous, Hypochondriac, or Hysteric* (Edinburgh, 1760), 96.

28. Eric Rothstein takes the unsympathetic view that Bramble "is sick because of his physical excess when young and emotional excess when old" (*Systems of Order,* 121). There are plenty of references to Bramble's carousing youth. In Bath, Quin often reminds Bramble of their "tavern-adventures" (50), and Charles Dennison was a "fellow-rake at Oxford" (320); that Bramble in his early manhood was "obliged to provide for nine bastards, sworn to him by women whom he never saw" (28) suggests that he was no stranger to what Mandeville called "venereal ferment" (a prime cause of hypochondria); and, of course, upon the discovery of Humphry Clinker's parentage Bramble exclaims: "You see, gentlemen, how the sins of my youth rise up in judgement against me" (318).

pect of hypochondria that we have not yet discussed. From the time of Sydenham the disease was understood as the male equivalent of female hysteria, "since however much antiquity may have laid the blame of hysteria upon the uterus, hypochondriasis (which we impute to some obstruction of the spleen or viscera) is as like it, as one egg is to another" (85).[29] The titles of those works by Mandeville and Cheyne that deal with the subject suggest the longevity of this understanding. In stressing the identity of the two disorders, Robert Whytt admits that "in women, hysteric symptoms occur more frequently, and are often much more sudden and violent, than the hypochondriac in men," but he explains this by the "more delicate frame, sedentary life, and particular condition of the womb in women" (195). Given the isomorphic relationship between hysteria and hypochondriasis, male sufferers became identified more generally with female traits: they were feminized. This process can be clearly seen in the testimony of one sufferer, speaking on how the disease affects his character and reactions to life: "I have read much and am near Fifty five, my Sight is very clear. When I am at the best, I can see, that the long habit of my illness has chang'd my very Humour: formerly I fear'd nothing, and had the constancy of a man; From what I have related you may gather what Temper I was of besides; but now I am full of Doubts and Fears, I'm grown peevish and fretfull, irresolute, suspicious, every thing offends me, and a trifle puts me in a Passion" (42). In his account of the changes wrought upon him by his hypochondriacal condition, Mandeville's Misomedon significantly evokes distinctions based on gender. Formerly he was courageous and had "the constancy of a man." Now he is doubting and fearful, cannot be decisive, and is overly con-

29. Ancient understandings of hysteria attributed it to a wandering womb, which the patient could force back into place by use of foul-smelling and nauseating substances, or entice back by the use of fragrant suppositories. Sydenham's expression that hysteria could extend to both sexes was, though not the first, "by far the most explicit . . . His alliance of hypochondriasis and hysteria was perfectly logical. After it was introduced by Smollius in 1610, hypochondriasis became the subject of many treatises, in which the hypochondrium was accorded a role similar to that of the uterus in hysteria. Just as 'uterine suffocation' gave rise to many physical and mental disorders in women, so *suffocatio hypochondriaca* caused numerous derangements of the abdominal viscera and, specifically of the spleen" (Ilza Veith, *Hysteria: The History of a Disease* [Chicago: University of Chicago Press, 1970], 144).

cerned with trifles. In short, he now suffers from the inconstancy to which women, in particular, are subject.

Bramble's seemingly confident exegesis of his bodily signs is, in fact, tainted by his culture's deep uncertainty over marks of gender. According to G. J. Barker-Benfield, a "persistent and fundamental concern" of the culture of sensibility was "the meaning of changed manners for manhood": warnings abounded that effeminacy was the inevitable effect of luxury.[30] Twentieth- century literary debates over whether figures such as Yorick and Harley are celebrations of or satires on "the man of feeling" reflect, Barker-Benfield says, "the eighteenth century's own ambivalence over the meaning of refining manhood" (142). James Carson offers an ingenious account of that ambivalence at work in *Humphry Clinker*. He argues that, having accorded moral value to the figure of the "feminized," benevolent Matthew Bramble, Smollett must "demarcate a limit on acceptable transformations of masculinity," which he does by including in his novel the "nightmare figure" of the castrato Tenducci—an index of the frightening effects of female luxury.[31] My own sense of the novel would lead me to reverse Carson's argument: Bramble's implication in the processes of luxury—the nature of his illness, his consumption of texts, and the generous gifts to his womenfolk—works to dissolve the gender differences on which critiques of luxury (including Bramble's own) depend. Traditionally, luxury was seen as driven by women, and we have seen that such a view is supported by important incidents in *Humphry Clinker,* but the novel does not leave the typology of luxury intact.

Two kinds of discourse are crucial to Bramble's narration of his physicality: medical discourses that treat of sensibility and hypochondria, and the social and moral discourse of luxury. As we have seen, Bramble's control of each discourse is inevitably limited; various kinds of slippage occur that associate him with the very processes—or the very sex—from which he wishes to dissociate himself. *Humphry Clinker* begins with a quarrel over interpretation, when Bramble, stubborn and constipated, tells his physician he does not know what he is doing. Conflicts over what bodies mean, and what they need, also occur outside the relatively pro-

---

30. *Culture of Sensibility,* 104.
31. "Figure of the Castrato," 40.

tected space of private correspondence. Bramble's sense of what his body means is contested, not only by his doctor, but in public. At Hot Well Bramble draws the attention of a quack, vying for patients, who offers an unflattering diagnosis: "Perhaps, indeed, your disorder may be *oedematous,* or gouty, or it may be the *lues venera.* If you have any reason to flatter yourself it is this last, sir, I will undertake to cure you with three small pills, even if the disease should have attained its utmost inveteracy . . . Sir, I have lately cured a woman in Bristol—a common prostitute, sir, who had got all the worst symptoms of this disorder" (19). Even the most refined bodies can be subjected to crude interpretations, and Bramble finds himself suspected of venereal disease and associated with a prostitute. Obviously rattled, he discusses the unsolicited consultation with Lewis: "Sure I have not lived to the age of fifty-five, and had such experience of my own disorder, and consulted you and other eminent physicians, so often, and so long, to be undeceived by such a—" (24). Bramble has only recently asserted that there are "no mysteries" in physic, but this incident makes clear that he does believe in mysteries, which he, through reading, study, and consultation, has learned to decipher. The idea that his body is plainly legible obviously unnerves Bramble, especially if the signs are what the quack takes them to be. If the quack has no authority for his opinion, while Bramble does, and if Bramble can deny the symptoms the quack claims to see, then the quack's diagnosis should just be dismissed. There is a comic insinuation that the quack may be right. More than that, though, there is the important spectacle of Bramble's assurance being shaken: "Let me know what you think of this half-witted Doctor's impertinent, ridiculous, and absurd notion of my disorder—So far from being dropsical, I am as lank in the belly as a grey-hound" (25). Having opened the novel by disputing with Lewis, Bramble now wants Lewis's authority to reinforce his own.

A more poignant misunderstanding of Bramble's bodily signs occurs when he goes for a swim attended by Humphry Clinker. Stung by the cold, Bramble "could not help sobbing and bawling out" (183). Clinker takes this to mean that Bramble is drowning and comes to his assistance, dragging him ashore. The result is that Bramble "cannot walk the street without being pointed at, as the monster that was hauled naked a-shore upon the beach" (184).

Bramble is Smollett's most sophisticated creation, the one who
draws most fully on his society's resources as he self-consciously
elaborates an account of his own body. In the cold water Bramble is
forced to abandon these refinements and reverts to the natural language of sobs and bellows. Suddenly, his body becomes a strange,
monstrous object on the shore. Yet the episode undercuts any tendency towards primitivism by the simple expedient of having
Humphry be wrong. Comic and touching, the scene makes two significant points: natural language offers no greater interpretative
certainty than developed linguistic signs; and what bodies are has
as much to do with the viewer as with the signs viewed. Unlike other
scenes of this kind in Smollett—I am thinking especially of the half-
dead, naked Roderick lying on the beach—this one admits that it is
not only malice and self-interest that interferes with the interpretation of bodily signs. Affection can be a hilarious misreader as well.

That bodies achieve meaning only within local context is
demonstrated by the meeting of the Bramble entourage with the
half-naked form of the novel's eponymous hero: "We had scarce entered the room at Marlborough, where we stayed to dine, when
[Tabitha Bramble] exhibited a formal complaint against the poor
fellow who had superseded the postilion. She said, he was such a
beggarly rascal, that he had ne'er a shirt to his back; and had the
impudence to shock her sight by shewing his bare posteriors, for
which act of indelicacy he deserved to be set in the stocks" (81).
Tabitha Bramble, herself so clearly a victim of repression, presents
Clinker's appearance as a failure of bodily regulation. Her complaint invokes both abstract categories (a standard of delicacy) and
the possibility of force (through the stocks). Tabitha, of course, often and unconsciously offends against delicacy herself—constantly
exposing in correspondence skin that decency demands she keep
under wraps. In contrast to his sister, Matthew Bramble invokes
the Sermon on the Mount, turning Clinker's plight into a satiric device: "Heark ye, Clinker, you are a most notorious offender—You
stand convicted of sickness, hunger, wretchedness, and want" (82).
Bramble here exposes, and rails against, the way in which class determines the significance of bodies. Because he is an impoverished
orphan, Clinker's illness, in contrast to Bramble's own, cannot be
an index of social corruption: he becomes "poor and shabby" and is
turned away by his landlord employer as a "miserable object" that

"would have brought a discredit upon my house" (82). Clinker's own justification is that his physical appearance is entirely beyond his own control: "[N]ecessity has no law, as the saying is—And more than that, it was an accident—My breeches cracked behind, after I had got into the saddle . . . I ha'n't a shirt in the world, that I can call my own, nor a rag of clothes, an please your ladyship, but what you see—I have no friend, nor relation upon earth to help me out—I have had the fever and ague these six months, and spent all I had in the world upon doctors, and to keep soul and body together" (81).

Humphry Clinker writes no letters. His body is presented to us entirely through the words of others, yet Smollett names his book for the naked postilion and directs our attention towards this silent enigma. What is it that Clinker expedites?[32] Most obviously, Humphry is Bramble's "clinker," the mistake or error whose unexpected appearance forces Bramble to recognize the "sins" of his youth. More subtly, clinkers are coals that won't burn, that resist the transmutation of fire. Clinkers give neither heat nor light; they are matter with which nothing can be done. To think of the body as a clinker is to think of it as matter that does not signify. Of course, Humphry Clinker's real name turns out to be Matthew Loyd—which is also the name of Matthew Bramble. Bramble tries to master his body's passage from sentience to significance; Clinker cannot ascribe any significance to his sentience. Yet these positions are closer than they seem. Bodies are neither entirely matter nor entirely discourse. We may say of bodily signs, as Win Jenkins does of marriage, "who nose but the frolick may go round."

The expedition of Humphry Clinker is never quite completed. We do not accompany the travelers back to Brambleton-

---

32. Michael Rosenblum sees Clinker as the incarnation of the spirit of disorder within the novel ("Smollett as Conservative Satirist," *English Literary History* 42 [1975]: 576). That Humphry's "self-realization and emancipation from the hopelessness and anonymity of his previous life are possible only within the master-servant relationship as literary tradition represents it" (John Richetti, "Representing an Under Class: Servants and Proletarians in Fielding and Smollett," in *The New Eighteenth Century*, ed. Felicity Nussbaum and Laura Brown [London: Methuen, 1987], 98) is a mark of Smollett's nostalgia for an organic society. In contrast, J. V. Price argues that Humphry's radicalism cannot be contained in a novel where "social rank and condition give no reliable guide as to behaviour, manners, or morals" (*Expedition of Humphry Clinker*, 60).

hall, even though plans for return fill the last pages. Our suspicions that felicity will not perfectly survive that return are supported by Win's news that the travelers' "satiety is to suppurate" (352). Expeditions end. *Humphry Clinker* is about the comedy of the sign, but bodies, unlike other bundles of signs, dissolve. Bramble nearly dies in the novel, not from the illness to which he has devoted so much time, but from drowning, an event that is foreshadowed twice on his travels—at Scarborough where Humphry Clinker pulls him out of the sea when he is in no danger at all, and on the crossing from Fife to Leith when the storm is so violent "the boatmen themselves began to fear" that landing would be impossible. Finally, right at the end of the novel, the coach overturns in a flood. Only the intervention of Humphry Clinker, who dives into the coach, brings Bramble's lifeless body up, and carries him ashore "as if he had been an infant of six months" (313), saves Bramble's life. Death will not always be played with, but for the moment the "frolick may go round."

You must unbend, you know. Why you might take to some light study; conchol-
ogy now; I always think that must be a light study. Or get Dorothea to read you
light things, Smollett—Roderick Random, Humphry Clinker; *they are a*
little broad, but she may read anything now she's married, you know. I remem-
ber they made me laugh uncommonly—there's a droll bit about a postilion's
breeches. We have no such humour now. I have gone through all these things, but
they might be rather new to you.

George Eliot, Middlemarch

Mr. Brooke, the scatty avuncular presence in George Eliot's *Mid-*
dlemarch, neatly summarizes the nineteenth-century attitude
to Smollett: his work is a little "broad," and its raw physicality
and split breeches are not suitable reading material for an unmar-
ried woman.[1] Brooke genially expresses prejudices from which
Smollett's work has never really recovered. This fiction is light,
boisterous, and a little rude. At the same time, Brooke's appreciation, though vague, seems real enough and is infused with nostalgia
for a vanished sensibility: "We have no such humour now." Behind
Brooke's recommendation, too, we can sense George Eliot's appreciation of Smollett's achievement. Brooke is, after all, speaking to
Casaubon, the arid, dogmatic, would-be author of *The Key to All*
Mythologies—a title that has been, since the publication of *Middle-*
march, a byword for futile scholarly endeavor and empty system
making. Casaubon marries an ardent, beautiful, young woman because his eyes are failing and he needs a reader. So completely do
his own intellectual constructions imprison him that he almost
becomes a tragic figure. Brooke, in his good-hearted and obtuse
way, thinks it possible that Casaubon might "laugh uncommonly"
at *Humphry Clinker.* That in itself is a comic notion. More seriously, though, the passage suggests that the desiccated, blinkered
Casaubon would find in Smollett's work the vigor, appetite, and

1. George Eliot, *Middlemarch* (New York: New American Library, 1964),
280.

fellow-feeling that his own life so rigorously excludes and so desper-
ately needs.

   Our own "going through" of Smollett has been rather different from that Mr. Brooke imagines for Casaubon, and some might
feel that the "humour" of Smollett's writing has not been appreciated as it might be. Certainly, the Smollett emphasized here is one
who speaks to various problems in contemporary criticism. Our
own historical moment and Smollett's are consonant in that both
are self-consciously aware of the body, and its involvement in social
and political narratives. As we have seen, eighteenth-century
thinking about the body is divided between the mechanism of Descartes and the vitalism of Whytt, between attempts, like that of
Locke, to define what the body is, and insistence, as in satire, that it
is enough to know the body works. For those eighteenth-century
writers concerned in representing the body, the crucial oppositions
were those between speculation and experiment, theories of the
body and the body as a social form. Smollett knew the range and
depth of these debates and what was at stake in representations of
the body, yet he also knew that materiality and discourse are, in a
certain sense, incommensurate. "The social body constrains the
way the physical body is perceived. The physical experience of the
body, always modified by the social categories through which it is
known, sustains a particular view of society. There is a continual
exchange of meanings between the two kinds of bodily experience
so that each reinforces the categories of the other. As a result of this
interaction the body itself is a highly restricted medium of expression."[2] Each of Smollett's novels offers us a different version of the
"exchange of meanings" between physical and social bodies. In
his first novel, *Roderick Random,* the body of the hero is regularly
treated as a strange, threatening form. Roderick's traumatic entrance into society reveals the disjunctions between sensation and
sociability. Throughout his career Smollett's work demonstrates
his knowledge of how the social body "constrains" the physical
body, and his awareness that the body is, as Mary Douglas observes,
"a highly restricted medium of expression." The body is an effect of
discourse and material sanctions. In *Peregrine Pickle* Smollett
shows how the law renders female sensibility monstrous and per-

2. Douglas, *Natural Symbols,* 93.

verse. But Smollett insists that bodies are not only effects. One of his narrators is an atom, an insignificant particle of matter that translates English politics into a material history, detailing how the state exerts control over the body. In his final novel, *Humphry Clinker*, Smollett shows how bodies are always subject to interpretation, and how such interpretations are always unstable. *Humphry Clinker* expedites the recognition that bodies are not only, or primarily, what they are said to be.

Even as he recommends Smollett, Mr. Brooke knows that this is writing from a different culture: "We have no such humour now." Bodies, like humor, are shaped by historical particularities, and Smollett's versions of the corporeal are no longer ours. We are, however, still thinking through a problem he approached with passion and moral courage. How is matter represented with feeling?

INDEX

Mrs. Baynard, 173–74; the body as sign in, xxvii, 162–84; Bramble, xxvii, 163–64, 165, 167–68, 168 n.10, 169–70, 171–78, 178 n.28, 180–84; changed meaning of manhood in, 180; Clinker as incarnation of spirit of disorder, 183 n; Clinker as sin of Bramble's youth, 164, 183; Clinker complained against by Tabitha, 182–83; Clinker rescuing Bramble from drowning, 181, 184; Clinker's Christian primitivism, 127 n; death in, 96; Dennison, 173, 178 n.28; epistolary technique of, 165, 165 n.4; Jenkins, 165, 166, 170, 183, 184; Lewis, 168, 168 n.10, 181; Lismahago, 172–73, 174; on London, 48; meaning of "clinker," 183; Jery Melford, 165, 166, 167, 172, 174–75; Lydia Melford, 165, 166, 170, 175, 176, 177; misogyny in, 172, 174 n.20; multiple viewpoints in, 165; on Scotland, 174–75, 174 n; as Smollett's one indisputably canonical novel, xxvii, 165; solidity of the protagonist in, xix; Squinkinacoosta, 172, 173; Tabitha, 165, 166, 170, 171, 172, 173, 174–75, 176, 182; therapeutic function of, 167, 167 n.8; Twyford, 164; women in, 163, 165–66, 170–76, 173 nn. 19, 20
Ezekiel, 159

F

Fathom (Smollett). See *Adventures of Ferdinand Count Fathom, The*
feminism: on bodies, xxi–xxii; and Smollett's misogyny, xxix
Fielding, Henry: *Amelia*, 122; *Jonathan Wild*, 99; the mock-heroic in, 101

Fizes, Antoine, 33, 42
Flynn, Carol Houlihan, xxix
Forster, James R., 134 n
Forty-five Rebellion, 135, 139–42
Foucault, Michel, xx–xi, xx n.16, xxi n.17, xxix, 23, 131, 139
Frank, Arthur W., xxi
Fraser, Nancy, xx n.16
Fuss, Diana, xxii

G

Garrick, David, 12
Gassendi, Pierre, 147, 150, 151
George II, 135, 152–53
Gil Blas (Lesage), 51–54
Gothic tales, 111
gout, 167, 168
Grant, Damian, 98 n
Greaves (Smollett). See *Life and Adventures of Sir Launcelot Greaves, The*
Greenberg, Janelle, 72 n.2
Greene, Donald, 13 n
Griffith, Ralph, 22
Gulliver's Travels (Swift), 8, 156–57
Guzmán de Alfarache (Alemán), 125–27

H

Halifax, George Savile, marquis of, xxiv
Haller, Albrecht von, 22
Hardwicke, Philip Yorke, earl of: Marriage Act of 1753, 75–77, 77 n.11, 82; repression of the Forty-five rebels, 135, 139–40
Harrison, C. T., 147 n.19
Harth, Erica, 76
Hawes, Frances Anne (Lady Vane), 70, 83, 84–88, 84 n.20, 91, 93, 94
Hazlitt, William: on *The Adventures of Ferdinand Count Fathom*, 98, 110; on the generosity of Smollett's characters, 54; "On the English Novelists" on Smollett, xix–xx

women, 185; Swift on, xxix; wife
beating, 38, 123. *See also*
marriage
wonder, 51

Y

Yates, Frances A., 146 n.16
Yorke, Philip. *See* Hardwicke, Philip
Yorke, earl of